8 —
do

Turkey Beyond the Maeander

Turkey beyond the Maeander

George E. Bean

John Murray

© Jane Bean 1971, 1980

First published 1971 by Ernest Benn Limited

This edition first published in 1989
by John Murray (Publishers) Limited
50 Albemarle Street, London W1X 4BD

Printed in Great Britain
by The Bath Press, Avon

British Library Cataloguing in Publication Data

Bean, George E. (George Ewart), *1903-1977*
    Turkey beyond the Maeander.
    1. South-west Turkey – Carian antiquities.
    Sites – Visitors' guides
    I. Title
    915.62

    ISBN 0-7195-4663-X

George E. Bean—a memoir

I first met George Bean in Izmir in 1948 soon after he settled in Istanbul as the teacher of ancient Greek in the University there; and in the next ten or twelve years I was lucky enough to make half a dozen journeys with him in Western Asia Minor. These were archaeological reconnaissances, in which he in particular took over the study of the ancient inscriptions that we found. By this time the younger generation of archaeologists were starting to go round the countryside in jeeps, pausing in the villages only for long enough to enquire whether there were any ancient remains. George was quite different. He was of course enormous—broad in the shoulder and almost six foot six inches tall; and to that imposing exterior he added a perfect command of educated Turkish. Arrived in a village we would take our seat at the coffee-house and for half an hour he would converse in his deep voice with the local dignitaries about crops and topics of the day before mentioning what had brought us there. At first I used to get impatient; but I came to see that by his unhurried procedure he was winning the confidence of villagers and officials and so ensuring that they would do all they could to help us in our search. More than once we came to a village where previous travellers had found nothing and in the end had to stay a couple of days before we exhausted all that came to light.

It was hard work because there was hardly any public transport and our travelling was done on foot. George put up with a good deal of hardship; in a Turkish bus the luggage space at the back was often the only place he could be fitted into, and in hotels he never found a bed that didn't contort him. As he said, things were not made for a full-grown man. But I don't remember him ever being put out of countenance; he took everything in his stride. He was of course a keen sportsman, who had reached the third round in the doubles at Wimbledon and captained Surrey at badminton for ten years.

George E. Bean—a memoir

His travels covered the coastal regions of Asia Minor from Bithynia right round to Cilicia. For twenty-five years he was spending a large part of his vacations in this way. The number of inscriptions that he found and published must run into four figures; in this he had the advantage of an exceptionally thorough knowledge of ancient Greek which he had perfected in the years when he was teaching scholarship Greek at St Paul's. He was very much concerned with ancient sites and their identification, to which he was able to add by his discovery of inscriptions or coins and careful study of the ancient authors. He was a natural choice to collaborate with Sir William Calder on a classical map of Asia Minor in the 1950s, and he was out in Turkey working on a revision of it shortly before he died. Few scholars have discovered and named so many ancient sites as he did.

His later travels were mainly in Southern Asia Minor, where he worked on behalf of the Austrian Academy; and it was from 1964 on that he started on the archaeological guide-books of which this is one. During a quarter of a century he became known in many hundreds of Turkish villages and no one ever forgot him. On the occasions when I have crossed his tracks more recently I have heard of the gigantic, almost legendary figure of Bin Bey and been treated with awe and warm hospitality when it was discovered that I was a friend of his.

His guide-books speak for themselves because he had the gift of writing lucidly and with authority. What his readers may not perceive is that behind the modest *persona* of the books lies an eminent scholar whose massive output in learned journals and monographs makes his name one of the big ones in classical topography and epigraphy.

Edinburgh   J. M. Cook
May 1979

vi

Foreword to the second edition

Although *Turkey Beyond the Maeander* was originally published after George Bean's other books, *Aegean Turkey* and *Turkey's Southern Shore*, it has required more extensive revision than either of them for this new edition. The reason for this was anticipated in his foreword, where he refers to the excavations in progress on many of the larger sites. These have continued, often with notable results, and have substantially enlarged our knowledge of Iasus, Halicarnassus and the Halicarnassus peninsula, Cnidus, Caunus, Aphrodisias, and Hierapolis. Furthermore, recent research, much of it arising from the excavations, has brought important developments in our understanding of the history of Caria at all periods. I have attempted to take note of this recent work in revising the text, and also in making alterations and additions to the plans. A number of new photographs have been added to illustrate the new discoveries. Needless to say, the same conditions apply now as did when the first edition was published. New discoveries continue to be made, and further research is constantly modifying the historical picture.

It has not been possible to revisit many of the sites covered in the book, so that the very latest information on the actual physical condition of the monuments, or the state of the roads that lead to them, has not always been available. However, I have been much helped in this respect, and in other matters, by the detailed observations of Mr D. Boyd, which he sent to George Bean after extensive travels in Caria in 1972, many of which were incorporated in his review of the first edition, published in the *Journal of Hellenic Studies*, vol. 94 (1974). I must also acknowledge a deep debt to Professor W. Radt, of the German Archaeological Institute in Istanbul, whose accounts of Kuyruklu Kale and of the Halicarnassus peninsula have formed the source for the additions and corrections to chapters 3, 9, and 10, and whose published plans have been the basis for the new figures. In addition I am grateful to Mr Stuart

Rossiter and Professor Kenan Erim for supplying recent photographs: Plates 63, 64, 76, and 83 by courtesy of Mr Rossiter; Plates 69, 70, 72, 74, and 75 by courtesy of Professor Erim (photographs by M. Ali Dugenci).

The area covered by this volume has in the past been less popular with tourists than the northern part of the West coast, with the great city sites of Pergamum, Ephesus, and Miletus, and the southern shore around Antalya. In recent years, however, it has come into its own. Increasing numbers visit the large sites of Hierapolis and Aphrodisias, while on the coast Bodrum and Marmaris have developed into major tourist resorts. It is hoped that the book will guide visitors to the many fascinating places within easy reach of these centres, and also serve to introduce the adventurous to the less accessible and rarely visited sites in the interior of the country. Not the least of the attractions of these is the opportunity they offer even the layman to make valuable observations which can contribute to our understanding of the history and culture of the region.

Swansea   Stephen Mitchell
May 1979

Foreword to the first edition

The region dealt with in the present work lies immediately to the south of that covered in my earlier book *Aegean Turkey*, corresponding almost exactly with the ancient Caria and largely with the present vilâyet of Muğla. Tralles and Nysa are actually north of the Maeander, but are included for the traveller's convenience.

It is a fascinating country, with a character of its own. Apart from the large cities, more or less purely Greek, it is full of smaller places that never entirely lost their Carian nature. I have not attempted to include all of these, and my selection is to some extent arbitrary; even of those included many, I fear, will not often be visited. But those excluded will be visited even less.

On many, even most, of the larger sites excavations are at present in progress, so that this book must inevitably be in some degree out of date even before it appears. This is obviously unavoidable; were I to wait till these excavations were finished, others would no doubt have begun. With hardly an exception I have myself visited all of the places discussed, many of them repeatedly, most of them recently, but some not for many years; if changes are found to have occurred, I ask the reader's indulgence.

I have followed the same method of presentation as in *Aegean Turkey* and *Turkey's Southern Shore*, and have observed the same lower limit of time, in general about A.D. 300; some critics have complained that readers would welcome a continuation into Byzantine and Turkish times, but in this matter I must stand firm. Such merit as these books possess must derive largely from their dealing with places and periods with which I am familiar.

Turkey is becoming steadily more popular with tourists. Roads and hotels are constantly improving, as also are facilities for camping; but in the area treated in the present volume (with one or two exceptions, such as Aphrodisias and Hierapolis) busloads of visitors are still a rarity. A word of warning to campers may not be amiss.

The organized camping sites are for the most part adequate and often good; but it is most unwise to set up camp by the wayside or in remote parts. Every year unpleasant cases of molestation occur when this rule is disregarded, and fatalities are by no means unknown.

It may be well to draw travellers' attention to the new and severe law in Turkey concerning antiquities. Since 1973 all finds must be delivered by the owner of the property to the appropriate museum, and may not be bought, sold, or exported. Any foreigner found in possession of any antiquity, whether bought or found, is at once suspected of intending to take it out of the country, and if brought to the notice of the police, is liable to arrest and imprisonment. Souvenir-hunting is accordingly illegal and strongly to be discouraged.

As before, I have written primarily for the traveller, actual or potential; for a comprehensive treatment of the country scholars must await the publication of Professor L. Robert's vast work *La Carie*. One volume of this was produced in 1954, with the expectation of others to follow in quick succession, but so far nothing more has appeared.

I may, I hope, be forgiven for not repeating here, in connexion with the use of ancient buildings, what I have already said elsewhere; similarly in the historical summary matters previously dealt with are here briefly dismissed. It may, however, be worth while to repeat again the rules for pronouncing Turkish names. These are: in general, consonants are pronounced as in English, vowels as in German, with these exceptions: c = English j; ç = English [t]ch; ş = English sh; ğ after soft vowels = English y, after hard vowels it merely lengthens them. The dotless ı resembles the indeterminate vowel-sound in the English bor*ough* or *a*gain. In speaking Turkish names the stress should be spread more evenly over the syllables than is done in English; in particular, the penultimate syllable is rarely stressed.

The photographs were taken by me; the text-figures are by my wife.

Contents

George E. Bean—a memoir		v
Foreword to the second edition		vii
Foreword to the first edition		ix
List of Plates		xiii
List of Illustrations in Text		xvii
Glossary		xix
1	Historical	1
2	Mylasa	13
3	Around Mylasa	25
	Euromus	
	Olymus	
	Chalcetor	
	Hydae	
	Peçin Kale	
	Ceramus	
	Kuyruklu Kale	
4	Labraynda	38
5	Iasus	48
6	Cindya and Bargylia	62
7	Stratoniceia	67

Contents

8 Lagina and Panamara   72
    Panamara

9 Halicarnassus   78

10 The Myndus Peninsula   91
    Myndus
    The Six Lelegian Towns
    Caryanda

11 Syangela-Theangela   103

12 Cnidus   111

13 The Rhodian Peraea   128

14 Caunus   139

15 Alabanda   152

16 Alinda and Amyzon   161
    Amyzon

17 Gerga   171

18 Tralles and Nysa   177
    Nysa and Acharaca

19 Aphrodisias   188

20 Hierapolis   199

21 Laodiceia and Colossae   213
    Colossae

Short Bibliography   225
Index   229

List of Plates

[*In one section between pages 44 and 45*]

1   Mylasa. Baltalı Kapı
2   Mylasa. Temple of Zeus (Carius?)
3   Mylasa. Wall of the precinct of Zeus Osogos
4   Mylasa. Berber İni
5   Mylasa. Gümüşkesen; Roman tomb
6   Euromus. The Temple
7   Peçin Kale. Early Wall
8   Ceramus. City Wall
9   Labraynda. Andron of Idrieus
10   Labraynda. Fountain-house
11   Labraynda. The Sacred Way
12   Labraynda. Temple of Zeus Labrayndus
13   Iasus. Street and Houses
14   Iasus. The Land-Wall
15   Iasus. The Theatre
16   Bargylia. The Theatre
17   Iasus. Newly-excavated Mausoleum
18   Stratoniceia. The Sarapeum
19   Stratoniceia. City Gate
20   Stratoniceia. Tombstone in the Museum
21   Halicarnassus (Bodrum). 'Ox-hide' ingot
22   Bargylia. Altar
23   Bodrum. Block of frieze from the Mausoleum
24   Bodrum. Castle and Harbour
25   Bodrum. The Castle Ramp
26   Bodrum. The Castle of the Knights

List of Plates

27 Lagina. Gate of the Temple Precinct
28 Alâzeytin. Lelegian houses
29 Alâzeytin. Compound farm building

[*In one section between pages 140 and 141*]

30 Theangela. Door of cistern
31 Myndus. 'Lelegian' Wall
32 Loryma. The Fortress
33 Theangela. Tomb (of the dynast Pigres?)
34 Cedreae. Wall and Tower
35 Cedreae. The Theatre
36 Amos. View from Acropolis
37 Cnidus. Round Temple, probably of Aphrodite, in 1969
38 Caunus. Rock-tombs
39 Idyma. Rock-tomb
40 Caunus. View over the Harbour; western acropolis on left
41 Caunus. The Long Wall
42 Caunus. Newly excavated building
43 Alabanda. The Theatre
44 Alabanda. Council-House
45 Alabanda. Aqueduct
46 Alinda. Market-hall and Agora
47 Alabanda. Temple of Apollo Isotimus in 1939
48 Alinda. Half-buried Stage of the Theatre
49 Alinda. The Theatre
50 Alinda. Interior of the Market-hall
51 Alinda. Aqueduct
52 Alinda. Tomb in use as a house
53 Alinda. Tower in the City Wall
54 Bridge at İncekemer
55 Gerga. Inscribed rock
56 Gerga. Pyramidal Stele
57 Gerga. Speaker's Platform (?)
58 Gerga. Colossal statue on western hill
59 Gerga. Temple
60 Gerga. Fountain-house (or tomb?)

[*In one section between pages 204 and 205*]

61 Nysa. The Theatre
62 Nysa. The Library
63 Aphrodisias. General view of site

64   Aphrodisias. Odeum
65   Aphrodisias. The Stadium
66   Acharaca. The Charonium (?)
67   Aphrodisias. Sarcophagus
68   Aphrodisias. Temple of Aphrodite
69   Aphrodisias. Theatre and fourth-century piazza
70   Aphrodisias. Theatre
71   Aphrodisias. Columns of the Agora
72   Aphrodisias. Section of carved balustrade depicting Ninos in
     Roman dress
73   Aphrodisias. Baths of Hadrian
74   Aphrodisias. Bust of Aphrodite of Aphrodisias
75   Aphrodisias. Statue of Flavius Palmatus, vicar of Asia (fifth
     century A.D.)
76   Hierapolis. Triumphal Arch and Main Street
77   Aphrodisias. Sarcophagus
78   Aphrodisias. Bull's Head
79   Hierapolis. Petrified Cascades
80   Hierapolis. The Sacred Pool
81   Hierapolis. Sculpture in the Theatre
82   Hierapolis. The Plutonium
83   Hierapolis. Burial tumuli
84   Laodiceia. Water-tower, showing remains of pipes
85   Laodiceia. The Aqueduct
86   Amyzon. The City Wall

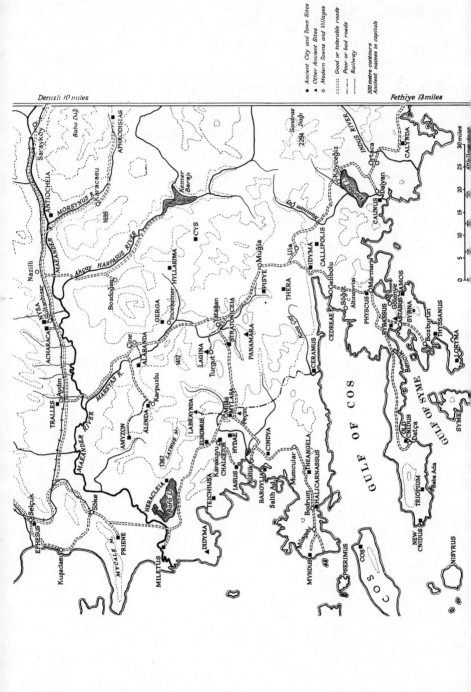

Denizli 10 miles   Fethiye 13 miles

■ Ancient City and Town Sites
▲ Other Ancient Sites
○ Modern Towns and Villages
⋯⋯⋯ Good or tolerable roads
⋯⋯⋯ Poor or bad roads
━━━ Railway
━━━ 500 metre contours
CAPITALS Ancient names in capitals

Sarayköy
Baba Dağ
APHRODISIAS
Karacasu
ANTIOCHEIA
MORSYNUS M.
1699
MAEANDER
Nazilli
Akçay HARPASUS RIVER
Bozdoğan
NYSA
Sultanhisar
ACHARACA
CYS
Kemer Barajı
Sandras 2294 Dağı
INDUS RIVER
Köyceğiz
Ortaca
CALYNDA
HYLLARIMA
GERGA
Incekemer
Çine
ALABANDA
1412
Çatağan
PISYE
Muğla
Ulla
DYMA
CALLIPOLIS
Gelibolu
CEDREAE
Söğüt
Altınyayla
PHYSCUS
Marmaris
BYBASSUS
Göltürk
TRALLES
Aydın
MARSYAS R.
Karpuzlu
LAGINA
Turgut
STRATONICEIA
PANAMARA
THERA
CERAMIUS
Koca çay
CASTABUS
LAMOS
SYRNA
Bozburun
HYDISANUS
MYCALE M.
MAEANDER RIVER
AMYZON
ALINDA
367 LATMUS M.
LABRAYNDA
EUROMUS
Milas
Beçin
CINDYA
THEANGELA
AMOS
Bencik
OLD CNIDUS
Datça
LORYMA
SYME
EPHESUS
Selçuk
Söke
HERACLEIA
Bafa G.
TEICHIUSSA
Karakuyu
CHALCETOR
IASUS
HYDAE
Küllük
BARGYLIA
Salih Ad.
Müsgebi
Mumcular
HALICARNASSUS
Bodrum
MYNDUS
GULF OF SYME
TRIOPIUM
Baba Ada
NEW CNIDUS
PRIENE
Kuşadası
DIDYMA
MILETUS
PSERIMUS
COS
GULF OF COS
NISYRUS
GERGA
PANAMARA

GULF OF COS

C O S

30 miles

List of Illustrations in Text

1	Districts of Asia Minor	4
2	Plan of Mylasa. *After A. and T. Akarca*	21
3	Ceramus. Sculptured Base	34
4	Ceramus. Inscription at Kurşunlu Yapı	35
5	Plan of Kuyruklu Kale. *After W. Radt*	37
6	Plan of Labraynda. *After the Swedish Publication*	42
7	Labraynda. Male Sphinx, in the depot	46
8	Plan of Iasus	55
9	Bargylia. Causeway and Acropolis Hill	64
10	Plan of Bargylia	65
11	Plan of Stratoniceia. *After P. Trémaux, 1874*	70
12	Lagina. Plan of the Temple	74
13	Plan of Halicarnassus	87
14	Bodrum. Stone Anchor in Museum	89
15	Map of the Myndus Peninsula	91
16	Myndus. Harbour and Peninsula from the Acropolis Hill	93
17	Plan of Myndus	94
18	Plan of Pedasa (Gökçeler)	96
19	Plan of Alâzeytin Kale (whole complex). *After W. Radt*	105
20	Plan of Alâzeytin Kale (circular compound farm buildings). *After W. Radt*	106
21	Theangela. Plan of the Fort at D (Tetrapyrgon)	107
22	Plan of Theangela	108
23	The Cnidian Aphrodite	116
24	Plan of New Cnidus	124
25	Loryma. Plan of the Castle	134
26	Loryma. Pyramidal Block	136
27	Plan of Caunus	148
28	Plan of Alabanda	156
29	Alabanda. Theatre	157
30	Alabanda. Council-House	158

31	Plan of Alinda	163
32	Alinda. The Second Acropolis	167
33	Gerga. Plan of the Village Centre	172
34	Gerga. Plan of the Temple	173
35	Gerga. Statue	175
36	Gerga. Base	175
37	Plan of Nysa	181
38	Nysa. Plan of First Floor of the Library. *After Graefinghoff*	184
39	Nysa. Dolphin and Boy at the School at Sultanhisar	185
40	Acharaca. Plan of the Temple (conjectural)	187
41	Plan of Aphrodisias. *By courtesy of Professor K. T. Erim*	191
42	Aphrodisias. Part of the Inscription over the North Gate	192
43	Aphrodisias. Plan of the Baths (approximate only)	197
44	Map of the Environs of Denizli	200
45	Plan of Hierapolis	205
46	Hierapolis. Relief in the Theatre	209
47	Hierapolis. Plan of the Martyrium of St Philip	210
48	Plan of Laodiceia	218
49	Laodiceia. Plan of the Nymphaeum	220

Glossary

Acroterium. An ornament placed at one of the angles of a pediment.

Analemma. The end wall of the cavea of a theatre.

Anta. A short projecting wall, treated as a pilaster; *in antis*, 'between antae', used of the columns of a temple or other building.

Ashlar. Masonry of squared blocks in horizontal courses.

Basilica. [1] In Roman architecture, an oblong building with central nave flanked by colonnaded aisles and an apse at one end, used for public business. [2] A church of this form.

Caesareum. A building devoted to the worship of the Roman emperors (the Imperial cult).

Cavea. The auditorium of a theatre.

Cella. The main chamber of a temple, in which the cult-statue stood.

Conventus. A provincial court of justice, or the place where this was held.

Deme. A subdivision of a city's territory; a village.

Dentil frieze. A frieze consisting of a row of alternate square projections and square spaces.

Diazoma. A horizontal passage across the cavea of a theatre.

Epistyle. Architectural members laid on top of a row of columns.

Exedra. A semicircular recess or alcove furnished with a bench.

Geometric. The more elaborate style of decorated pottery which succeeded protogeometric and lasted from about 900 to 700 B.C. Frequently the whole pot was covered with bands of geometric patterning, and stylized animal and human figures begin to appear towards the end of the period.

Hellenistic period. The period from the time of Alexander to that of Augustus.

Hypocaust. Under-floor heating. See *Aegean Turkey,* p. 191.

Glossary

Isodomic. Laid in courses of equal, or almost equal, height; applied to ashlar masonry.

Naiskos. A term used to denote the central chamber of a Greek temple, especially one of modest size (cf. *cella*).

Neocorus. Title given to a city by virtue of the possession of a temple of the Imperial cult.

Odeum. A small theatre-like building used for musical recitals, lectures, or rehearsals.

Opisthodomus. The rear chamber of a temple, often used to house the temple-treasure.

Palaestra. An open court for athletic exercise.

Parodoi. The side-entrances to a theatre, between the cavea and the stage-building.

Pediment. A triangular space like a gable, set over a colonnade or other architectural feature.

Peribolus. The enclosure round a temple.

Pilaster. A rectangular column.

Podium. A solid base on which a structure is erected.

Pronaos. The front chamber of a temple, usually on the east.

Propylon. The entrance gate of a sacred enclosure leading to a temple.

Proscenium. A colonnade erected between the orchestra and the stage-buildings of a Greek theatre.

Proto-geometric. The style of pottery prevalent in the archaic Greek world between 1050 and 900 B.C. The decoration is characterized by simple bands of geometric patterning between large reserved areas.

Return Wall. A wall turning at right-angles from the end of another wall.

Skene. The stage-building which formed the backdrop of a Greek theatre.

Stele. A narrow slab of stone set upright and generally bearing decoration or writing or both.

Stylobate. The stone pavement on which a row of columns stands.

Tetrastoon. An open square surrounded by four stoas, or colonnades.

1 Historical

Who were the Carians?

Ancient Greek belief was that they lived originally on the islands of the Aegean and from there migrated to the mainland of Asia. The Cretan account, as reported by Herodotus, was that they were subjects of Minos, king of Crete, not tributary but manning his fleet when required to do so, and were called at that time Lelegians; later, when the Dorians and Ionians spread from Greece to the islands, they expelled the Carians to the coast of Asia. Strabo's account is similar. Thucydides agrees that they were islanders and says they practised piracy, but disagrees in regarding them as having been expelled by Minos himself. For their occupation of the islands he advances a piece of archaeological evidence: when the island of Delos was 'purified' during the Peloponnesian War—that is, all burials were removed from it—more than half the dead were recognized as Carians both from the manner of their burial and from the armour buried with them. This evidence has not in fact been confirmed by modern archaeology; the early culture of the Cyclades (of which Delos is one) shows a character not Carian but Cretan and Mycenaean.

The Carians themselves, however, would have none of this. They maintained that they had always lived on the mainland and had always been called Carians, and they advanced their own evidence: there was at Mylasa an ancient sanctuary of Carian Zeus, to which, besides Carians, only Mysians and Lydians were admitted; these, they claimed, were historically akin to themselves, and had never been other than mainlanders. Scholars today are much inclined to believe that in this matter the Carians were in the right.

However this may be, the Carians in early times appear to have been a maritime folk; there was in antiquity a strong tradition of a 'Carian thalassocracy', dated by Eusebius (about A.D. 300) to the latter part of the eighth century B.C. Nothing whatever is recorded

1

either of the leaders of this rather nebulous sea-power or of its achievements.

In Homer's *Iliad* the Carians appear as allies of the Trojans; he calls them 'barbarous of speech' and places them around Miletus and Mt Mycale. Homer, as Thucydides noted, never speaks of 'barbarians' in the usual sense of non-Greeks; presumably then he is not distinguishing them from other Trojan allies who spoke Greek, but merely refers to the exceptional harshness of their language. (As a coincidence it may be remarked that the dialect of Muğla today is the harshest in the west of Turkey.) Strabo rejects this explanation, but only on the inadequate grounds that Carian included many Greek words mixed with it.

Homer's location of the Carians around Miletus and Mycale is confirmed by Herodotus, who places Miletus, Myus, and Priene in Caria and, writing in the present tense, says that they speak a common language, which was presumably Carian. Now in Herodotus' time, and no doubt also in Homer's, these were Greek cities and members of the Ionian League, whose official language was certainly Greek; evidently there was still a considerable element of the former Carian population who continued to speak in their own tongue. The Milesians themselves, according to Pausanias, believed that their country was originally occupied by Carians, until some Cretan refugees from Minos arrived under their leader Miletus, after which the two races merged.[1] In any case these cities were normally reckoned Ionian, and the boundaries of Caria were quite clearly defined, on the north by the Maeander and on the south by the present lake of Köyceğiz.

Closely associated with the Carians at all times were the Lelegians. In the ancient literature these people appear in many parts of the Greek world, east and west of the Aegean; but in many cases they were used, like the 'Pelasgians', merely as a stopgap, and were put in when in fact nothing was known. A certain amount, however, seems to be established firmly enough. Herodotus and Strabo agree that Lelegian is an earlier name for the Carians; elsewhere they are distinguished, and in fact there can be no doubt that they were distinct. For Homer they are clearly so; he places them far from Miletus in the southern part of the Troad, where their king, Altes, holds the city of Pedasus on the Satnioeis. From here, after the Trojan War, they moved southward, leaving traces of their presence on the way,[2] till they settled finally in the Carian country around Halicarnassus. Here they founded eight cities, of which the ruins, with their distinctive masonry, still remain; of these some account is given below in Chapter 10. One of them bears the name Pedasa, an obvious echo of the city of Altes.

In their relations with the Carians all accounts agree that they held a subordinate position. Pausanias calls them 'a part of the Carian race'; Strabo says they served the Carians as soldiers and became scattered all over Greece, so that the nation disappeared; Philip of Theangela, itself a Lelegian city, calls them servants of the Carians and compares them with the Spartan helots. Culturally too they seem to have been inferior; not a single Lelegian inscription has ever been found, and to judge by the ruins of their cities their interests were confined to the mere business of living and dying; nothing is found but houses, walls, and tombs.[3] Some attempts have been made by modern scholars to explain the name, of which perhaps the most attractive connects it with the Luwian *lulahi*, 'barbarian'; but nothing is certain. In the absence of inscriptions their language is equally unknown.

It is not impossible that the Lycians also were for a time at home in Caria. It was generally agreed in antiquity that the Lycians came from Crete with Sarpedon, brother of Minos, when he was expelled by the latter; and a tradition with the respectable authority of Ephorus recorded that they made their way first to Miletus, of which they were the founders. From here they will have moved, perhaps some centuries later, to the country which they finally occupied. Now the Lycians called themselves in early times Termilae, and some scholars have thought that the syllable mil-, recurring in Miletus, Mylasa, and Milyas (the old name for Lycia), marks their passage southwards. If the statement that they founded the Carian town of Idrias, later Stratoniceia, has any real basis, it will go to support this theory.

One or two Carian customs are mentioned. They are said to have taught the Greeks the use of crests on helmets and of handles on shields, which previously were worn slung over the shoulder; and it was their practice not to take their women with them to dinner. This last, however strange it may have seemed to the Greeks, would raise no eyebrows in Turkey.

The Carian language is still not perfectly understood. This is chiefly due to the paucity of the material; only about three dozen inscriptions in the Carian language and script have so far been discovered, many of them very short and fragmentary. In recent years some progress has been made towards decipherment, but what is most needed are lengthier texts than those we have at present. The script is certainly alphabetic, not syllabic; some of the letter-

3

forms are identical with Greek, others are peculiar to Carian. It is still disputed whether the language is Indo-Germanic or not, and the meaning of hardly a single word has been convincingly determined.

Of the successive waves of migration, Aeolian, Ionian, and Dorian, from Greece to Asia after the Trojan War, the Dorian was the last and southernmost. It occupied the islands of Rhodes and Cos and a few places on the mainland. A league of six cities was formed, known as the Dorian hexapolis; it included Cos and the three cities of Rhodes, and on the mainland Cnidus and Halicarnassus, and it met periodically at the festival of Triopian Apollo on the territory of Cnidus. Other Dorian settlements, such as Iasus, were not included. The degree of fusion between the newcomers and the native population seems to have varied. At Halicarnassus the Carian names known from the inscriptions form half of the total, whereas at Cnidus they are virtually unknown.

But this Greek colonization touched only the coast. The interior remained Carian, and Caria was a land of villages. When the country begins to feature in our historical records, we find a few places that may fairly be called cities—Mylasa, Alabanda, Alinda, Ceramus, and no doubt others—and for the rest a great number of villages grouped in local federations, each containing a principal village

Fig. 1 Districts of Asia Minor

4

together with the smaller places in the neighbourhood. By the sixth century at least there had developed also some kind of national federation; at least, as Herodotus tells us, when danger threatened from the Persians, the Carians met to decide their policy at a spot called White Pillars, which appears to have been a regular meeting-place. The common sanctuary of the federation was the temple of Zeus Carius at Mylasa. In the earlier records we hear simply of 'the Carians'; the word 'federation' occurs only later.

In the course of the seventh and sixth centuries the Lydian kings had subjugated all the Greek cities of the west coast, including the Dorian cities of Caria. In 546, however, Croesus, the last king of Lydia, was defeated by the Persians and his kingdom came to an end. The Persians at once set about replacing the Lydian rule with their own, and sent to the west coast an army under their general Harpagus. Having dealt with Ionia, Harpagus advanced into Caria, where he met with opposition only from the little Lelegian town of Pedasa; the Greek cities gave no trouble.

A generation later the Ionians organized a revolt against the Persian king, and with some hesitation the Carians joined them. The revolt was wretchedly conducted and failed utterly, ending ignominiously with the capture of Miletus in 494. The Persians then sent an army south under Daurises to suppress the rebel Carians. At their meeting at White Pillars the Carians decided on resistance, but were defeated beside the river Marsyas; reassembling at Labraynda, where some Milesians joined them, they resolved to fight again. A second defeat cost them the loss of Mylasa, but still did not break their spirit; when Daurises advanced southward to attack the Carian towns around Halicarnassus—and no doubt primarily the Pedasans, who had given trouble before—he contrived to become benighted, and his force was ambushed by the Carians and destroyed.

A few years later came Darius' invasion of Greece, which failed at Marathon, and ten years later again, in 480, the second attempt by Xerxes, defeated at Salamis and Plataea. The Athenians thereupon established their maritime league, known as the Delian Confederacy, which later turned into an Athenian empire; in this virtually all the cities and towns of the Aegean coast, Caria included, were enrolled. Each was required to pay a fixed sum in tribute (or in a few cases supply ships), with the avowed object of preventing a revival of the Persian power on the coast. The sums at which the various places were assessed give a fair indication of their relative wealth and importance at that time.

The defeat of Athens by Sparta in the Peloponnesian War (404 B.C.) put an end to the Delian Confederacy. The Spartans attempted for a time to keep the coast of Asia under their own control; but they had not the qualities to manage an overseas empire, and in 387 B.C., by the treaty known as the King's Peace, all the cities of Asia were recognized as belonging once more to the Persians.

About this time, following an Athenian naval victory over the Spartans in 394 B.C., a group of Aegean cities formed an alliance among themselves, apparently with the object of securing independence from Persians, Spartans, and Athenians alike. The members were Rhodes, Samos, Ephesus, Cnidus, Iasus, and Byzantium. This league, if it may be so called, is not recorded by any historian, but is known only by the coinage which it issued. It did not survive for long; even before the King's Peace it seems to have been dissolved.

The vast Persian Empire was divided into regions called satrapies, and the first satrap of Caria was a man of Mylasa by the name of Hyssaldomus; he was succeeded by his son Hecatomnos, and in 377 by the latter's son Mausolus. Mausolus was an able, energetic, and ambitious man, and he took advantage of the great distance of his satrapy from the Persian capital to make himself virtually an independent ruler, though he never actually took the title of king. He was not unopposed in Caria itself, for we hear of plots against his life, and on one occasion in 367 'the Carians'—that is evidently the Carian federation—sent an envoy to the Great King, possibly to complain of his conduct. The King, however, took Mausolus' part, and in the other cases the plotters were punished with death or exile.

Mausolus' capital was at Mylasa, the principal city of inland Caria and his own home town. Seeing, however, the much finer position of Halicarnassus, he decided to rebuild that city on a much grander scale and make it his headquarters. This was one of the first steps in the great plan to which his life was devoted, nothing less than the Hellenization of the whole of Caria. The old Lelegian towns of Myndus and Syangela he rebuilt on new sites with a greatly enlarged area; the others he suppressed and transferred their inhabitants to Halicarnassus. At the extremities of his satrapy he fortified Latmus and Caunus with splendid walls.[4] He was active also in the Greek cities of the coast; we have decrees passed in his honour at Iasus and even at Ionian Erythrae, though they give no details, but merely refer to him as a benefactor. Inner Caria, too, would no doubt have been treated in similar fashion, but Mausolus died com-

6

paratively young in 353 B.C., and this part of his work remained uncompleted.

Nor was much done in this way by the members of his family who followed him. He had two sisters and two brothers; the elder sister, Artemisia, was also his wife, and it was she who built his tomb, the Mausoleum. They had no children, and Artemisia succeeded to the rule of Caria; within a few years, however, she died of grief, and the elder brother Idrieus came to power. He married the younger sister Ada, but he, too, quickly died, whereupon the younger brother Pixodarus expelled Ada to exile in Alinda and took command himself. It seems that Pixodarus had not the title of satrap, but ruled unofficially; the official Persian appointee was a man of the name of Orontobates, and Pixodarus called him in to share the government. When Pixodarus, too, died before long, Orontobates was left in control, and this was the position when Alexander arrived in 334.

Alexander's conquest of the Persian Empire proceeded with remarkable speed and success. Only in a few places was he vigorously resisted, and one of these was Halicarnassus. After its capture (below, pp. 83–4) he brought back Ada, with whom he had already had friendly dealings (below, p. 161–2), and handed over the whole of Caria to her.

How long Ada's restored rule lasted is not known. By the time that Alexander's successors had begun to fight for the country, she had disappeared. Alexander died at Babylon in 323, leaving the vast territory he had conquered without a ruler. His generals proceeded to divide it among themselves, but before long they grew dissatisfied with the region allotted to them, and for a generation they warred constantly against one another. Prominent among them, and among the most ambitious, were Antigonus and Lysimachus, but their successes were not lasting; eventually three permanent kingdoms were established, those of Macedonia with Greece, of Egypt under the Ptolemies, and of Syria under the Seleucids, with kings named either Seleucus or Antiochus. Western Asia Minor, not falling clearly within any of these, continued to be a bone of contention among all of them.

To these three powers two others must be added, namely the kingdom of Pergamum, established soon after 280 B.C., with kings named Eumenes or Attalus, and later the Rhodians, who had built up a considerable sea-power. The history of Asia Minor during the third century is exceedingly confused, and consists largely of a struggle between the Ptolemies and Seleucids; their main interest

7

was naturally concentrated on the Greek cities, whose support was useful to them, and many places changed hands more than once. Some account of the fortunes of the individual cities will be found below.

As the power of Egypt and Syria weakened during the course of the century, the others began to take a hand. The Rhodians had acquired a considerable area of territory on the mainland opposite their island, and Attalus I of Pergamum, after breaking the Seleucid authority, had by about 227 B.C. extended his rule as far south as Caria, though without establishing himself firmly. At this point, perhaps in order to check any further progress by Attalus, Antigonus III of Macedon, called Doson, made an expedition into Caria. This was not a conquest; he met with no opposition and was well received by the cities, which acted independently. In effect he found the country without a ruler, apart from the somewhat enigmatic figure of Olympichus. This man had been a general of Seleucus II, and had held the country around Mylasa in his name. About 245 B.C. Seleucus decided to grant Mylasa freedom and ordered Olympichus to evacuate the district. This, however, he failed to do, for whatever reason; instead, he seems to have made himself into an independent dynast. Antigonus left him undisturbed, and when Philip V became king of Macedon in 220, Olympichus maintained good relations with him. His authority was in any case very limited, and the cities did not recognize him as their ruler. How long he lived is not known, but by 201 at least he has disappeared from the scene.

In that year Philip himself came to Caria. By a series of raids in the Aegean and the Black Sea he had incurred the hostility of Rhodes and Pergamum, and these combined to defeat him in a sea-battle off Chios. Philip thereupon took an army into Caria, where at least he expected to be well received, in view of the previous good relations established by Antigonus. His campaign, however, was badly mismanaged; he found himself beleaguered in Bargylia by the Pergamene fleet for the whole winter, and was glad to escape the following spring (below, p. 63).

It is during the third century that we first hear of a second Carian federation, known as the Chrysaoric League. This was common to all Carians and was organized on the old village-system, so that each city's voting strength depended on the number of villages on its territory. The League met to discuss its affairs at the sanctuary of Zeus Chrysaoreus near Stratoniceia (below, p. 68). Its relation to the old Carian League is not clear, but since the latter continued at least down to the first century B.C., the two federations must have existed simultaneously. When the Chrysaoric League was first founded is not known; it may well have been older than the foundation of Stratoniceia, but the earliest actual evidence for it is a newly discovered inscription of 267 B.C.

Philip V's restless energy soon brought him into conflict with the growing power of the Romans, who were just beginning to interest themselves in the affairs of Greece. In 197 B.C. a pitched battle ended with the defeat of Philip, after which the Roman commander ostentatiously declared that all Greek cities, both in Europe and in Asia, should be free.

Antiochus III of Syria, however, was not impressed by this proclamation. In the same year, 197, in a rapid campaign he overran the south and much of the west coast of Asia Minor in a determined effort to regain the old Seleucid empire. His activity had the result of bringing the Roman armies for the first time into Asia, and in 190 at the crucial battle of Magnesia-under-Sipylus Antiochus was utterly defeated. By the treaty of Apamea which followed, Caria and Lycia were given to the Rhodians and the rest of western Asia Minor to Eumenes of Pergamum.

Rhodian control continued for twenty years and was bitterly resented from the start. The Lycians especially resisted continuously, and in 167 B.C. the Carians, too, organized a revolt (below, p. 16). The revolt failed, but in the same year the Roman Senate issued a decree declaring Caria and Lycia free.

Freedom lasted until 133 B.C., when Attalus III bequeathed the kingdom of Pergamum to Rome. This unprecedented gesture, which has been compared with that of a captain scuttling his own ship, was not allowed to pass unchallenged. A certain Aristonicus, claiming kinship with the royal house, at once attempted to secure the kingship for himself. After some successes he was suppressed by the Romans, who thereupon, in 129 B.C., organized the Pergamene territory as the province of Asia. In this province Caria (but not Lycia) was included.

The Roman provincial government was highly unsatisfactory, chiefly owing to the cupidity of the governors and of the Roman merchants and bankers who found abundant opportunities for enriching themselves. Accordingly, when in 88 B.C. the king of Pontus on the Black Sea, Mithridates VI, decided to overrun the province, he was in most places welcomed as a liberator. By his command all the Romans in the province, together with their families, were ruthlessly butchered, to the number, it is said, of 80,000 persons. The

Roman defence was at first feeble, but in 85 Mithridates was finally worsted in the field and expelled from Asia. His second attempt twelve years later did not reach as far as Caria.

The civil wars in Rome during the first century B.C. cannot be recounted in detail here. The murder of Julius Caesar in 44 B.C. was followed by a bad time for the provincials. The 'tyrannicides' Brutus and Cassius, finding themselves for the moment in supreme power, and regarding the provinces in the usual way as a convenient source of wealth and manpower, proceeded to the east to raise money and troops. Back in Rome, however, Mark Antony had roused the people's feelings against the murderers, and in 43 he, together with Octavian, the great-nephew of Caesar, and Lepidus, another of Caesar's supporters, were appointed 'Triumvirs for the ordering of the State'. Their first act was to proscribe the enemies of Caesar. Brutus and Cassius, faced with inevitable war, redoubled their exactions from the provincials, requiring from them a levy equal to ten years' normal taxes. The clash came in 42 B.C. at the battle of Philippi, where Antony and Octavian were victorious, both Brutus and Cassius being killed.

The victors then divided the world between them, the east falling to Antony. This change proved no blessing to the provincials. Antony at once adopted an arrogant, quasi-royal style, taking the title of 'Latter-day Dionysus', and among other things repeating Brutus's demands for the equivalent of ten years' taxation. Before long, however, he fell under the spell of Cleopatra, queen of Egypt, and betook himself to the pleasures of the palace at Alexandria.

Asia was thus left unguarded, and this afforded an opportunity for an event without parallel in Roman history. Brutus and Cassius, when the showdown with the Triumvirs was imminent, in their desire to raise forces had gone so far as to approach the Parthians, Rome's most formidable enemy, for assistance. They sent as their envoy a young man by the name of Labienus. He proved a good negotiator, but before he could bring them aid from this source Brutus and Cassius were dead. Nevertheless, the Parthian king was persuaded to send a force against the Romans, and Labienus was put at its head (40 B.C.). The undefended province of Asia quickly fell a prey to the barbarians under their Roman commander, though resistance was offered in a few places (below, pp. 17, 214); Caria in particular suffered severely. In face of this inroad Antony found himself obliged to leave Cleopatra's side; in 39 he sent a strong force to Caria to deal with it. Labienus hastily withdrew to Cilicia, whither he was pursued, brought to battle, defeated, and put to death.

Free again to return to the charms of Alexandria, Antony proceeded to excesses which finally led to his downfall. Led on by the
ambitious Cleopatra, he declared her children by Caesar and himself nominal rulers of the various regions of the east, and himself as
virtual monarch of the inhabited world. This was too much for
Octavian, who resolved that his old ally must be suppressed. War
followed, and at the sea-battle of Actium in 31 B.C., at which
Cleopatra was present, she and Antony were decisively defeated.

This was the end of the Roman Republic; in 27 B.C. the Empire
was founded, with Octavian, who then received the title of Augustus,
as the first Emperor. The condition of the eastern provinces at once
improved. To Caria, which had suffered more than most, the new
Emperor showed himself a good friend; and in general, from now
on during the long period of peace which followed, the cities were
able to develop their industries and resources and conduct their
local affairs in comfort. They were still, as before, under the orders
of the governor, except nominally those which were recognized as
'free', 'friends and allies of the Roman People'; but we now hear
far less of the exactions and injustices which had disfigured the
Republican administration. Most of them grew rich and prosperous,
and adorned themselves with the fine buildings whose ruins stand
today.

In Caria the smaller, inland cities were at last able to enjoy the
benefits of civilization which Mausolus had not lived to confer on
them. Their inhabitants were mainly the old Carian stock; the
official language, since Alexander's conquest, was Greek; and as
time went on, Roman merchants and others made their way
further and further into the interior. Brigandage was still a menace,
and continued unruliness in the remoter parts required the establishment of Roman military colonies, though none are known in
Caria itself. But the general picture, for the first two centuries of
the Empire, is one of contentment and prosperity. Of the provincial
Commonalties and their relations with the Emperor, of the worship
of the Emperors, and of the multitudinous festivals celebrated
annually or quadrennially all over the east, enough has been said
elsewhere.[5] In such a long period free from war the cities had
naturally little individual history. For the most part an occasional
earthquake or a visit from the Emperor is about all there is to
record.

Decline set in in the third century. Under a rapid succession of
Emperors, some barbarian, many incompetent, most short-lived,
the power of the Empire was gradually weakened. The process was

accelerated in the middle of the century, first by an appalling plague which raged over the whole Empire for fifteen years, and second by the troublesome inroads of the Goths, who at one time made their way as far south as Miletus. Towards the end of the century the Emperor Diocletian made a reorganization of the provinces, by which Caria became for the first time a separate province.

Christianity was on the whole slow to take hold in Caria. The region was not visited by St Paul, and the only early churches seem to be those of Laodiceia and Colossae on the extreme fringe of the country. It was not, it appears, until Christianity was officially adopted by Constantine that the new religion made any real headway in Caria. The subsequent fortunes of the country belong to Byzantine and Turkish history and are not the business of the present work.

Notes

1 Minos was traditionally dated to the middle of the fifteenth century.
2 Miletus, for example, was called Lelegeïs.
3 Even sanctuaries are very rare.
4 For Latmus and the later city of Heracleia see *Aegean Turkey*, p. 211; for Caunus, see below, p. 143.
5 See *Aegean Turkey*, pp. 16–17.

2 Mylasa

Only three cities of inland Caria are considered 'noteworthy' by
Strabo; they are Mylasa, Alabanda, and Stratoniceia. The first two
of these names, with their old Anatolian endings in -asa and -nda, are
sufficient proof of very early foundation; Stratoniceia, on the other
hand, Greek in name and foundation, was not yet 300 years old in
Strabo's day.

A theory held by certain scholars was mentioned above[1] which
connects the name of Mylasa with the passage of the Lycians from
Miletus to their final home in the south. This theory is by no means
proved, and there is nothing else to suggest a Lycian origin for
Mylasa, which is indeed generally thought of as the most Carian
of all cities. Stephanus of Byzantium in his *Ethnica* (below, p. 170)
says that she took her name from a certain Mylasus, son of Chrysaor
and a descendant of Sisyphus and Aeolus—an impressive but un-
substantial genealogy. Apart from this obvious fabrication nothing
is recorded of the city's origin. Its earliest historical mention is at
the beginning of the seventh century, when a Mylasan by name
Arselis is said to have helped Gyges in his contest for the throne of
Lydia; even at that early date Carians were serving as mercenaries.

Under Persian rule from the middle of the sixth century the
individual cities were governed by tyrants appointed with Persian
approval, and in 500 B.C. the tyrant of Mylasa was a certain Oliatus,
son of Ibanollis. In the Persian fleet led by Aristagoras, tyrant of
Miletus, against the island of Naxos[2] this Oliatus served as a ship's
captain; following the failure of the attack Aristagoras determined
upon revolt against the Great King, and began by capturing by
means of a trick a number of the captains, tyrants of their various
cities, including Oliatus. What was done with him does not appear,
as he is not mentioned again, but Mylasa, like most of the Carians,
joined in the revolt; and a few years later, when the Persian army sent
to suppress them was ambushed and destroyed, the Carian leader
was a brother of Oliatus named Heraclides. Whether this man had

13

succeeded his brother as tyrant of Mylasa is doubtful; he is heard of once again, when he is said to have fought at Artemisium. Scholars are divided in opinion as to whether this refers to the battle fought by the Greeks against the Persians in 480 B.C. or to another Artemisium in Spain; in any case it seems evident Heraclides felt it wise to escape from Persian vengeance by withdrawing from Asia.

In the Confederacy of Delos, founded in 478, Mylasa may or may not have been an original member; her situation comparatively far inland, and the flight of Heraclides, suggest the probability that she had fallen back into Persian hands. Later she was included, and from 450 to 440 paid regularly a tribute of one talent or rather less. This assessment, though lower than that of several of the Lelegian towns on the Myndus peninsula, indicates that Mylasa was even at this early date the leading city in her own district; her neighbours Euromus, Hydae, and Chalcetor were all assessed at a much lower figure. After 440 the Athenians removed all these places from the list of members, and by the end of the century, if not much earlier, the whole of inland Caria was once more under Persian control.

The days of Mylasa's greatness followed in the early fourth century under the dynasts (officially Persian satraps) Hyssaldomus, Hecatomnos, and Mausolus; Mylasa was at once their home town and their capital. The spectacular career of Mausolus has been described above, but his rule was not unopposed at home. An inscription found at Mylasa records three decrees passed by the Mylasans in 367, 361, and 355 B.C.; we read in the first that a certain Arlissis, sent by the Carian League on an embassy to the Great King, abused his trust and plotted against Mausolus, for which he was put to death and his property made over to Mausolus himself; in the second, that the sons of Peldemos had insulted the statue of Hecatomnos and had their goods put up to public sale; in the third that one Manitas son of Pactyes had attempted the life of Mausolus during the annual festival at Labraynda and had been lynched on the spot, that a further investigation had revealed that another man named Thyssus was involved in the plot, and that the property of both was sold for the benefit of Mausolus.

Among the many changes introduced by the Hecatomnids, and especially Mausolus, it is not improbable that we should count the foundation of the city on its permanent site at Milâs. There are reasons for believing that until the fourth century Mylasa stood on the great rock of Peçin, some three miles south of Milâs. This question will be discussed more fully below, but it may be noticed here that the site at Milâs is a most unusual one for an early Carian

14

city, quite unlike the hilltop positions that were generally chosen. Her situation on the plain at the foot of a considerable mountain was thought surprising in antiquity, and a certain Roman governor is said to have exclaimed, 'If the man who founded this city felt no fear, had he at least no shame?' On the other hand, the proximity of the adjacent mountain had the advantage that it afforded an abundant supply of good-quality marble, so that the city was unusually well equipped with fine public buildings. A professional harpist named Stratonicus, whose *bons mots* were famous, once gave a recital in Mylasa, and noticing the great number of temples, prefaced it not with the usual words 'Oyez ye peoples', but with the change of a single letter, 'Oyez ye temples'—as it might be 'Oyez ye steeples'.

In connexion with Alexander's campaign no special mention is made of Mylasa, except that the Athenian statesman Phocion, whose policy was consistently pro-Macedonian, is said to have been offered by Alexander the revenues of four cities in Asia Minor, one of which was Mylasa. Phocion, however, declined.

Even after the transference by Mausolus of the capital to Halicarnassus, and the great enlargement of that city, Mylasa continued to be the chief centre of her own district. She had from ancient times possessed the sanctuary at Labraynda, and the recent Swedish excavations on that site have thrown considerable light on conditions in the third century. Under Ptolemy II the region was claimed as part of the Egyptian empire, and its affairs were conducted by the Chrysaoric League with Ptolemaic support; the League may possibly for a time have held its meetings at Mylasa, before being moved to Stratoniceia. But the Egyptian control was very weak, and Antiochus II of Syria (261–246 B.C.) had little difficulty in reconquering the country; and one of the first acts of his successor, Seleucus II, was to declare Mylasa a free city. Not that this meant in practice very much. 'Freedom' implied really little more than freedom from occupation by a garrison and the right to administer its own territory, subject always to interference at the king's pleasure. But Seleucid rule was hardly stronger than the Ptolemaic, and some twenty years later the Macedonian king Antigonus Doson (229–221 B.C.) occupied Caria. He was well received at Mylasa, and friendly relations with Macedonia continued during the early years of his successor, Philip V. A letter from Philip, written in 220, was found at Labraynda confirming the Mylasan possession of the sanctuary. Later, in 201 B.C., after Philip's defeat at sea by the combined fleets of Rhodes and Pergamum, he made his way to Caria; during the

15

following winter, beleaguered in Bargylia and at his wits' end for the means of feeding his army, he was helped by the Mylasans with supplies. Failing, however, to obtain further assistance, he turned upon the city and made an attack on it, though without success. It appears that the Mylasans had reverted to the Seleucid cause under Antiochus III, who a few years afterwards occupied the country almost without resistance.

Some years later, in 189 B.C., after the defeat of Antiochus, when the Roman delegates at Apamea gave Caria to the Rhodians, they expressly declared Mylasa to be free from payment of tribute. Despite this relief the Mylasans were no more pleased than the other Carians with Rhodian rule, and in 167 B.C. they organized a rebellion. Seizing 'the cities in Euromus' (that is, Euromus itself, Olymus, Chalcetor, and perhaps some others) they obtained help from Alabanda; but their combined forces were promptly engaged and defeated by the Rhodians at Orthosia. The rebellion was evidently spreading, for Orthosia lies away to the north-east beyond the river Marsyas. But all this was at once rendered meaningless by the Roman decree in the same year that the Rhodians should withdraw and Caria be left free.

During the comparatively peaceful period which followed, Mylasa, now somewhat overshadowed by her neighbour Stratoniceia, took occasion to improve her standing. Already as early as 209 B.C. she had requested and obtained from Miletus a treaty of 'isopolity', that is a grant of reciprocal citizenship; she now proceeded to bring all the cities in her neighbourhood under her own control by means of treaties of 'sympolity'. The men of Euromus, Chalcetor, Hydae, Olymus, and Labraynda now became citizens of Mylasa, and were allotted to one of the three tribes of that city. These tribes were a very ancient institution at Mylasa; back in the fourth century we find decrees ratified by 'Mausolus and the three tribes', and their names are thoroughly Carian: the Otorcondeis, the Conodorcondeis, and the Hyarbesytae. They were subdivided into clans, with equally outlandish names, and these again into families.

Quarrels about territory were always common between Greek cities, and in 143 B.C. when Priene and Magnesia disputed a piece of land, Mylasa was selected by the Roman praetor to act as adjudicator. This was something of a compliment for a Carian city, and shows the extent to which she was by this time accepted into the Hellenic sphere. Mylasa herself had about the same time a similar quarrel with Stratoniceia, which was referred for settlement to Rome.

In the Roman province of Asia, Mylasa, like Alabanda, was

chosen as the seat of a *conventus*, that is a centre where the provincial governor held assizes; and in general relations with Rome
were good and friendly. Nevertheless, Mylasa could not escape from
the effects of the unsatisfactory government under the Roman
Republic, and by the middle of the first century B.C. the city was in
debt to a Roman banker named Cluvius and unable to meet her
commitments.

At this same period Mylasa's affairs were controlled by two distinguished citizens by name Euthydemus and Hybreas. 'Both', says
Strabo,

> were orators and popular leaders. Euthydemus inherited from his
> family great wealth and distinction, to which he added personal
> ability, and so attained to great honour not only in his own
> country but all over Asia. Hybreas, on the other hand, was left
> by his father a pack-mule and its groom; with these for a time
> he made his living, then after studying under Diotrephes of
> Antiocheia he returned home and served under the clerk of the
> market. Having by this means made a little money he entered
> politics, and rapidly acquired influence, both in Euthydemus' life-
> time and more especially after his death, becoming indeed the
> city's leading statesman. Euthydemus, however, while he lived,
> was by far the more dominant, and used his power for the city's
> good; so that even though there was a touch of the tyrannical in
> his methods, this was fully compensated by the resulting benefit.
> In this connexion a saying of Hybreas was much applauded:
> 'Euthydemus', he said, 'you are a necessary evil for our city, for
> we can live neither with you nor without you'. Hybreas, despite
> his great reputation and his services to his city, came to grief by
> his opposition to Labienus [above, p. 10]; for when the Parthians
> were already in control of Asia, and Labienus arrived with a
> Parthian army, most of the cities, being peaceable and unarmed,
> submitted to him, but Zeno of Laodiceia and Hybreas refused
> and roused their cities against him. Hybreas furthermore provoked
> Labienus, a foolish and irascible youth, by a certain answer he
> made: when Labienus declared himself emperor of Parthia,
> 'Then', said Hybreas, 'I call myself emperor of Caria'. Labienus
> thereupon attacked the city. Hybreas himself he failed to capture,
> as he had withdrawn to Rhodes, but he wrecked his house with
> all its fine belongings, and ravaged the whole city. When he had
> gone from Asia, Hybreas returned and set about restoring his
> own fortunes and those of Mylasa.

17

It was nevertheless some time before Mylasa recovered from this disaster. In 31 B.C., when Augustus (then called Octavian) after his final victory at Actium was sojourning in Samos, the Mylasans sent an embassy to him reminding him of the citizens they had lost as prisoners slaughtered by Labienus, of the holiest of their temples destroyed, of their territory ravaged and their farms burned. Augustus' reply was engraved on stone by the Mylasans, from which it may be inferred that it was favourable; but the stone is now broken and we do not know what help he may have given. It is, however, likely that it was at this time, or soon after, that the temple of Rome and Augustus was erected which was still standing in the eighteenth century. Some years later the city was still in financial straits and compelled to borrow money from its own citizens.

Under the Empire, here as elsewhere, prosperity returned, and Mylasa, like the other cities, has little or no individual history. Coinage continues down to the third century, and later the city was the seat of a bishopric under the metropolitan of Aphrodisias.

The principal deity of Mylasa was Zeus, who was worshipped under three titles, two of them with an alias. The first is Zeus Carius, whose cult was the most important in early times before the advent of the Hecatomnids. He had, as Herodotus tells us, an ancient sanctuary at Mylasa, to which, besides Carians, their traditional kinsmen the Lydians and Mysians were also admitted, but no others, even if they spoke Carian. He was the god of the 'Commonalty of the Carians', a league which survived, though with reduced importance, at least down to the first century B.C. His temple and sanctuary have been identified by some scholars with the great enclosure on the east slope of the hill of Hisarbaşı in Milâs (below, p. 22); but it has recently been proposed to locate it on the rock of Peçin outside Milâs on the south.

The second is the Zeus of Labraynda, called either Zeus Labrayndus or Zeus Stratius. He, too, is mentioned by Herodotus, who notes that Zeus was not worshipped elsewhere under the title Stratius. His cult, though ancient, was a purely local affair until it was adopted wholeheartedly by the Hecatomnids, who greatly increased the splendour of the sanctuary at Labraynda (described by Herodotus as a large and sacred grove of plane-trees), raised the cult to be the most revered in Mylasa, and stamped the figure of the god on their coins. On these he is shown standing, in Greek dress, with a double axe (*labrys*) over his right shoulder and a long spear in his left hand. These weapons mark his character as Stratius, or 'military'. Later coins, however, show the actual cult-statue of wood which stood in the temple. This is of very archaic appearance, reminiscent in some ways of the Ephesian Artemis; the bearded deity stands stiffly with his feet together, swathed from the waist downwards in a criss-cross of bands like a mummy; in his hands are the double axe and spear, on his head is a cylindrical headdress (*polos*); he wears a necklace and a kind of breastplate with numerous breast-like pro-tuberances. The last three of these features are essentially feminine, and consort oddly with the beard and the weapons; and it has been suggested that the Zeus of Labraynda must at a very early date have been in a manner fused with a female deity who preceded him. The crossed bands have been compared with the network pattern on the omphalos-stone at Delphi, which would mean that Zeus at Labraynda had oracular functions; this question will be mentioned again below (pp. 44–5), but others prefer to see a connexion with the Egyptian Osiris. From the fourth century onwards Zeus Labrayndus, or Stratius, was an outstanding deity of the Carians.

The third is Zeus Osogos,[3] the only one of the three who is strictly Mylasan. He was more particularly the god of the tribe Otorcondeis, but his cult was in effect the most important in Mylasa itself, and his renown extended over all Caria and even beyond. He stands on a par with Zeus Labrayndus; on the coins of Mylasa the two gods' attributes are often combined, and the same man might on occasion be priest of both. His sanctuary stood just outside the city (below, pp. 22–3) and was remarkable for a strange phenomenon; it possessed a spring of salt water, though the sea is ten miles away. It appears that the water had originally been fresh, but had changed its nature; Theophrastus rather naïvely attributes this change to the frequency of thunderbolts in the region. Whether because of this phenomenon, or perhaps more likely because the Carians had once been a maritime people, Zeus Osogos had to a great extent the character of a marine deity; his special attributes are the trident and the crab, and some scholars have sought to explain the Carian name Osogos by a connexion with the sea.[4] The trident was the emblem of the sea-god Poseidon (inherited by Britannia), and the Greeks, always ready to identify barbarian deities with their own, combined his name with that of Zeus and called the Carian god Zenoposeidon. This composite name excited remark in ancient times as a curiosity. Athenaeus tells a pleasing story in this connexion. A certain musician by name Dorion paid a visit to Mylasa, but had difficulty in finding lodging; he sat down to rest in a sanctuary outside the gates, and seeing the sacristan about his duties asked the name of the god. 'Zenoposeidon', was the reply. 'No wonder then', said Dorion, 'that a mere mortal cannot find a bed, when even the gods have to double up'.

Zeus Osogos possessed, besides his temple and sanctuary, a considerable landed estate. A series of inscriptions dating to the first century B.C. record the sale of land to the temple by private owners; in most cases the ex-owner then rents the land from the temple for his own use. This practice, which was common around Mylasa and elsewhere, reflects the general shortage of money among the citizens in the early years of the province of Asia. The temples, however, seem to have managed well enough.

Mylasa has suffered the usual fate of a city continuously inhabited since antiquity, and very little now remains of the many temples and other buildings mentioned by Strabo. Of the city walls nothing at all survives, though they are known to have existed, and for their position we have three clues only: the handsome gate now called Baltalı Kapı; the fact that the temple of Zeus Osogos stood 'in front of' (outside) the city; and the situation of the numerous tombs, which may be supposed to have lain, as usual, outside the walls. The position of the gate suggests that the wall may have run up to the Topbaşı Hill (and perhaps also to the Yeldeğirmeni Hill), then southwards and round between the Augusteum and the present Orta Okul, then bending northwards past the foot of the Hıdırlık Hill.

The unusually weak situation of the city has been noticed above; but it was to some extent compensated by a subsidiary fortification on the Hıdırlık Hill just to the west. The upper part of this hill was enclosed by a ring-wall whose line may still be followed, except in the south-eastern part, where it has disappeared. It is 8 feet thick and stands up to 8 feet high in places; the masonry is a very irregular ashlar. There are no surviving traces of buildings in the interior. This fortified enclosure must have served as a refuge for the people in time of danger.

Baltalı Kapı, dating probably from shortly before the Christian era, still stands virtually intact (Pl. 1). It takes its name from the double axe which is represented on the keystone of the arch on the outer (northern) side. The decoration of the piers consists of a row of flutes surmounting a row of palmettes. An aqueduct was carried over the gate, but this dates from a later period.

Of the many temples originally possessed by Mylasa, scanty remains of one only may now be seen. This has one column still erect and stands on the east slope of the Hisarbaşı Hill in the middle of the town. The column (Pl. 2), a handsome specimen of the

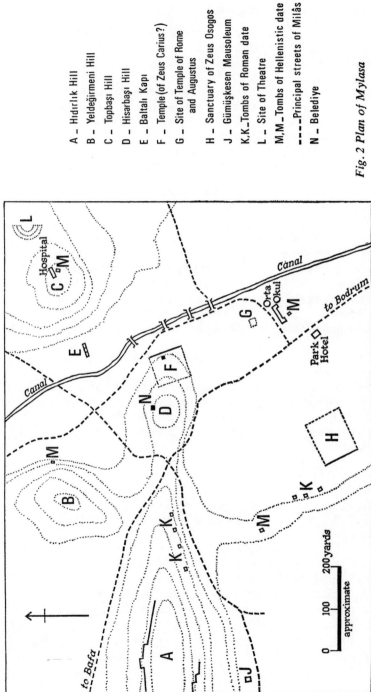

A - Hıdırlık Hill
B - Yeldeğirmeni Hill
C - Topbaşı Hill
D - Hisarbaşı Hill
E - Baltalı Kapı
F - Temple (of Zeus Carius?)
G - Site of Temple of Rome and Augustus
H - Sanctuary of Zeus Osogos
J - Gümüşkesen Mausoleum
K,K - Tombs of Roman date
L - Site of Theatre
M,M - Tombs of Hellenistic date
------- Principal streets of Milâs
N - Belediye

Fig. 2 Plan of Mylasa

Corinthian order, stands on a podium some 11 feet (3·35 m.) high
of which only the east face is now visible. A flight of steps on the
north side could be seen until recently. There is a panel on the
column as if for an inscription (such as we find on the columns of
the temple at Euromus), but it never seems to have been properly
smoothed and was clearly never inscribed. The temple was surrounded as usual by an extensive precinct. The eastern wall of this,
overlooking the canal, still stands for the whole of its length, about
100 yards (91·4 m.), to a height of eleven courses in places; the
masonry is a regular ashlar. This temple, like the Baltalı Kapı,
probably dates to the reconstruction of the city after the sack by
Labienus in 40 B.C. It is not known with certainty to what deity it
belonged. All probability points to Zeus, and a fragmentary dedication was found close by inscribed 'to Zeus . . .', but the distinguishing epithet was broken away. Not, surely, Zeus Osogos, whose
precinct stood outside the city; presumably then Zeus Carius or Zeus
Stratius. Most scholars are inclined to prefer the former. These
arguments for the identification of the temple and the line of the
city walls might all be worthless if we follow Strabo rather than
Athenaeus, when he states that the temple was not 'in front of the
gates' (and therefore outside the city), but in the city. However,
Strabo is not here making a topographical point, and is probably
simply stating that the temple belonged to the city, and was not
necessarily within the walls.

The temple of Zeus Osogos has quite disappeared, but its position is known; it stood outside the city wall on the south-west. Not
a single stone of the temple itself has ever been seen in modern
times, but a part of the wall of the surrounding precinct still exists.
It stands to the west of the Güveç Dede Türbesi in the quarter of
Hacı İlyas; all this part of the town is now built over, and the wall is
mostly hidden among the houses and gardens. It is a fine polygonal
wall, still some 10 feet (3·05 m.) high in places, constructed of large
blocks; one of its stones measures 9 feet by 3 feet 8 inches (2·74 by
1·12 m.) (Pl. 3). Masonry of this kind dates normally to the fifth
century B.C. Nothing more can be seen today, but formerly, when
this was open ground, there stood a row of columns extending at
right-angles from near the south end of the wall; in 1881 there were
fourteen, in 1933 only two. These belonged to a stoa which once
surrounded the precinct. Four of them were inscribed with the names
of priests of 'Zeus Osogos Zeus Zenoposeidon'; another recorded
that a certain ex-priest of Zeus presented eight columns to Zeus
Osogos. The style of the script, and the Roman names of the priest,

show that this colonnade must date to the Imperial period. At the house of Ismail Hakkı Bey, close beside the wall, the writer in 1970 saw two column-stumps, much battered and nearly buried, but said to be each about 6 feet (1·83 m.) long; whether these may be remnants of the stoa in question he could not determine. Of the famous spring of salt water nothing has ever been seen.

A third temple, that of Augustus and the deified Rome, was seen and described by early travellers. Sir George Wheler's companions in 1675 saw 'a fair temple of marble', with the dedication on the architrave. His drawing shows six Ionic columns on the front, with leaf decoration at the top and bottom of the shafts. The position of this temple, a little north of the present Orta Okul, has recently been determined by means of an inscription, but nothing of it now remains.

A theatre was, of course, an essential feature of all Greek cities of any size. That of Mylasa was situated on the east slope of the Topbaşı Hill, outside the city; but all that survives is the hollow in the hillside. Excavations on the west side of this hill brought to light theatrical masks, and showed furthermore that a shrine of Nemesis must have stood close by. A small collection of antiquities has been gathered in the park on Topbaşı Hill.

Otherwise the visible ruins of Mylasa are restricted to tombs. Two of these at least are well worth a visit. The best known is that called Gümüşkesen, on the western fringe of the town (Pl. 5); it is now approached by a broad road. It is a handsome two-storeyed building, whose date is not firmly established. Estimates vary from the first century B.C. to the second century A.D. A proper architectural study is needed for more precision on this point. The upper storey is surrounded by an open colonnade, with a square pilaster at each corner and two partially fluted oval columns on each of the four sides; the decoration is similar to that of the Baltalı Kapı. The roof is formed of five layers of blocks, with each layer placed diagonally across the angles of the one below, and decreasing upwards in size to form a shallow pyramid. The underside is adorned with plants and geometric shapes, and is thought to have been originally painted. The lower storey, the actual grave-chamber, has a wall of broad-and-narrow masonry and contains four pillars supporting the floor of the upper storey. The door is on the west side towards the north end, and is now closed with a grille, which is usually kept locked. An interesting feature is a small funnel-shaped hole in the floor of the upper chamber, evidently intended for the pouring of libations to the dead man in the tomb below.

To see this it is necessary either to clamber up to the upper storey or to find the guardian who holds the key.

Some two miles to the south of the town at a spot called Süleyman Kavağı, on the left of the road from Milâs to Güllük, is an interesting rock-tomb, well deserving of a visit. It is cut in the east face of a fair-sized hill, just below the summit, looking directly across to Peçin Kale, some fifteen minutes' climb from the gate of the modern cemetery by the roadside. It is known locally as Berber İni or Berber Yatağı (Pl. 4).

The tomb is in two parts, a rock-cut façade in temple form, with two engaged unfluted Doric half-columns flanking a false door, with architrave and pediment above, and below this the tomb itself, with its own plain door. The doorstone is lying outside. Inside are two long benches on right and left; they measure 12 feet (3·66 m.) by three (·91 m.). At the back is a much smaller chamber, again with its own door; the floor is sunk 16 inches (·41 m.) below that of the outer chamber, and on either side is a ledge some 5 inches (127 mm.) wide and 15 inches (·38 m.) above the floor. This sunken pit is 5 feet 8 inches (1·73 m.) long by internal measurement.

There is no inscription, but it has been suggested that this fine tomb, unique in this region, may be that either of Hyssaldomus or of Hecatomnos. The great man would be laid in the rear chamber, while the roomy-benches in the outer chamber would be reserved for his relatives or dependants. On the spot the writer felt some doubt of this, chiefly owing to the modest dimensions of the inner chamber, which Miss Akarca even calls an 'alcove for votive offerings'; if the dead body was laid in a coffin (let alone a sarcophagus), he must have been of distinctly short stature. On the other hand, it is unlikely that he would be required to mix with the others in the outer room. But in fact it seems probable that in tombs of this kind it was usual simply to lay the embalmed corpse on the floor or benches; in countless similar tombs in various parts of Asia Minor the writer cannot remember ever having seen any sign of a sarcophagus on the benches. There is also presumably the possibility that the actual grave is not in the tomb at all, but hidden somewhere close by. The question therefore remains open.

Notes

1 See above, p. 3 and *Lycian Turkey*, pp. 21–2
2 See *Aegean Turkey*, p. 185
3 Or Osogoa; the form varies in the sources.
4 The element -og- has been compared with Okeanos, the ocean, and with the island Ogygia. This cannot be considered established.

3 Around Mylasa

Of the smaller cities in the neighbourhood of Milâs, namely Hydae, Chalcetor, Olymus, and Euromus, all the sites are known, but with the exception of the last their ruins are unspectacular. All were independent cities in early times, and all were enrolled in the Confederacy of Delos, with much lower assessments for tribute than Mylasa. Most of their names had at that time a somewhat different form. They were all, towards the end of the second century B.C., united with Mylasa in a 'sympolity', that is, a mutual community of citizenship (above, p. 16). By such an arrangement each city in principle kept its independence, but in practice it was common for one of them to exercise a preponderance which might on occasion amount to subjection or even absorption; and such was undoubtedly the case with Mylasa. Otherwise these smaller cities have little or no individual history; they merely shared in the fortunes of the country as a whole.

Euromus

Some seven or eight miles (11·3 or 12·9 km.) from Milâs towards Bafa, at Ayaklı, close to the road on the east side, the traveller's eye is caught by the columns of a temple, still standing to the number of sixteen. This was at first thought to be the temple of Zeus of Labraynda, but in fact marks the site of Euromus. This was the most considerable city in the region after Mylasa in early times. It controlled the northern part of the plain, and seems at one time to have given its name to a wide area, for the historian Polybius once refers to 'the cities in Euromus'. These presumably included Olymus and Chalcetor. In the fifth century the name appears as Kyromus or Hyromus; the Greek form Euromus, 'strong', is likely to date from the Hellenization of the country which resulted from Mausolus' policy. At the same time it is remarkable that as early

25

as the fifth century B.C. and as late as the first the city's name appears sometimes in the form Europus.

In the revolt of Mylasa against the Rhodian domination in 167 B.C. Euromus and her neighbours were forcibly involved (above, p. 16); the Mylasans seized their cities, presumably in order to suppress any local opposition. The Mylasan success was short-lived, but the sympolity which followed before the end of the century was of more account. It seems to have offended the men of Heracleia, Euromus' neighbours on the north; an inscription tells us that they had raided the territory of Euromus and carried off sacred and private property; a Euroman citizen who had suffered in this way complained to the authorities in Mylasa, who thereupon sent one of their citizens as ambassador to Heracleia and succeeded in obtaining satisfaction. It is noticeable that the Euromans do not act on their own account, but prefer to apply to Mylasa; and the inscription observes that the ambassador 'secured the interests of the city'— that is of Mylasa. The inequality of the sympolity is very evident.

This union of the two cities did not last. Quarrels broke out; another inscription records that on one occasion the Mylasans, alleging apparently that the Euromans had broken some agreement, demanded from them an indemnity of fifty talents, and Euromus felt obliged to turn to the Romans and the Rhodians.

Having recovered her independence, Euromus appears to have flourished, for the extant ruins, battered though they are, attest considerable prosperity. The coinage extends from the second century B.C. to the second A.D.

On the ground today the outstanding feature is the temple, which is among the half-dozen best preserved in Asia Minor (Pl. 6). It is in the Corinthian order, and dates from the second century A.D. It had originally eleven columns on the long sides and six on the short; of these, sixteen are still standing complete with their architrave, in groups of eight, five, and three. The three on the south side, and the south-west corner column, are unfluted, no doubt because the work was never quite finished. Most of the columns, on the west and north sides, have a panel with a dedicatory inscription; five were presented by a certain Menecrates, state physician and magistrate, together with his daughter Tryphaena, and seven by Leo Quintus, also a magistrate. On the south side a piece of the cornice with a lion's head water-spout is still in place. An excavation, begun in 1969, has revealed the foundations of an altar in the usual position in front of the temple on the east, and has made a start on clearing the jumble of blocks in the interior. It is now possible to make out the walls of the *naiskos*, and the niche which held the base of the cult-statue. Around the temple a complicated sequence of associated buildings has been revealed by the rather limited trenches of the excavators. They include a large late Hellenistic altar, and among the finds was a quantity of archaic architectural terracottas, which suggest that the sanctuary should be dated at least as early as the sixth century B.C. Among the most interesting discoveries is an inscription of Hellenistic date recording an honorific decree to be set up in the temple of Zeus Lepsynus. This tells us not only the name of the god who possessed the temple, but also that the present building is not the first to be erected on the site, as indeed the archaeologists have shown. The epithet Lepsynus is new and, like Osogos, un-Greek. The excavation continues.

The temple is outside the city, which occupied the ground to the north. A hundred yards from the temple, on a slight rise, is a handsome round tower in good ashlar masonry, belonging to the city wall; the wall itself may be followed from here, curving round northwards over the hillside, with other towers at intervals. It is in general 8 to 9 feet (2·44 to 2·74 m.) thick, having two faces with headers and rubble filling. A wall of this quality can date little, if at all, after 300 B.C. It enclosed a considerable area, nearly a quarter of a square mile; some distance to the north it descends into the plain, crosses a ridge, and comes down to the road, then runs southward parallel to the road on its west side for 700 yards (640 m.) before turning east to join the round tower near the temple.

In a recess in the hillside, a little above the plain, is the theatre, quite large but badly ruined; it faces west. Five rows of seats remain visible, best preserved on the north; of the stage-building a corner of the substructure survives, with five or six courses standing. The agora, or market-place, stood on the flat ground surrounded on all four sides by a stoa, some of whose columns are still erect. Further west is another stoa. On one of the pillars is a long inscription, very hard to read, recording the financial services to the city of a certain Callisthenes and mentioning an alliance with Iasus. Close to the road is a large, rather shapeless building of late date, probably a baths. Finally, beside the path leading from the road to the temple, are several underground tomb-chambers handsomely constructed and roofed in the Carian manner with huge slabs. Other buildings in more or less ruinous condition will be noticed, but nothing more is identifiable.

Olymus

Although nothing now remains visible above ground, the site of Olymus is fixed with certainty by the great number of inscribed and other ancient stones which are found a little below the surface. It lies five miles north-north-west of Milâs and three miles east of Euromus across the hills, at or near the village of Kafaca (Kafcı). In the Delian Confederacy the city's name appears as Hylimus.

The principal deities were Apollo and Artemis, who shared a temple; they were worshipped under the title of 'gods of the people of Olymus'. The site of this temple is recognizable as a mound rising a few feet above the ground, but it has never been excavated. The form of the cramps joining the blocks found here suggests a date in the Hellenistic period. The temple possessed a considerable area of land, much or most of which was obtained by purchase from private owners; these frequently continued to work the property as tenants of the temple. Numerous leases of this kind have been discovered.

It is possible that the city itself was situated on the hills above the village, although no ruins have been found; in this case the temple was outside the city, like that at Euromus and that of Zeus Osogos at Mylasa, and many others.

Chalcetor

About six miles (9·65 km.) from Milâs on the way to Bafa a road turns off to the left to Karakuyu and the ruins of Chalcetor. This was never a city of any consequence; apart from its membership of the Delian Confederacy all we know of its history is that it was instructed by one of the Hellenistic kings to enter into sympolity with another city; the name of the second city is lost, but is likely to have been Euromus. This might help to explain Polybius' curious phrase 'the cities in Euromus'. Later, of course, both were united with Mylasa. The name Chalcetor is to all appearance Greek, meaning 'with heart of bronze'; but it is likely to be a Graecized form of an earlier Anatolian name.

Shortly before reaching Karakuyu the road passes through the necropolis of Chalcetor; the villagers will readily act as guides. The acropolis of the city is on a pine-clad hill of fair height called Yaz Tepesi, from which a ridge runs down to the modern road; it is about half an hour's climb. Nothing is preserved apart from the ring-wall, well built of squared blocks in the Lelegian manner. Two other fortresses defended the city; they are something over a mile away by the hamlet of Köşk, and are called respectively Asar and Kale. Their walls of dry rubble are surprisingly thick, as much as 12 and 15 feet (3·66 to 4·57 m.), but are nowhere preserved to a height of more than 5 feet (1·52 m.).

At the foot of the ridge, close to the road, are the scanty remains of the temple of Apollo. Lying on the ground are a large block with dentil frieze and a fluted column-drum, Ionic or Corinthian, 5 feet (1·52 m.) high and 2 feet (·61 m.) in diameter, but little more. Here was found the inscription recording the sympolity, and another including the name Chalcetor; and in 1968 the writer found there a Carian text in three lines which has not yet been interpreted.

The tombs in the necropolis are of various types. Some are underground chambers like those at Euromus, solidly constructed of stone blocks, with roofing slabs up to 9 feet (2·74 m.) in length, and in some cases with layers of small stones on top. Others are shallow graves, quite plain, and in one place a sarcophagus with disc-and-festoon relief is standing in the middle of a field.

Hydae

Recorded in the Delian Confederacy in the form Kydae, and united later in a sympolity with Mylasa, this small city has no other history. Its site, unknown until 1933, is located in the valley of the Sarıçay west of the Sodra Dağı at the village of Damlıboğaz. The name is certainly Anatolian,[1] and occupation of the site was much earlier than the earliest record, as is proved by a small hand-made jug found at Damlıboğaz and dating to the third millennium B.C. This is now in the museum depot at Milâs. As at Olymus, the city's principal deities were Apollo and Artemis, who here also shared a temple; they were called 'ancestral gods', which may indicate that they are old Carian deities assimilated to the Greek. Here as elsewhere the river was deified, and the coinage shows a river-god representing the Sarıçay; its ancient name was the Cybersus.

Not very much remains to be seen on the spot. The acropolis hill, directly above the village, is of moderate height; the summit carries a ring-wall now largely reduced to a pile of stones, but standing in places up to 8 feet (2·44 m.) The entrance is on the south-east, and outside the wall on the south-west are one or two plain rock-tombs. Other tombs, some dating to the Hellenistic period, are frequently found by digging in the village.

On the plain in front of the village is a flat heap of ruins, only

29

a few feet high, which it has been thought may represent the temple of Apollo and Artemis. The plan of the building is not now easy to make out, and the identification must be regarded as quite uncertain.

Peçin Kale

The visitor to Milâs who is not unduly pressed for time should not fail to spend half a day on a visit to Peçin Kale. About three miles to the south of Milâs this great flat-topped rock rises abruptly from the plain to a height of some 700 feet (213·4 m.); it is easily ascended on the west side by a paved and stepped road of Turkish construction. The place was an important stronghold of the Menteşe dynasty in the fourteenth century, and the extensive summit carries, in addition to the powerful fortress, a number of Turkish buildings, among which the *medrese* of Ahmet Gazi is especially worth a visit.

But ancient remains also are not lacking. Below the castle on the east is a short stretch of early wall in handsome bossed ashlar masonry (Pl. 7); whether this is part of a ring-wall or merely a terrace wall cannot now be determined. And just inside the entrance to the castle, on the right, a flight of six solid marble steps is preserved, which is recognized to have belonged to an ancient temple, and one of fair size. It is accordingly clear that there was here at least a sanctuary in ancient times, and it has generally been thought that the importance of Peçin in antiquity amounted to no more than this. Miss Akarca in her book on Milâs remarks that Peçin was not then a place of any consequence. But recently Professor J. M. Cook has shown reason to revise this estimate, and to believe that this was in fact the site, or at least the citadel, of Mylasa until the fourth century B.C. Professor Cook's arguments are briefly as follows.

Sherds found on the site range in date from the seventh to the early fourth centuries, and include a good proportion of Attic black-glazed vessels, indicating a site of some importance by Carian standards. Recent excavations of a cemetery here have produced a good deal of proto-geometric and geometric pottery of local Carian manufacture, confirming the antiquity of the site. The wall and temple-steps are not accurately datable, but sherds of Hellenistic and Roman date are remarkable by their absence. On the other hand, an obsidian blade-core picked up in the writer's presence in 1968 suggests occupation on the site as far back as the Early Bronze Age around 2000 B.C.[2]

Among the ancient historians Herodotus tells us only that there was in Mylasa an ancient sanctuary of Zeus Carius, but Strabo has rather more to say; he speaks of Mylasa and her two sanctuaries of Zeus Osogos and Zeus Labrayndus, then continues:

> these then are peculiar to the city, but there is a third sanctuary of Zeus Carius, common to all Carians and shared by the Lydians and Mysians as kinsmen. It is said [*or* there is said] to have been a village in olden times, with the ancestral home and palace of the Hecatomnids.

The editors of Strabo have always assumed that the subject of the last sentence is the city of Mylasa (which in Strabo's day was of course at Milâs); but the historian seems to be distinguishing the village from the city of his own time; and it is much more satisfactory to suppose that he is recording a tradition that Mylasa, with the temple of Zeus Carius, once stood on the hill of Peçin. The temple is then the one whose steps are still to be seen, the same which is recorded by Herodotus.

If this is right, it is virtually certain that the move down to the new site at Milâs was made by Mausolus. In accordance with his policy of Hellenizing Caria he moved the position of a number of cities, notably Myndus and Syangela. And Peçin is a far more suitable town-site than Milâs for the Carians of early times, who chose invariably to live on hill-tops. One other piece of evidence may be suggestive. An ancient writer passing under the name of Aristotle informs us that Mausolus at one time collected contributions to pay for the erection of a city wall, the city being then unfortified—as it would naturally be if the site was in fact a new one.

Professor Cook is careful to observe that this suggestion is not yet proved beyond a doubt. If it is right, pre-Mausolan remains at Milâs should be lacking in any considerable quantity. A few early pieces have in fact been reported from there, but not enough excavation has been done to determine the presence or absence of a fifth-century city. The temple on Hisarbaşı, as was said above, is likely to have been a temple of Zeus, most probably Zeus Carius; but this is not to say that in Herodotus' time his temple did not stand at Peçin; if it was wrecked (for example) by Labienus in 40 B.C., it might well be rebuilt in the city. It may indeed have been built there when the move was made; so at Cnidus, which changed her site about the same time, new temples were at once erected on the new site.

31

Until further evidence appears, therefore, we may regard it as probable that when Mausolus embarked on his scheme to change the Carian way of life to something more Hellenic, he began with his home-town Mylasa.

Ceramus

The north side of the Gulf of Cos towards its east end is formed by the mighty wall of the Kıran Dağ rising sheer from the sea to over 2,000 feet (609·6 m.) and leaving no room for a road along the shore. Only at one point is this wall broken, where the Koca Çay makes its way down from the plateau above and has formed an alluvial plain or delta at its mouth. Despite its length of over twenty miles (32·2 km.) this river dries up in summer, and much of the water from the plateau finds its way to the sea by underground channels. In a corner of this plain are the ruins of Ceramus. The delta has spread since antiquity, and the walls still standing on the flat ground are quite deeply buried in their lower parts; it is likely that Ceramus stood originally on or near the sea. Being somewhat difficult of access the site was rarely visited; the best method was a boat trip from Bodrum. But in this case the return journey is apt to be rough, when the wind gets up in the afternoon. Now, however, the village of Ören is linked by a regular minibus service from Milâs, making a long journey much shorter. The ancient name survives in the form Gereme, which is nowadays applied to the country around; the village itself is called Ören, meaning 'ruins', and has the rank of a *nahiye*.

For a city of her size Ceramus is peculiarly devoid of any history. Nothing is known of her foundations, and she was evidently Carian in origin; although her name is identical with the Greek word for 'pottery' or 'tile', this is agreed to be a coincidence only. The city had, however, become in some degree at least Hellenized by the sixth century, as archaic statuary of Greek type has been found there; whether this was due to the city's own initiative or to an unrecorded Dorian settlement is unsure, but in the Hellenistic period (the earliest for which we have evidence) the Doric dialect was not used in the inscriptions. Ceramus was a member of the Delian Confederacy, paying a talent and a half, and later of the Chrysaoric League, of which indeed she was among the more important members, owing to the large number of villages on her territory. To what extent Mausolus interested himself in Ceramus there is nothing to show, but he can hardly have been indifferent.

With the rest of Caria, Ceramus was given to Rhodes in 189 B.C. and taken away again in 167; to the period following this belongs the one fragment known of the city's individual history. We learn from an inscription that Ceramus had entered into a sympolity with another city, unnamed but almost certainly Stratoniceia, whose territory must have adjoined hers. Things went badly, however, and Ceramus found herself 'in a difficult situation'; no doubt, as so often happened, the stronger partner began to assert herself unduly; at all events Ceramus found it necessary to apply to Rhodes for an alliance; this was secured by the good offices of the man honoured in the inscription. The choice of Rhodes is interesting, and suggests that the Ceramians at least bore no lasting grudge against their recent masters who had proved so unpopular elsewhere. In the Mithridatic War it appears that Ceramus took the king's side, and was punished by being given in 81 B.C. to Stratoniceia.

The coins range in date from the second century B.C. through the Roman Imperial period. Some of them show a youthful god standing clad in a short tunic and carrying a double axe and a spear; this is evidently a local deity, hard to identify with any Greek god; we shall meet him again below. In some cases he appears together with Zeus Chrysaoreus, the principal deity of Ceramus.

Almost the only Ceramian of any distinction was the runner Polites, who won the stadium, diaulus, and long-distance races at Olympia on the same day. In later times Ceramus was one of the many bishoprics attached to the metropolitan of Aphrodisias.

The ruins of Ceramus have suffered sadly in recent years from the depredations of the local inhabitants, and much of what was recorded earlier in this century is no longer to be seen. The city-wall could until recently be followed in all its length; at present a long stretch is visible high up on the rocky mountainside on the east of the city, and on the flat ground on the south it is still standing in part. The masonry is in general polygonal (Pl. 8), but in some places the upper part was built of squared stones; the unusual effect was accentuated by the difference in material, the polygonal work being of grey limestone, the squared masonry of a yellowish pudding-stone. But of the upper parts virtually nothing now remains. There were numerous gates, mostly arched but in a few cases rectangular; some of these survive. The polygonal work need not imply an early date, nor the arches a late one; the whole wall was no doubt built at one time in the early Hellenistic period. Outside the gates the roads were flanked with tombs in the usual way; some are sarcophagi, others of 'Carian' type sunk into the ground.

33

On a low hill, very dry and stony, just outside the village, at a spot called Bakıcak, is a site which has produced a good deal of early material. A platform with supporting wall of respectable ashlar masonry carries the foundations of a temple which has almost totally disappeared; only three large blocks remain, lying at different levels on the hillside, so that the form and order of the temple cannot be determined. There is, however, evidence to suggest that it was a temple of Zeus, in all probability Zeus Chrysaoreus. A block was found nearby with a relief of a double axe, the special symbol of Zeus in Caria. And in 1932 the villagers unearthed on the spot a youthful male head in marble, of archaic date and of the type known as *kouros*. It has been attractively suggested that this is the head of the young god who appears on coins in company with Zeus. The head is now in the museum in Smyrna. Other archaic fragments have been found in the same place, and the antiquity of the temple is beyond doubt.

Below the platform on the west a terrace wall was later constructed, the space between it and the platform being divided into chambers by cross-walls; and below this again, at a much lower

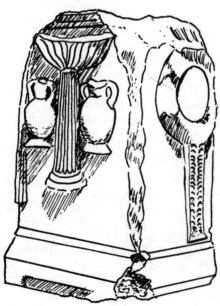

Fig. 3 Ceramus.
Sculptured Base

ЄΥϹЄΒΗϹ
ΙЄΡЄΥϹΜΑΥΡΧΡΥ
ϹΑΝΤΑϹΓΟΙЄΡЄΥϹ
ЄΥϹЄΒΩϹΤΑΠΡΟϹΤΟΥϹ
ΘЄΟΥϹΚΑΙΤΟΥϹΙЄΡЄΙϹ
ΠΑΝΤΑΔΑΨΙΛΩϹΚΑΙЄΚ
ΤЄΝΩϹЄ ΞЄΤЄΛЄϹΑΜЄ
ΤΑΚΑΙΤΗϹΓΥΝΑΙΚΟϹ
ΜΟΥΑΥΡЄΥΦΡΟϹΥΝΗϹ
ЄΥΤΥΧΩϹ

Fig. 4 Ceramus. Inscription at Kurşunlu Yapı

level, is a second terrace wall, the intervening space being again divided by two cross-walls now mostly destroyed. In the outer face of this lower wall are six large niches with round top. Along the upper terrace wall runs a water-pipe. The purpose of this unusual complex is not clear.

One other temple is known at Ceramus. It lies outside the city-walls about a quarter of a mile (402·3 m.) to the east, at the foot of the mountains, and is known as Kurşunlu Yapı. Here the destruction has been particularly lamentable, and the building is now a sorry sight. The temple stood on a platform with supporting wall, which until recently stood to its full height of 20 feet (6·10 m.) with a cornice at the top. The cornice is now completely destroyed. Of the temple itself, in the Corinthian order, many architectural members are lying around; their excellent quality shows that the building must have been very handsome. On no other site has the writer been more depressed by the vandalism which is still only too rife in Turkey. The temple walls were decorated with reliefs showing a round shield enclosed in a wreath, with their inscriptions still legible. One of them reads: 'With good fortune. I, the pious priest Marcus Aurelius Chrysantas, zealously and openhandedly performed my duties towards the gods and the other priests, together with my wife

35

Aurelia Euphrosyne'. The other is similar. Modesty was a quality not expected in documents of this kind.

Other ruins of Roman and Byzantine date meet the eye in various parts of the site, but their purpose is unknown. On the south side of the city, beside a Turkish cemetery, is a small Byzantine church with some remnants of wall-paintings.

Ceramus was not without water, as springs issue at the foot of the mountains, the water coming apparently underground from the plateau above; but a more satisfactory supply was obtained by means of an aqueduct leading from the north. But of this also hardly anything survives.

Kuyruklu Kale

A further site worthy of mention in the vicinity of Milâs is the hill-top castle known as Kuyruklu Kale. It is sited on the first of the higher hills east of Milâs, some 600 feet (183 m.) above the level of the plain, south-west of the small village Yusufca köyü. It is visible from Mylasa itself, and of course has a commanding view of the plain below. The name of the site can be translated as Scorpion Castle, and it is interesting to note that Strabo remarks on the abundance of scorpions in the region between Mylasa and Alabanda. Strabo also remarks that in early days Mylasa was not a powerful city but a village settlement. The population, one would gather, lived scattered over the countryside in small settlements, not concentrated in a single spot. However, their rulers must have needed defensible strong-points from which to exercise control, and it is suggested that Kuyruklu Kale performed just such a service for the ruler of Mylasa. The site (Fig. 5) is oblong in shape, measuring about 450 metres from east to west, and 250 from north to south. At least three phases of masonry can be identified. The first is pre-Hellenistic in date, made of unworked slabs and blocks. The main circuit is in this style, and did not apparently have the additional protection of towers. The best stonework in the castle is the fine squared masonry, apparently of early Hellenistic date, which is to be seen especially in the outworks on the north side, and in the square towers placed at intervals along the circuit. The final phase of building took place in medieval times, largely along the line of the pre-Hellenistic wall, and is to be distinguished by the use of mortar between the stones. At the east end of the fortress there was an inner citadel, also dating to the pre-Hellenistic period but with later modifications. It contained two cisterns. It has been proposed

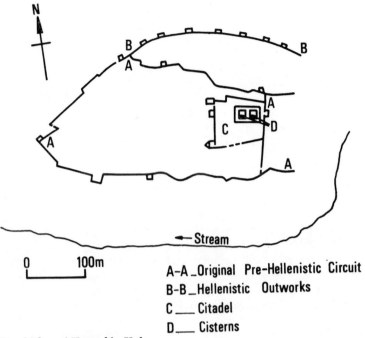

A-A _ Original Pre-Hellenistic Circuit
B-B _ Hellenistic Outworks
C ___ Citadel
D ___ Cisterns

Fig. 5 Plan of Kuyruklu Kale

that the earliest building phase should be dated to the late fifth or
early fourth century B.C., and ascribed to one of the predecessors of
Mausolus who controlled the region then. The fine Hellenistic addition may have been the work of Eupolemus, a follower of Alexander
the Great, who was probably in control of much of Caria between
320 and 300 B.C. Kuyruklu Kale, with its strong fortification and
commanding position, could well have been his power base.

Notes

1 Even though the next village is called Yaşyer, 'Wet Place', it would be a
  mistake to connect the name Hydae with the Greek word for water.
2 Professor Colin Renfrew of Sheffield University, for whose expert advice
  I am very grateful, reports that it is a worked-out blade-core of a type
  common in Greece and the Cyclades, but rare in the eastern Aegean. It
  is likely to have come from the island of Melos, with a possible range
  of date from 3000 to 1500 B.C.

4　Labraynda

Soon after 499 B.C. a Persian army under Daurises marched south to suppress the Carians who had supported the revolt of the Ionian cities. A battle was fought by the river Marsyas; the Carians were defeated with heavy losses and retired to the sanctuary of Zeus Stratius at Labraynda. Here they debated whether to surrender to the Persians or to quit Asia altogether, but on the arrival of reinforcements from Miletus they decided to stand and fight again. Again they were defeated, and Mylasa fell into Persian hands. Herodotus describes the sanctuary as a large and sacred grove of plane-trees, and remarks that the Carians are the only people known to sacrifice to Zeus Stratius.[1]

His description is far from doing justice to the site as it appears today, and in fact the splendid buildings recently cleared by the Swedish excavators were not erected till more than a hundred years later. They are due to the Hecatomnid rulers Mausolus and his brother Idrieus, who adopted the cult of Zeus Stratius, or Labrayndus, and raised it to an importance which it never afterwards lost (above, pp. 18–19). Herodotus makes no special mention of a temple, and it may well be that there was none at the time of the battle of Labraynda. After Idrieus practically no changes were made until the first century A.D.

The sanctuary belonged from early times to Mylasa, the nearest city and Mausolus' capital, and was in fact joined to it by a Sacred Way, paved with stone and eight miles (12·87 km.) long, by which at festival time the procession made its way up. At the same time, the priest of Zeus had a certain measure of independence, and was responsible for the administration of the temple lands. According to Strabo he was appointed for life from among the notables of Mylasa, but this rule seems to have been abandoned in the course of time and the priesthood became annual.

Mylasan possession of the sanctuary was not, however, altogether undisputed. In the early part of the third century the country was dominated politically by the Chrysaoric League, centred on Stratoniceia and supported by the Ptolemies. An inscription recently found at Labraynda records a meeting of the League in the nineteenth year of Ptolemy II (267 B.C.), though not apparently held at Labraynda itself. Soon after this, however, Antiochus II of Syria (261–247 B.C.) overran the country and brought it under Seleucid control. His successor, Seleucus II, was friendly to Mylasa and granted the city her 'freedom', at the same time confirming her possession of Labraynda. But the priests of Zeus were jealous of their limited independence, and before long, about 240 B.C., we find a priest by the name of Corris complaining to Seleucus that the Mylasans were usurping his privileges and otherwise misbehaving. The king was sympathetic and sent instructions to his governor Olympichus to restrain them. The Mylasans, however, indignantly denied the priest's accusations, whereupon Seleucus held an investigation; the upshot was that Corris was judged to have lied and Mylasa to be in the right.

Twenty years later this incident was almost exactly repeated. In the meantime the Seleucid control had weakened, and Olympichus, though ordered by Seleucus to evacuate the district and leave it to Mylasa, had neglected to do so and had made himself into an independent dynast. This was the situation when the Macedonian king Antigonus Doson occupied Caria in 227 B.C. He established good relations both with Mylasa and with Olympichus, and the latter, after the king's departure, seems to have acted as representative of Macedonia in the region. While Antigonus was in Caria, another priest of Zeus, apparently named Hecatomnos, approached him with similar complaints to those of Corris, and obtained from him a letter conveying a favourable reply. Knowing, however, that his claims were in fact false, he suppressed the letter for six years until the king died. When he finally produced it, the Mylasans immediately protested to Antigonus' successor, Philip V, complaining at the same time that the officials of the Chrysaoric League were attempting to appropriate Labraynda in an effort to recover their old dominance. Philip's response was wholly in favour of Mylasa; he sent orders to Olympichus to exclude the Chrysaorians and to restore the sanctuary to the city. This decision was final and, so far as we know, Mylasan possession of Labraynda was never again seriously questioned; the village and sanctuary continued as before to be a part of the Mylasan state.

Early in the first century A.D. a number of buildings were added to the precinct, including baths at the east end and a stoa at the west, the building E on the plan, and probably also the well-house L. Much later a second baths was built on the south side. In the fourth century most of the western part was ruined by a disastrous fire; but the place was not abandoned, and in early Byzantine times a church was built between the eastern baths and propylaea, largely with material taken from those structures, which by that time must have already collapsed. This church was in its turn destroyed by fire, perhaps about the eleventh century.

Not very much is known about the cult of Zeus at Labraynda. Of the god himself, with his two titles Stratius and Labrayndus, an account was given above (pp. 18–19); his name is sometimes coupled with that of Hera. It is possible that his sanctuary contained an oracle; of this more will be said later. There is also some evidence that athletic contests were held, and in fact a stadium has recently been recognized on the slope above the temple.

The site of Labraynda is remarkable for its steepness, necessitating numerous artificial terraces, and for its abundance of water, from which at present the town of Milâs is supplied. The sanctuary is set on a steep hillside, with an acropolis on the summit several hundred feet higher up. The acropolis comprises a fortress about 100 yards (91·4 m.) in length, containing several buildings, all badly ruined and overgrown. Since Labraynda was never a city, only a village, it is thought that this fortress may have been built by Ada while she was maintaining herself in semi-royalty at Alinda. The altitude is well over 2,000 feet (609·6 m.). A passage in a letter from Olympichus to Mylasa reads: 'I restore to you the place and its territory and revenues; and I hand over to you also Petra by Labraynda'. It has been suggested that Petra, 'the rock', may be identified with this acropolis. Although the acropolis must surely be included, if not in the 'place', at least in the territory, it might nevertheless be separately mentioned because Olympichus had maintained a garrison there. But there are at least two other fortresses within a mile or two, and Petra may equally well be one of these.

The material used generally on the site is the local stone, a kind of gneiss; the marble used for facing and other purposes was brought from the Sodra Dağı above Milâs, but is not of first-rate quality.

Herodotus, as was mentioned above, speaks only of a grove of plane-trees; and there are today some fine trees of this kind close to the sanctuary. The earliest temple of Zeus, built perhaps some time in the fifth century, was a simple affair of the type called *in antis*, consisting merely of a pronaos with two columns between the antae, and a cella behind. In the following century this was converted by Idrieus into the building whose foundations have recently been excavated. The walls of the old temple were allowed to stand, with the addition of two short antae at the west end, with two columns between, forming a very shallow opisthodomus; and the whole was surrounded by an Ionic colonnade having eight columns on the long sides and six at front and back. These unusual proportions are due to the fact that the building was not planned for itself but was merely a conversion of an existing structure (Pl. 12).

Though the temple was completed and dedicated to Zeus by Idrieus (part of his dedicatory inscription has been found), it is likely that he was only carrying out a plan conceived by his brother, for it was Mausolus who initiated the great transformation of the sanctuary. Two dedications by him have come to light, namely those of the North Stoa and the Second Andron (F and D on the plan); in each case the god's name appears as Zeus Lambrayndus. If the name is, as is generally supposed, connected with the word *labrys*, a double axe, the 'm' is intrusive, and in fact this form does not occur after the fourth century. In the Hellenistic inscriptions it is consistently Labraynda, and this is also the form found most usually in the manuscripts of the ancient writers from Herodotus onwards. The later inscriptions have commonly Labraeynda, showing that the word had four syllables, not three. The more familiar form Labranda has only inferior authority.

The most conspicuous building on the site is the First Andron (C, Pl. 9), dedicated by Idrieus. This building, which stands in part to its full height apart from the roof, has always been visible, and before the Swedish excavations was supposed to be the temple of Zeus. It is virtually identical in shape and size with the Second Andron built by Mausolus, which is identified as an andron by its inscription. The word means 'a room for the men', that is a sort of men's club-house, though no doubt of a more or less religious character. It would be used for banquets at the festival and doubtless for other social occasions. In form it is strikingly similar to the old fifth-century temple, though larger, and is remarkable for its unusually large door and for the number and size of its windows. There are no fewer than ten of these, two in the antechamber, three in each side of the main room, and rather surprisingly two in the wall between the two rooms. This wall is exceptionally thick, over 6 feet (1·83 m.), and the windows are more like passages. The building is thus particularly well lit, an obvious advantage when artificial

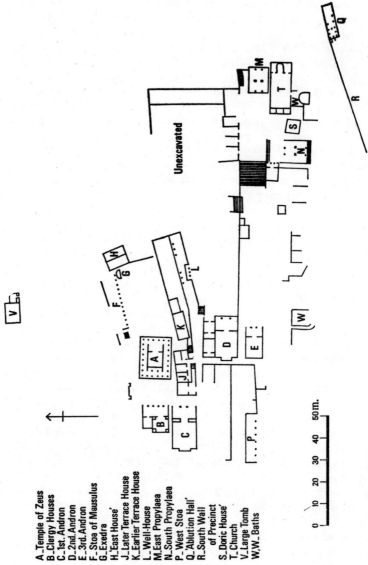

A. Temple of Zeus
B. Clergy Houses
C. 1st. Andron
D. 2nd. Andron
E. 3rd. Andron
F. Stoa of Mausulus
G. Exedra
H. 'East House'
J. Later Terrace House
K. Earlier Terrace House
L. Well-House
M. East Propylaea
N. South Propylaea
P. West Stoa
Q. 'Ablution Hall'
R. South Wall
   of Precinct
S. Doric House'
T. Church
V. Large Tomb
W,W. Baths

Unexcavated

| | | | | | | | |
|0|10|20|30|40|50 m.|

Fig. 6 Plan of Labraynda

lighting was so inadequate. The windows are fitted with grooves for fixing shutters against the wind and rain. A further peculiarity, found also in Mausolus' andron, is the rectangular niche at the back of the main room. It forms a projection behind the building, and on the inside begins about 7 feet (2·13 m.) from the floor. Its purpose is uncertain; possibly it held statues. The Second Andron differs from this only in being less well preserved and in having no windows in its north wall, owing presumably to the buildings, called 'annexes' by the excavators, which flanked it on that side. A most unusual feature of the building was the use of Ionic column capitals with a Doric entablature above them, almost unparalleled in a building of the fourth century B.C.

Adjoining the First Andron on the north is a group of two rooms with a porch and four Doric columns in front; the inscription on the architrave designates them as 'Houses', that is probably dwelling-quarters for the temple clergy. They are quite well preserved, with the back wall standing to its original height. Like the andron, they were dedicated to Zeus Lambrayndus by Idrieus. At a much later date the roof of the larger room was replaced by a dome of tiles, supported by piers placed in each corner of the room. The smaller room too was used in Christian times, when a marble altar was set against its back wall.

The early terrace-house K was apparently standing in the fifth century B.C., but was demolished in the course of the great reconstruction by the Hecatomnids. It was replaced by the later terrace-house J, which is still quite well preserved, with four rooms and a corridor in front. These were perhaps store-rooms. They are backed against the temple terrace, to which stairs lead up, so that the roof of the house formed a sort of continuation of the terrace.

The eastern part of the temple terrace is an open space bounded on the north by a stoa and at the far end by the 'East House', H on the plan. This house dates back to the fifth century, but little or nothing is known about it. The stoa, on the other hand, was dedicated by Mausolus. It is not completely excavated owing to the modern road which passes just above. The semicircular exedra standing in front of its east end is a much later addition.

In front of the Second Andron is another open terrace flanked on the north by a handsome terrace wall with a well- or fountain-house in its middle (Pl. 10). Behind this wall is another stoa, built by Idrieus, but the fountain-house with its three columns was not added before the first century A.D. At the east end of this terrace is a vast building which has not been excavated; its nature is accordingly not known, though it is conjectured to have been a royal palace. At the other end, beside the Second Andron, is the Third Andron E. This, though similar in form to the other two, is of much inferior workmanship and is poorly preserved; it too dates to the first century A.D. Of the same period also is the West Stoa P.

The south-east corner of the precinct, on a lower level, must have been in the fourth century B.C. just as impressive as the western part, though it is now much less well preserved. From the terrace above a splendid staircase leads down to a central courtyard with magnificent entrance gateways (propylaea) on the east and south, to which the Sacred Way led up. The stairway is almost 40 feet (12·2 m.) broad, with twenty-three steps, most of which are still in place. The two entrance gateways appear to be contemporary, both being due to Idrieus. The reason for thus providing two similar entries of such grandeur so close together is not clear, and it has been suggested that the East Propylaea was built first and almost immediately destroyed by an earthquake or other calamity, being replaced by another on the same plan but in a different place. The respective levels of the two structures and the adjoining buildings give some support to this idea.

Close to the South Propylaea on the east are the ruins of a small building called by the excavators the 'Doric House'. It faced north, with four Doric columns on the front, and may possibly have been a treasury; it dates, like the propylaea, to the time of Idrieus. When in Roman times a baths was built just to the east, the house was incorporated in it in such a way that its western half became the tepidarium of the baths, while its eastern half was demolished and made to form part of the hypocaust. The façade was reduced to two columns, the Doric flutes being chiselled away to produce plain round shafts—a remarkable indication of the taste of the times.

Still further down to the south-east, at a level some 100 feet (30·5 m.) below that of the temple terrace, is the long wall R which seems to have formed the southern boundary of the precinct, and set against it is the interesting building Q. This was in two storeys, the upper containing three rows of seven monolithic granite columns, more than half of which are still standing; the lower storey is filled with a mass of fallen blocks and architectural members. There seems to have been no wall in the upper storey, but merely an open hall forming a kind of canopy to the lower storey. This building has not (at the time of writing) been cleared out; the Swedish excavators have dubbed it an 'Ablution Hall', but the French scholar A. Laumonier offers a more interesting interpretation. Aelian, in his

1 Mylasa. Baltalı Kapı

2   Mylasa. Temple of Zeus (Carius?)

3   Mylasa. Wall of the precinct of Zeus Osogos

4   Mylasa. Berber İni

5 Mylasa. Gümüşkesen; Roman tomb

6 Euromus. The Temple

7 Peçin Kale. Early Wall

8 Ceramus. City Wall
9 Labraynda. Andron of Idrieus

10   Labraynda. Fountain-house
11   Labraynda. The Sacred Way

12 Labraynda. Temple of Zeus Labrayndus

13 Iasus. Street and Houses

14 Iasus. The Land-Wall

15 Iasus. The Theatre
16 Bargylia. The Theatre

17 Iasus. Newly-excavated Mausoleum
18 Stratoniceia. The Sarapeum

19   Stratoniceia. City Gate
20   Stratoniceia. Tombstone in the Museum

21   Halicarnassus (Bodrum).
     'Ox-hide' ingot

22 Bargylia. Altar
23 Bodrum. Block of frieze from the Mausoleum

24 Bodrum. Castle and Harbour
25 Bodrum. The Castle Ramp

26 Bodrum. The Castle of the Knights
27 Lagina. Gate of the Temple Precinct

28 Alâzeytin. Lelegian houses
29 Alâzeytin. Compound farm building

work on the Nature of Animals, observes that there are in the sanctuary of Zeus at Labraynda, in a fountain of limpid water, tame fish
adorned with necklaces and earrings of gold. Pliny confirms this,
and adds that the fish come when called and readily accept food
from all hands. Is it not possible that they were housed in this curious
building Q? Though it is not explicitly stated, there can be no doubt
that these fish were sacred to the god, and it may even be that he
issued oracles by means of them. Ancient fish-oracles are well
known; there was one, for example, at Sura in Lycia, where the
response was favourable or otherwise according to whether the fish
accepted or rejected the morsels offered them. There is some slight
evidence that Zeus Labrayndus had oracular functions. The crossed
bands on the god's statue, which have sometimes been compared
with the Delphic omphalos-stone, were mentioned above (p. 19);
and there has been found at Labraynda a dedication by a certain
chresmologus, or pronouncer of oracles. He may have been attached
in a professional capacity to the sanctuary; but this is by no means
certain, since itinerant oracle-mongers were commonly called by this
name. The matter must therefore remain undecided, at least until
building Q has been excavated.

The recently discovered stadium lies above the temple to the north,
running east and west across the slope. It is in poor condition, only
the two extremities being preserved about 200 yards apart. At the
west end is a solidly built structure spanning a gully, with a tunnel
through it to permit the passage of the winter rain-water; at the
east end still less is preserved.

Many tombs are to be seen around the sanctuary, placed mostly
in the ancient fashion along the roads leading to the site. They are
more than mere villagers' tombs, and reflect the universal desire,
not only in ancient times, to be buried as near as possible to some
holy spot. As would be expected, they are numerous along the
Sacred Way. In general they are of two types, either chamber-tombs
in a rock-face or large boulder, or sunk into the rock and covered
with a massive lid. The finest of all, however, is a built tomb on the
slope above the temple; a short but steep path leads up in a few
minutes from the terrace. The tomb is in three parts, a forecourt
and two funerary chambers one behind the other. The walls, outside
and in, are superbly constructed of beautifully finished ashlar. The
door to the forecourt is at the east end of the south wall; it was
closed with a slab on its inner side, as will be explained. The floor
of the forecourt was paved only in the part in front of the tomb.
The doorway into the tomb itself was closed by a huge stone slab

45

Fig. 7 Labraynda. Male Sphinx, in the depot

which is now standing in the forecourt; it is estimated to weigh about six tons. The outer chamber contained two sarcophagi, one on each side, of which only broken fragments remain. From here another door leads through to the larger inner chamber, in which are three sarcophagi, one on each side and a very large one at the back, all well preserved. Both chambers are roofed with a 'corbelled' vault, the blocks being cut away in a curve on their under sides to produce the effect of a true vault. The inner corner stones are so cut as to form part both of the back and of the side walls. Over both chambers is an upper storey, equally solidly built but less carefully finished and only about 4 feet (1·22 m.) high; it is entered by a window-like opening overlooking the forecourt. It is roofed with ten slabs of stone 14 feet (4·27 m.) in length, and even longer blocks, over 17 feet (5·18 m.), are to be seen above the entrance to the outer chamber.

Nearly everything about this tomb is remarkable, and not least the arrangements for burial. Originally, it appears, the largest sarcophagus stood alone in the inner chamber, no doubt in a more or less central position; at the same time the two sarcophagi were installed in the outer chamber. These would be the tombs of the owner himself and two of his dependants. The chamber doors were then closed and a slab set in position on the inner side of the door to the forecourt, after which the whole forecourt was filled with earth and sand. At some later time the tomb was opened and the other two sarcophagi introduced to the inner chamber, the large sarcophagus being pushed back to the corner where it now stands; the forecourt was then filled up again. Despite the impressive precautions the tomb has at some time been broken into by treasure-seekers. A further remarkable feature is that the original sarcophagus is too large to be taken through the doors, so that the tomb must have been built around it. Little evidence has been found to determine the date of construction, but certain sherds unearthed in the forecourt suggest a period not later than the fourth century B.C. As to the identity of the owner, nothing whatever is known.

Stretches of the Sacred Way are preserved here and there. It is paved with long blocks of stone placed transversely, a method quite unlike the Roman. It resembles the Roman roads, however, in running very straight, in spite of the steep gradient; there are cuttings and embankments in places. The width is in general about 25 feet (7·62 m.). The piece shown on Pl. 11 is close beside the modern road, about a quarter of a mile west of the sanctuary.

Note

1 Zeus Stratius was in fact worshipped, at least in later times, at a number of places in the northern part of Asia Minor.

5 Iasus

Until recently the most convenient way of reaching Iasus was by
chartering a boat from the port of Güllük, and this can of course
still be done. But in recent years a road has been opened from the
Milâs–Bafa highway, turning off through the village of Karakuyu;
buses use this road, and it is perfectly passable for a car. The
site of the ancient city is now partially occupied by the village of
Kuren.

A professional musician once visited Iasus and gave a recital in
the theatre. In the middle of his performance a bell rang, indicating
that the fish-market was now open. The audience at once rose in
a body and departed, except for one old man who remained seated
with his hand cupped to his ear. The musician approached him and
said, 'I must thank you, sir, for the compliment you have paid to
me and my art; for when the bell rang everyone else rushed away'.
'What?' said the other, 'did you say the bell had rung?' 'Why yes'.
'Then, sir, by your leave—' and he too hurried away.

Strabo tells this story to illustrate the character of the city; for,
he says, the soil being poor, the inhabitants live mainly by the produce of the sea. Fish were abundant, as they still are, witness the
big fishery (*dalyan*) at the head of the gulf. The great marsh, now
largely reclaimed, at the mouth of the Sarıçay to the north-east of
Güllük was in antiquity sea; an inscription tells us that two citizens
of Iasus persuaded Alexander the Great to restore to the city
possession of the 'Little Sea', that is without doubt the area of the
marsh. For a city dependent on its fisheries the matter was of importance, and the two citizens were suitably rewarded with immunity
from taxation and a front seat in the theatre. A gastronomer of the
fourth century B.C. observes that the visitor to Iasus will find there
prawns of great size but scarce in the market; and the present-day
visitor to Güllük will inevitably be offered fish for his dinner.

Since 1960 Italian archaeologists have been digging at Iasus. The excavations are still in progress at the time of writing, but have already revolutionized our knowledge of the city's early history.

According to the Greek foundation-legend Iasus was colonized by Peloponnesians from Argos. Their coming was not unopposed, and the local Carian inhabitants inflicted such losses on them that they were obliged to call in help from the son of Neleus, the founder of Miletus. As a result of this Milesian influx the city became Ionian instead of Dorian. The settlement by Argives is very likely to be historical; Homer gives to Argos the epithet Iason, and there was a small town of Iasus in the Peloponnese. The leader of the colonists was later supposed to be a man of the name of Iasus, and he is represented, with the title Founder, on Iasian coins; in this particular case there is perhaps slightly less reason than usual to regard him as mythical. The recent excavations have produced quantities of Minoan pottery in the buildings of the Middle Bronze Age levels, providing archaeological evidence for a Cretan connection, as there was at Miletus.[1] Above these there are Mycenaean pottery and buildings.

Strabo says that Iasus stood on an island lying close to the mainland. At present this island is joined to the mainland by a shallow isthmus, and it is not unlikely that it was so also in antiquity; the term 'island' is sometimes used to denote a peninsula.[2] To the ancients Iasus is to all appearance an island-city, and nothing would lead one to expect, on the mainland, the splendid stretch of fortification-wall, two miles (3·22 km.) long, which in fact is still standing there. Of this wall and its significance more will be said below.

The Greek settlement was certainly on the island. It was at one time suggested that until the fifth century B.C. the city stood on the mainland, defended by the fine wall just mentioned; but the buildings and sherds discovered on the island by the excavators show continuous occupation there from Mycenaean and even earlier times until the end of antiquity. The meagre remains inside the mainland wall will be described later. The foundation-legend involving the son of Neleus would place the Argive colonization somewhere about the ninth century; the excavators' discoveries show that long before this there was civilized occupation on the site, so that the Greeks' arrival might well be strongly resented and resisted.

After it nothing is heard of Iasus until the fifth century, when the city was enrolled in the Delian Confederacy. Tribute was assessed at one talent, the same as that, for example, of Mylasa; when the assessments were revised—that is in most cases raised—in 425 B.C., the Iasian figure was increased to three talents, but whether this was ever actually paid is not known.

In 412 B.C. disaster overtook the city. At that time the Spartans and Persians were acting in concert against the Athenians, whereas Iasus, still an ally of Athens, was in the hands of a certain Amorges, a Persian noble who was in revolt against the Great King. The satrap Tissaphernes then persuaded the Spartan admiral to attack Iasus. The Iasians were taken by surprise, supposing the advancing ships to be Athenian, and their city was captured and sacked; the booty, says Thucydides, was very rich, for the place was wealthy 'from of old'. The tribute of one talent (or even three) does not suggest great riches, but a trade in salted fish was a profitable business in classical Greece, and the recent excavations suggest a reasonable level of prosperity. After the capture the city—though Thucydides calls it rather a 'town' or 'place'—was handed over to Tissaphernes, together with Amorges himself and all the prisoners, slave and free; for these latter he agreed to pay a gold stater per man.

Spartan vindictiveness seems not to have been satisfied with this. It is recorded that the Spartan commander Lysander, shortly before the final defeat of the Athenians in 404 B.C., destroyed the city of 'Thasos in Caria, an ally of Athens', slaughtering 800 adult males and selling the women and children as booty. No city of Thasos in Caria is known or can ever, it seems, have existed; most scholars have accepted that the place in question was really Iasus. Since the population must have been much reduced after the events of 412, the figure 800 is surprisingly high, and gives an impression of considerable importance for the city in its normal state.

All pretence of Spartan control of this region was, however, ended for good by the Athenian naval victory under Conon near Cnidus in 394 B.C. The interesting attempt, immediately after this, by a group of Aegean states to form an independent league (known only by the coinage it issued) was mentioned above (p. 6); equally interesting is the inclusion of Iasus. Here again we receive the impression that Iasus was no inconsiderable city, for her partners— Rhodes, Samos, Cnidus, Ephesus, and Byzantium—were all places of size and importance. But the league had a short life; the King's Peace in 387 confirmed the Persian possession of all the cities in Asia.

For Mausolus' relations with Iasus we have only once piece of direct evidence, an inscription recording the punishment of certain persons there who had plotted against him. The city was of course within his district as Persian satrap, and in his plan for the Hellenization of Caria he can hardly have failed to include it; it is not unlikely that it was he who caused the island to be fortified with the handsome wall which was standing till the end of the nineteenth century. At the time of writing, at least, the excavators' discoveries do not appear to contradict this suggestion. The inscription shows that Mausolus' authority was officially recognized but not universally accepted; Iasus had remained as long as possible faithful to Athens, and Mausolus' anti-Athenian policy was no doubt responsible for some disaffection in the city.

When Alexander arrived in 334 B.C. and laid siege to Miletus, the Iasians contributed one ship to the Persian fleet which attempted to relieve her. Iasus had never aimed at naval power, and her one ship was such a slow sailer that it was captured in a minor engagement. Ten years later, when Alexander was in Ecbatana, his armoury-commander was an Iasian named Gorgus; at the festival which Alexander celebrated there, when every kind of toasting and flattery was lavished on the king, this Gorgus is said to have outdone all the rest. This is the same man who, with his brother Minnion, secured for his city the fishery in the Little Sea.

There was another Iasian who also found favour with Alexander. This was a boy who had the curious fortune to be loved by a dolphin. It was the custom at Iasus for the boys, after exercising in the gymnasium, to run down and bathe in the sea;[3] the dolphin would then come and carry the boy away on his back, then return him safely to land. This story is told in various forms, with different details and different names for the boy; one account says that Alexander, hearing of it, summoned the boy to Babylon and made him priest of the sea god Poseidon. Such tales of dolphins were common in antiquity, from Arion downwards, but this one was evidently firmly believed at Iasus, for the city's third-century coinage shows a boy swimming beside a dolphin, with an arm over its back.

New inscriptions found by the Italian excavators throw light on the city in the ill-documented period after the death of Alexander the Great. It apears that it had fallen into the hands of three privateers, Machaon, Sopolis, and Hieron, sometime between 320 and 310. The city now struck a bargain with them by paying them a sum of money, in return for which the place was to regain its freedom and independence. Machaon and his two colleagues, as well as the soldiers with them, were to be allowed to settle in Iasus, and to travel where and when they wished, provided that they obeyed the laws of the city. Meanwhile the Iasians were to swear loyalty to Alexander's erstwhile general Ptolemy, shortly to become

51

Ptolemy I Sotêr of Egypt, who controlled south-west Asia Minor in the late fourth and early third centuries. He was also to act as guarantor to the agreement. The inscription reveals vividly the insecurity of those unsettled times, when a city might fall victim to private opportunism, backed by force.

Towards the end of the third century Iasus, still a free city, became involved in the politics of that rather troubled time. Probably about 220 B.C., when Olympichus was established as an independent dynast in the region of Mylasa (above, p. 8), a subordinate of his, by name Podilus, was guilty of misbehaviour on the territory of Iasus; it seems that his troops had been oppressing or molesting the inhabitants. The Iasians complained of this to the Rhodians, who had helped them previously, and the Rhodians made a serious appeal to Olympichus on Iasus' behalf. In doing so they quoted the guarantees that the Macedonian king Philip V had given for the city's security. Philip was much interested in Caria, and when at the end of the century he conducted a campaign in the country, Iasus was one of the towns which he occupied. In 196, however, the Romans required him to withdraw his garrison and leave the city free.

No sooner was this done than Antiochus III of Syria stepped into the breach and by so doing brought the Roman armies to Asia Minor for the first time. At Iasus there was a division of loyalty; the town was held by the king's garrison, but a rival party supported Rome. These latter were compelled to leave the city and joined the Roman forces. In 190 B.C. the Roman commander Aemilius was contemplating an attack on Iasus, but the Iasian exiles serving with him put in a strong plea that the city be spared; they themselves, they declared, were the true representatives of the city's loyalty, the others having been merely coerced by the king's troops. It is doubtful whether this was really true, but the Rhodians joined in pleading for their 'friends and kinsmen', and Iasus escaped.[4]

From this period there is another important and interesting inscription, found reused in a building of the late Roman period. The first part comprises a letter from Laodice, the sister of Antiochus III, in which she demonstrates her concern for the city which had fallen on unexpected ill fortune, partly caused by the unwelcome domination of Philip V, and partly by an earthquake. In order to restore the fortunes of needy citizens, and to ensure the future prosperity of Iasus, she instructed a financial official, Struthion, to arrange for the delivery of 1,000 *medimni* of wheat to the city, every year for a ten-year period. This was to be sold at a fixed, low, price to the population, and the profits from the sale were to be used to provide dowries for the daughters of needy citizens, not exceeding three hundred drachmas in value. In recognition of this splendid generosity and the ingenious arrangement to restore the city's fortunes, the Iasians passed a decree to honour Antiochus III and Laodice. Antiochus is thanked for rescuing the city from slavery and driving out the garrison of soldiers (those of Philip), and sacrifices are to be offered to him at an altar associated with the cults of the main gods of the city. Laodice, appropriately for one who had taken thought for the marriage prospects of the girls of Iasus, was to be identified in a cult with the goddess Aphrodite and worshipped accordingly, special honours being paid to her by intending married couples. The arrangements for the cult of the two royal persons, linked as they were with existing cults of the traditional gods of the city, recall the detailed provisions of the decrees found at Teos in Ionia, also passed in honour of Antiochus III.[5]

Nothing is heard of Iasus under the Rhodian domination which followed Antiochus' defeat in 190 B.C., nor during the period of freedom after 168 B.C. until the formation of the province of Asia in 129. In the war with Mithridates (88 B.C.) Iasus evidently took the king's side, and did not escape punishment; the pirates were permitted by Sulla to sack the town before his own eyes.

Under the Empire, Iasus was not a city of great account, though she seems to have served as one of the customs stations in the province; we hear of a certain Pulcher who functioned there as agent for the tax-farmers. Coinage continued down to the third century, and later Iasus was the seat of a bishopric, attached, like the other cities of the region, to the metropolitan of Aphrodisias. The castle on the island is now thought to be attributable to the Knights of Rhodes.

The principal deities of the city were Apollo, Artemis Astias, and Zeus Most Great. The sanctuary of Artemis has been located in all probability at a site between the agora and the later castle, on the west side of the peninsula. Work to clear this area, and disentangle its problems, is still proceeding. The temple is said to have been 'hypaethral', that is, the cella was unroofed and the cult-statue of the goddess stood exposed to the weather. This, however, caused her no inconvenience, for when Zeus sent rain or snow, he was careful that none should fall on his daughter. The situation of the temple of Zeus is known approximately from the handsome inscription beside the East Gate which marks the limit of the temple precinct (below, p. 60). At least one other boundary-stone of the precinct is known, but it was not found in its original place. The importance of Apollo is clear from his pre-eminence on the coins, but of his temple nothing is known.

From the Argive colonization onwards Iasus was always a Greek city. The Carian element was very small; with one or two exceptions, such as Hyssaldomus and Bryaxis, the names of her citizens, and of her tribes, are exclusively Greek. The constitution from Hellenistic times was that of a normal Greek democracy. The chief magistrate was the stephanephorus, whose name was used for dating the year of his office; other magistrates mentioned in inscriptions are the prytaneis, who presided at the assemblies, the strategi, now only nominally military and charged rather with civil duties, and the prostatae concerned primarily with the register of citizens. Also recorded is the board of neopoeae, whose proper duty was to care for the upkeep of the temple; they function, however, in a different capacity in an interesting inscription concerning the method of payment of the fee due to citizens attending the assembly. On the sixth of each month (the regular day for the assembly) at daybreak a water-clock is to be set up in the form of a vessel holding nine gallons placed 7 feet (2·44 m.) from the ground, with a hole the size of a bean, and the water set running as soon as the sun is up. The neopoeae, six in number, one for each tribe, are to take their seats, each with a box in front of him having a slot of two fingers' length; the boxes shall be previously sealed by the prostatae. Each citizen as he enters is to give to the neopoea of his own tribe a ticket inscribed with his and his father's names, which the neopoea shall put into the box. The inscription breaks off at this point, so we do not know how or when the fee was actually paid; but it is evident that no citizen arriving after the water had run out was entitled to any pay. Inscriptions such as this, which give a sudden glimpse of life as it was lived in an ancient city, are unfortunately all too rare.

Certainly the most striking feature in the ruins of Iasus is the great land-wall which runs west and north from near the village for a mile and a half (2.41 km.), then turns south-westward for another half mile (804·7 m.). Beyond this point its course is not so obvious, but recently the thick undergrowth along the shoreline has been cleared and the full circuit of the land wall traced. This has put paid to much earlier speculation based on the assumption that the wall was never finished. It is well and elaborately built, with frequent jogs and round towers; its average thickness is about 6 feet (1·83 m.). The masonry is a very irregular ashlar, with many small blocks and others up to two tons in weight. Each tower is entered by a door

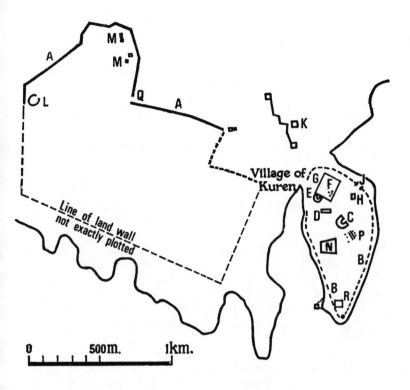

A,A _ Land Wall

B,B _ Island Wall, now destroyed

C _ Theatre

D _ Gymnasium and shrine of
    Artemis Astias

E _ Council House (or Odeum?)

F _ Protogeometric graves
    recently excavated

G _ Agora

H _ Building with mosaic floor

J _ Byzantine Gate

K _ Mausoleum

L _ Round Building

M,M _ Similar Buildings

N _ Castle

P _ Street and Houses

Q _ Main Gate

R _ Propylon and Temple of
    Demeter and Core

Fig. 8 Plan of Iasus

through the wall, and contains two sally-ports close against the outer face of the wall on right and left; in the wall of the tower are five v-slit windows. Each jog also contains a sally-port, so that the number of gates leading outside the wall is exceptionally high. The main entrance-gate (Q on the plan) is set in a recess near an angle of the wall, from which it is enfiladed; it is further protected by windows. Close beside each tower a stairway led up to the parapet (Pl. 14).

The date and purpose of the wall have given rise to much argument, much of it now outdated by recent discoveries. Previous suggestions that the construction of the fortifications was never completed must now be rejected. On the basis of a mid-fourth century tomb discovered outside but abutting the wall, the Italian excavators suggest a date then, or a little later, which would fit well with other fortifications in the region, notably the Mausolan walls at Halicarnassus, Heracleia, and Caunus. However, it must be stressed that there is a crying need for careful excavation of the foundations of these and other city walls in Caria, to establish a more precise and reliable chronology. The interior is thickly overgrown, but limited excavation has shown that it contained buildings, largely of the modest local Lelegian type. The presence of larger public buildings in the centre of the enclosed area should not be completely ruled out.

A good example of these Lelegian buildings, comparatively well preserved, has been recently excavated by the Italians; it lies near the point where the land wall breaks off (L on the plan). A wall about 3 feet (·91 m.) thick encloses a rough circle some 30 yards (27·4 m.) in diameter and ending on the north at two small buildings, one oval, one rectangular, which are standing up to 8 feet (2·44 m.) in height. Each has a door on the inner side. In the oval building is a staircase which led probably to a flat roof rather than to an upper storey. Its plan may be compared with the circular buildings of the Halicarnassus peninsula, especially those at Alâzeytin Kale, which are certainly animal compounds attached to dwelling-houses (below, p. 105). However, the staircase in the Iasus example is a feature difficult to explain. The two buildings are joined by a short wall between them, and also by a curved wall enclosing a semicircular space which was once paved; on this stood an olive-mill with a circular groove in its surface. Near the rectangular building, but outside the ring, is a stone deeply hollowed out, apparently a drinking-trough.[6] Black-glazed pottery and a coin found by the excavators suggest that this building was constructed about 400 B.C.

and collapsed about a century later. Similar structures have been noted in the northern bulge of the land-wall, also outside it and further to the south. J. M. Cook and the present writer have proposed to explain them as shepherds' shielings; the Italian excavators suggest rather small oil-factories. In any case they are clearly of a pastoral, not an urban character. As such they may be compared with the circular compound farm buildings which stood outside the fortification wall of Alâzeytin Kale (below, pp. 105–6).

According to earlier theories, which were elaborated before the full circuit had been discovered, it appeared likely that the long wall was built to defend not a city but a camp. On balance the evidence suggested a construction date in the late fifth or early fourth century. The camp, as it was believed to be, was no makeshift affair and evidently meant to be permanent, in which case the most probable builder was Amorges. He was maintaining a large army in revolt against the Great King and needed a secure base. At this point the Spartan assault of 412 took him by surprise and forced him to abandon his project unfinished and unused. However, this explanation is rendered obsolete by the revelation that the land was completed and probably belonged to the fourth, not the fifth, century. There is no need to doubt that its solid and well-built masonry was designed to enclose a city, or part of a city, not a temporary camp.

In the light of the many recent discoveries at Iasus the history of the occupation of the site will have to be reconsidered in detail. What follows is little more than speculation, but may perhaps form the basis for discussion. It now appears that the original site in the Middle and Late Bronze Age was on the peninsula, where buildings associated with, and dated by, Minoan and Mycenaean pottery have been found. However, during the proto-geometric and geometric periods the area of the classical agora on the peninsula was used for a cemetery (F), suggesting that the site of the town had been transferred elsewhere. The obvious conclusion is that much of the population could have moved to the Lelegian town on the mainland, although the peninsula, in particular the sanctuaries, need not have been completely abandoned. The buildings within the land-wall have not been dated, but they can be compared in style to the Lelegian settlements near Halicarnassus, which generally date between the seventh and fourth centuries B.C. At the end of this period, like the town of Latmus, a fortification wall was built, possibly by Mausolus.[7] However, not long afterwards, in the early Hellenistic period, the whole settlement was again moved back to the peninsula where it was laid out in the Greek style.

The sequence of occupation on the peninsula must be harmonized with this reconstruction, and it is not yet clear from the published reports whether this is possible. The earliest occupation was on the summit and dates back, as the Italian excavators have shown, to the Early Bronze Age at the end of the third millennium. Among their discoveries is that of an early ring-wall, of which they have uncovered a stretch below the mediaeval castle on the east side; it is about 2 feet 8 inches (·81 m.) thick, built of irregular blocks with small stones inserted between. Whether this is to be attributed to the Argive colonists or is even older has not been determined. Later, when the sea-wall was built, this early circuit became unnecessary and was used as a terrace wall; other terraces and houses occupied the slopes below. In particular, an area just to the south of the theatre has been cleared (Pl. 13), revealing a narrow main street flanked by a handsome wall and numerous houses. The wall is dated to the fifth century, but Mycenaean and archaic sherds have been found. If the fifth-century date for this wall is sound, it may cast some doubt on the interpretation suggested in the previous paragraph. On the other hand, we need not assume that the peninsula was completely abandoned when the main area of settlement was elsewhere.

The theatre is of good size, over 200 feet (61 m.) across, but in poor preservation; it faces approximately north-east. Texier saw twenty-one rows of seats still in place, but these are now entirely gone, only the rock-cut substructures remaining, and these covered with earth. The retaining wall of the cavea is of handsome bossed masonry, best preserved on the south side, where a broad staircase, recently excavated, leads up to the cavea. The stage-building is preserved in part, but belongs in its present state to a late reconstruction in Roman times. Four or five courses are preserved, but only the lowest is original; the rest was remade to form the back wall of the Roman stage. This contains three doors leading to rooms behind, which are mostly destroyed. The front wall of the Roman stage stands 18 feet (5·49 m.) further forward into the orchestra; this has a door in the middle which led under the stage, and on either side a group of three niches, one curved between two rectangular, with columns between. In the middle, between these two walls, is a row of columns which supported the stage.[8] This middle row is continued on the south side by a row of blocks which is perhaps the remnant of a ramp leading up to the stage; the first of these blocks is the base of a statue of Justice dedicated by a citizen to the People.

The walls of the theatre once carried an interesting series of inscriptions, dating to the second century B.C., recording special performances by flute-players and comedians paid for by the generosity of private citizens. These have long since been removed, but there remains on the north wall part of a long inscription in a single line recording the dedication of a section of the cavea and the stage to Dionysus and the People, also of the same century; the repair of this part of the cavea is in fact evident from the inferior workmanship.

On the flat ground to the north of the theatre was the city centre. Here again much has been revealed by the Italian excavators. To the west, a high wall with two arched doorways has always been visible; it is thought to be a gymnasium or palaestra. Let into the wall is an inscription in one line dedicating it to Artemis Astias. The agora (G) has been cleared by the excavators, and it is flanked on either side by stoas. In the south-west corner it is adjoined by a small theatre-like building (E), well preserved in its lower parts. The rows of seats are divided into three sections, with four stairways, and the 'orchestra' forms nearly a complete circle. On either side is an arched entrance approached down a flight of steps, and a vaulted corridor runs all round behind the seats. This building appears to be a council-house. In the east corner, there is another rectangular building, 13 by 17 metres square, which has been identified as a Caesareum. Two monumental architrave inscriptions from the stoas around the agora record dedications to Hadrian, Olympian Zeus, and the city of Iasus, and to Artemis Astias, the emperor, and the Homeland respectively. The first also mentions the name of Pomponius Marcellus, governor of the province of Asia towards the end of Hadrian's reign, and this dates the agora to the 130s A.D. The clear ground in the centre has given the excavators an opportunity to make deep soundings into the earlier levels of the site, and it is here that the geometric necropolis, as well as the Late and Middle Bronze Age buildings, have been found.

Of the elegant isodomic ashlar wall which surrounded the island very little survives. It was standing complete until late in the nineteenth century, when nearly all of it was removed to build quays and other structures in Istanbul. A small fragment remains at the southern tip, and more has been uncovered by the excavators near the gate at the north-east corner (J on the plan). This gate has been rebuilt more than once, and before the excavation only its latest form, a Byzantine arch, was visible. On a bastion of classical date close by is the inscription mentioned above marking the limit of the

59

precinct of Zeus; this appears to date to the fifth century B.C. A short distance to the south a tower in the wall is well preserved.

The site of the temple of Zeus is located with much probability at a point some 70 yards (64 m.) inside the gate, where a basilica was later erected. Under the basilica were found stylobates bearing the marks of columns; these are not all parallel and must belong to different buildings. The architectural fragments found are datable to the second century B.C., but an excavation beside the basilica on the north-east revealed walls and pottery dating from Mycenaean to Hellenistic times. This excavation is continuing.

At the southern tip of the peninsula there was a temple (R on the plan) dedicated to the goddesses Demeter and Core, approached from the direction of the sea by an impressive stepped gateway, or propylon. Next to it, in a splendid position overlooking the sea, one of the richer citizens of Iasus built himself a villa in the Roman period, with polychrome and black and white mosaics, and wall paintings which can still be seen.

Space on the island being restricted, burials were mostly confined to the mainland. There a multitude of tombs may be seen, ranging from prehistoric graves to the built tombs and mausolea of Roman times. The earliest date to the third millennium; over eighty of these have recently been excavated. In general they consist simply of four thin slabs, unworked, set up on edge. Similar graves on the island are also found. They are nearly all of less than a man's length. Mixed with and overlying these are later tombs; and the presence of walls and olive-presses indicates that the area was at one time inhabited. Here and there are tombs of 'Carian' type, that is a rectangular hollow sunk in the rock and covered by a separate lid. In the village are many built tombs of rather mean aspect, with more or less illegible inscriptions on the door-lintel; some of these have been converted into modern houses. Before the excavators got to work the most conspicuous tomb was a mausoleum of Roman date in two storeys, reminiscent of the Gümüşkesen monument at Mylasa but of different construction. This, however, is now eclipsed by the splendid mausoleum revealed by the excavations. This stands close beside the Roman aqueduct in the middle of a large square courtyard with walls containing blind arches. This enclosure was visible before the excavation, and had been variously supposed to be either a gymnasium or possibly the fish-market to which, in Strabo's story, the musician's audience hurried away. The mausoleum itself consisted of a tall temple-like chamber standing on a podium and approached by a flight of ten steps, of which six remain.

The order is Corinthian. Under the chamber, inside the podium, are numerous sunken graves in which bones were found; they were originally covered with slabs to form a lid. The monument has been partially restored to stand over 30 feet (9·14 m.) high (Pl. 17). It is of Roman date, but no inscription has come to light to tell the owner's name. Such a fine tomb in a spacious enclosure is a distinct rarity, and finds its closest parallel in the handsome mausoleum by the shore at Side in Pamphylia.[9] It has now been converted into an antiquarium to house some of the sculptural and architectural pieces found in the excavations.

Notes

1 See *Aegean Turkey*, p. 182.
2 A familiar example is the Peloponnese, the 'Island of Pelops'.
3 Sea-bathing does not appear to have been so much indulged in by the ancients as it is today; the same was true in Turkey until quite recently.
4 The 'kinship' depended on nothing more than the Dorian nationality of the original colonists of Iasus; but the Greek cities were always ready and willing to discover such ties of relationship even on the slenderest grounds.
5 See *Aegean Turkey*, p. 112.
6 So say the excavators; but in fact the hollow is only 5 inches (127 mm.) deep and 17 inches (432 mm.) in diameter.
7 See *Aegean Turkey*, p. 212.
8 These appear in the photograph (Pl. 15) encased with small stones put there by the excavators to protect them from damage.
9 See *Turkey's Southern Shore*, p. 74 and Pl. 41.

6 Cindya and Bargylia

Artemis Astias at Iasus was not alone in enjoying miraculous immunity from rain and snow. Exactly the same claim was made for her sister goddess Artemis Cindyas. Cindya was a purely Carian city of whose origins nothing is known, nor indeed do we hear much about it at any time, apart from Artemis herself. Early in the fifth century a certain Pixodarus, son of Mausolus, was living at Cindya and was probably a dynast there; his name and his father's leave little doubt that he was an ancestor of Hecatomnos and Mausolus, and he was distinguished enough to marry a Cilician princess. Later in the same century Cindya was assessed in the Delian Confederacy at the respectable figure of one talent, six times more than was paid by her neighbour Bargylia. In 425 B.C. the city was still under a dynast, and the assessment was raised to four talents.

The scanty ruins of Cindya crown the summit of a steep hill, some 600 or 700 feet (182·9 or 213·4 m.) high, directly above the village of Sığırtmaç, close beside the main road from Milâs to Bodrum. They comprise an outer wall, poorly preserved, enclosing a citadel whose walls stand in places up to 16 feet (4·88 m.) in height; the gate is on the north-west. The masonry is of dry rubble roughly coursed. Many fallen blocks are strewn over the interior, but nothing is standing.

By the third century B.C. Cindya had ceased to exist as a city and had become absorbed in Bargylia; Artemis was thenceforth the principal deity of Bargylia. The site of her temple has been located on a slight eminence close to the point where the road to the village of Kemikler leaves the main highway. Here were found many architectural fragments and two inscriptions, which leave no doubt of the identity, but nothing now remains beyond a few stones belonging to a Byzantine church which replaced the temple. The spot has not been excavated.

This complete reversal in the status of Bargylia relative to Cindya may no doubt be explained by the importance of sea-borne commerce in the Hellenistic period; at the same time it is likely to have been instigated by some ruling power, and we may not improbably see in it the hand of Mausolus or one of his successors. Only now did Bargylia become a Greek city. No claim was made for any early colonization from Greece. A legend grew up that the hero Bellerophon founded the city in honour of his friend Bargylus, who was killed by a blow from his winged horse Pegasus; and in memory of this, Pegasus was commonly shown on Bargylian coins. On the other hand, we hear from Stephanus of Byzantium that Bargylia was at one time called Andanus. Both names are equally un-Greek.

As was mentioned above, Philip V in 201 B.C. made Bargylia his base for a time, and passed the winter there with his fleet. He was far from happy, being both short of provisions and uneasy for his safety; the peculiar situation of the city made it only too easy for his ships to be trapped. In 196 he was ordered by the Roman general Lentulus to withdraw his garrison, and Bargylia was declared 'free'. This freedom was interrupted for twenty years when Caria was given to Rhodes after the battle of Magnesia, but was resumed after 167.

In 133 B.C. when the pretender Aristonicus was fighting the Romans for the kingdom bequeathed to them by Attalus III of Pergamum, he sailed to Myndus and took her by force. The Bargylians, who had contributed forces to the Roman side, viewed the situation with alarm, fearing that they might be next; and it seems that the city was for a time in real danger, from which it was saved by a miraculous epiphany of Artemis Cindyas. What form the divine intervention took the inscription, as usual, does not tell us. About the middle of the first century Bargylia was one of the five Carian cities who were in arrears with their debts to the Roman banker Cluvius.

On the coins the commonest types are Pegasus and Artemis Cindyas. The goddess is clearly an old Carian deity identified with the Greek Artemis; she is shown on the coins standing stiffly to the front, with her arms folded on her breast, wearing a long robe and a veil; sometimes a deer stands beside her. This portrait evidently represents the cult-statue in her temple. The coins begin in the early second century and continue into Imperial times. Under the early Empire the cult of Artemis was associated with that of Augustus, a compliment normally paid in the east only to the old Anatolian deities.

The site of Bargylia is very much denuded—remarkably so, since there is no habitation within miles. It is likely that here, as at Iasus and elsewhere, stones have been removed by sea for city-building in other parts. The ruins lie on a low hill at the angle of a boot-shaped inlet from the gulf of Mandalya, called on the Admiralty chart 'Bargylia Creek'. Its present name is Varvil Bay, preserving the ancient name in its mediaeval form, Barbylia. The early maps mark salt-pans at the southern tip of the peninsula, and until the present century salt was exported from here in quantities up to 2,000 tons a year; but this industry is now defunct. The inner part of the inlet, beyond the city, has become silted up by a small stream and is now marshy, but the outer part remains navigable for small boats; there is a landing-stage about a mile north of the ruins. At L on the plan a solid causeway leads across the inlet, but there is no proper road across the flat land to the east. Bargylia is a desolate spot.

Fig. 9 Bargylia. Causeway and Acropolis Hill

The hill has two summits, both quite low; the earlier remains, Hellenistic and Roman, are mostly on and around the northern, the rest being mainly Byzantine. Of the city wall nothing remains but an angle on the west slope of the southern hill and a few short pieces near the shore on the east (A,A on the plan). At the top of the northern hill are the foundations of a temple about 100 feet (30·5

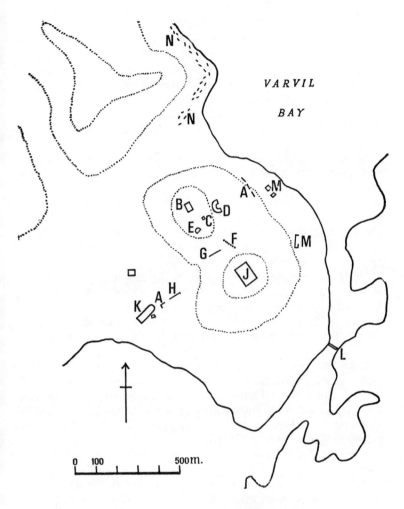

VARVIL

BAY

0   100   500m.

A,A _ City Wall   H_Byzantine Wall
B_ Temple   J_Byzantine Castle
C_ Altar   K_Church
D_ Theatre   L_Causeway
E_ Odeum   M,M_Byzantine Buildings
F_ Stoa   N_Necropolis
G_ Aqueduct

Fig. 10 Plan of Bargylia

m.) in length; it is orientated north-west to south-east, and is in the Corinthian order. Numerous architectural blocks have rolled from it down the slope to the south, including a pediment-block and columns partly concave-, partly convex-fluted. This temple is of Roman date, but to what deity it belonged is not known. Lower down the south slope is a small odeum facing south-east; Newton counted ten rows of seats, and the vaulted passage under them is still preserved.

Lying on the hillside between the temple and the odeum is a rectangular altar now broken into two parts. All four sides carry reliefs, showing respectively Artemis Cindyas in a long robe, with a bow in her left hand and with her right drawing an arrow from the quiver; Apollo, apparently lyre in hand; a male figure in a cloak, possibly the hero Bargylus; and a female figure carrying a cornucopia. These figures are now a good deal damaged, but still recognizable (Pl. 22).

On the east slope is the theatre, facing east over Varvil Bay. It is in poor condition, but an angle on the south side is well preserved (Pl. 16), and much of the stage-building no doubt exists under a mound of earth; the vaulted rooms of its ground floor are still visible. But of the rows of seats little or nothing survives, though the position of the diazoma is discernible.

South-east of the odeum the remains of a stoa are, or were, to be seen, running north-west to south-east for a distance of some 50 feet (15·2 m.) The columns are no longer standing, but their positions are shown by circular marks on the stylobate. Close by on the south-west is a short stretch of an aqueduct with neatly-formed arches of Roman date.

The southern hill is largely occupied by a Byzantine castle of no particular interest; and the church below on the west is unremarkable. To the south of the causeway a quay of uncertain antiquity can, or could, be seen above the surface when the water is low.

Tombs are mostly of sarcophagus type with slightly arched lids. Chamber-tombs are scarce.

7 Stratoniceia

Under the Prohibited Degrees a man may not marry his stepmother; but in the Hellenistic royal families these matters were otherwise regulated. Seleucus I, king of Syria, had a wife Stratonice whom in 294 B.C. he transferred to his son Antiochus; and it was this lady, his stepmother-wife, in whose honour Antiochus founded Stratoniceia. The date is not known, but must have been after 281, when the Seleucids first came into control of this country. Strabo says that they adorned the new city with costly buildings, which is natural enough; yet before very long they gave it away as a present to Rhodes. The date is again uncertain. Long after, in 166 B.C., a Rhodian envoy to the Roman Senate, pleading that Stratoniceia should not be taken away, claimed that the Rhodians had received her 'by the great generosity of Antiochus and Seleucus'. As only too often in the ancient writers, no indication is given as to which of the numerous kings of those names are meant; but the reference appears to be to the same Antiochus I and his son Seleucus, who were co-regents from 279 to 268.

Livy says that in 197 B.C., or a little later, the Rhodians 're-covered' Stratoniceia. They must presumably therefore have lost her at some period, though the event is not recorded; it occurred perhaps during the Carian campaign of Philip V in 201–198 B.C. Rhodian possession of the city was confirmed at Apamea in 188, but in 167 it was taken away for good.

In 88 B.C. the city was captured by Mithridates and punished for its resistance, but was compensated at the end of the war by Sulla, who treated it handsomely. Labienus, at the head of his Parthian hordes, attacked Stratoniceia in 40 B.C., but was successfully repulsed; he revenged himself by sacking the sanctuary of Hecate at Lagina, but failed in a similar attempt upon Panamara.

According to the ancient writers Stratoniceia was founded on the site of an old Carian town which was called first Chrysaoris then

Idrias; and by one account she was the first city founded by the Lycians. If this last tradition has any historical basis, it may go to strengthen the theory mentioned above (p. 3) by which the Lycians passed southwards from Miletus to their ultimate home. Both names, Chrysaoris and Idrias, must in fact have denoted a region rather than a town; Herodotus says that the Marsyas flows 'from the Idrias country' to the Maeander, and Strabo observes that the reason why the Idrians are not mentioned by Homer is that they are included in the Carians. In the tribute lists of the Delian Confederacy the Edrians (evidently a variant form of the same name) are assessed together with Euromus and the unknown Hymessus at the remarkably high figure of six talents. Chrysaoris is quoted by Pausanias as an earlier name for the site and territory of Stratoniceia, and in Hellenistic times Chrysaorian became a synonym for Carian, at least outside Caria itself.

The reason for this was the Chrysaoric League (above, p. 8), to which all Carians belonged. The temple of Zeus Chrysaoreus, where the League met to offer sacrifice and discuss its affairs, is said to have been close to Stratoniceia, and the new city, though not Carian but Macedonian, was admitted to membership by virtue of the many Carian villages on its territory. Herodotus speaks of a place called White Pillars, where he says the Carians met, near the river Marsyas; this has been thought to be the same sanctuary of Zeus Chrysaoreus, though he does not actually call it so, and there is in fact no actual reference to the Chrysaoric League before 267 B.C. The place has not been identified with certainty, though there are ancient remains at a spot some two and a half miles (4·02 km.) to the east of Eskihisar which would meet the conditions reasonably well.[1] The other Stratoniceian sanctuaries at Lagina and Panamara are discussed separately below.

As a Hellenistic foundation Stratoniceia was not divided like Mylasa into tribes and clans, but on the Greek model into tribes and demes. This was, however, a distinction without a difference, for the demes were in fact the old Carian villages, just like the Mylasan clans. Their names—Loboldeis, Londargeis, Korazeis, and others—are equally un-Greek.

Under the Empire, Stratoniceia is recorded as a free city and was very rich and prosperous. Stephanus says that she was 'founded' —that is, refounded, or rather embellished with new buildings—by Hadrian, and took in his honour the name Hadrianupolis; but this is agreed to be a confusion with another Stratoniceia in the neighbourhood of Pergamum. In Byzantine times the bishopric of

Stratoniceia was subordinate, like the others of the region, to Aphrodisias.

The ruins of Stratoniceia at Eskihisar are somewhat scanty in proportion to the size of the city, but what remains gives an impressive idea of the solidity and magnificence which they once possessed.

The acropolis hill lies to the south of the site, beyond the area shown on the plan Fig. 11; it is fortified with a ring-wall round the summit. But the inhabited city lay on the flat ground to the north, and is now partially occupied by the village of Eskihisar. Of the city wall F,F only insignificant ruins now remain; it was originally rather less than a mile in length. The main entrance was on the north at C; part of the arched gate is standing, in massive broad-and-narrow masonry, and just inside it a single unfluted Corinthian column survives from the row which originally stood there (Pl. 19). At the north-east corner of the site are the ruins of a powerful fort, D, overlooking a dip in the ground; it is solidly constructed of large squared blocks in regular courses, with some mortar, but in places additions or repairs show a very inferior masonry with many reused blocks and even column-drums.

In the present village, and almost in the centre of the ancient city, is the most impressive building on the site, the Sarapeum or temple of Sarapis, A, dating from the second or third century A.D. The outer walls are standing to a fair height (Pl. 18), in the same broad-and-narrow masonry as the north gate, but the interior is filled with earth and is now used as a garden. The north wall is covered, partly on the inside and wholly on the outside, with inscriptions in Greek and Latin; one of these, at the east end of the inner face, is an ex-voto to Helios Zeus Sarapis for salvation from war and foreign seas. Another records an oracle delivered by Zeus of Panamara; the Stratoniceians had asked, apparently on the advice of Sarapis, whether the barbarians would attack the city in the current year; the god reassures them. The occasion was evidently the invasion of the Goths in the middle of the third century A.D. A third is a very curious document; it consists of twelve very faulty verses, each of which contains as many letters as one of the months of the year, beginning with October; the number of days is written at the right in Greek numerals. At the same time the initial letters of the lines form an acrostic giving the name of the writer, Menippus. His purpose, as he explains, is to provide a mnemonic which may be useful to his less well educated fellow-citizens.

Just to the west of this building, in a maize-field, stands a solitary

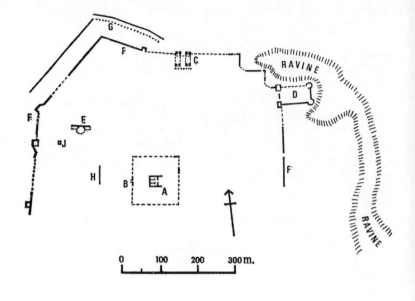

A _ Temple of Sarapis

B _ Gate of temple precinct

C _ Main City-gate

D _ Fortress

E _ Building of unknown purpose

F,F _ City Wall

G _ Colonnaded Street

H _ Agora

J _ Coffee-house of Eskihisar

The Acropolis hill and the Theatre lie further to the south.

Fig. 11 Plan of Stratoniceia

gate, B, with uprights and lintel. This was an entrance to the peri-bolus or precinct surrounding the temple, an enclosure over 100 yards (91·4 m.) square of which very little else survives. The gate carries no inscription.

To the west again lay the agora, or market-place, of Stratoniceia. Virtually **all that now remains** of it is a row of marble blocks, H on the plan, bordering one of the village lanes. To the north of this, beyond the coffee-house, is a building E of unknown purpose, comprising at present a long wall of large well-squared blocks, joined on the south side by part of a curved wall. This arrangement does not conform to the plan of any normal building.

At the north-east corner of the site (G on the plan) Trémaux in 1874 saw a colonnade beside a street leading in the direction of the city-gate at C. Something of this colonnade is said to survive, but the present writer has not seen it.

At the north foot of the acropolis hill, not shown on the plan, is the theatre, large and quite well preserved, but badly overgrown and poorly maintained. The cavea, facing north in the manner approved by Vitruvius, is divided by stairways into nine cunei; the single diazoma is now largely destroyed. The capacity is estimated as not less than 10,000. The stage-building too, or at least its foundations, is probably in quite good preservation; but it has not been excavated and the plan is not at present to be made out.

On the hillside above the theatre is a levelled area on which lie the ruins of a small temple in the Ionic order, identified from an inscription as devoted to the cult of the Emperors.

Across the main road from the school is a small museum which is well worth a visit. It contains mostly small pieces of Roman date, including epitaphs and several bearded heads from the angles of a sarcophagus; among the former is the quaint tombstone of a young man (Pl. 20) erected by his parents and brothers. But the most remarkable object is a Mycenaean stirrup-cup of buff with horizontal red stripes which is dated to the twelfth or eleventh century B.C. All the exhibits were found locally.

Note

1 They are described as lying beside the main Aydın road around a Turkish cemetery, with many broken marbles and two large blocks flush with the ground. The writer has not seen these.

8   Lagina and Panamara

Of all the deities who made up the Greek pantheon one of the strangest is surely Hecate. It is possible, though not proved, that she was of Carian origin; but in Greek mythology she is daughter either of Zeus or of a Titan. She is assimilated to, or even identified with, other goddesses, especially Artemis and Demeter; in one metrical inscription she is addressed as Ompnia, a special epithet of Demeter. She is thought of as an underworld deity, mistress of the dead and holder of the key to the door of Hades; she is the sender of bad dreams, ghosts, and spectres, but as sender can also defend men against them. Often she is accompanied by dogs, and dogs were sacrificed to her. The dog was indeed called 'the Carian sacrifice', and its association with the underworld is seen, for example, in the familiar case of Cerberus. At the same time Hecate is a moon-goddess, a roamer by night, haunting especially crossroads and forks in the road, and in these places she was worshipped by night, on the last day of the old moon, with offerings of cakes, fish, eggs, and cheese. A proper temple such as that at Lagina is therefore something out of the ordinary. In art she is represented sometimes with a single body (so at Lagina, and this seems to be her earliest form), or more often with three complete bodies or with one body and three heads. Her principal attributes are torch, dagger, whip, snake, and key. At Lagina she carries a torch in her left hand and a dish in her right; on her head is the cylindrical headdress called *polos*, with the horns of a crescent moon, and at her feet sometimes a dog. At Lagina also mysteries were celebrated in her sanctuary, and it appears that on occasion she might even deliver oracles.

How old the cult of Hecate at Lagina may be is not known. Our earliest evidence is an inscription recording a priest of Hecate and of Helios and Rhodes; this must clearly date from the Rhodian domination of 189–167 B.C. The temple itself, of which the ruins remain, is variously dated by scholars from about 125 B.C. to the time of Augustus; the choice lies most probably between the earliest date, after the war with Aristonicus and the foundation of the province of Asia, and one about 80 B.C. after the war with Mithridates. What stood in the sanctuary before this is unknown. In 88 B.C. Mithridates took Stratoniceia by force; after his defeat the decree of the Senate confirming the friendship and alliance of Rome and the inviolability of the sanctuary was engraved on the wall of the temple at Lagina; at the same time a festival was inaugurated with the double title of Hecatesia-Romaea. In 40 B.C. Labienus failed to capture Stratoniceia, but he sacked her temples, including that of Hecate; the inscription on the lintel of the propylon which is still standing refers in general terms to the help given after 27 B.C. by Augustus in restoring the cult after this disaster.

From 81 B.C. onwards the Hecatesia-Romaea were celebrated every fourth year with especial brilliance; in the intervals the Hecatesia alone were held annually. But these were by no means the only ceremonies in honour of Hecate. Very important was the festival of the Bearing of the Key, held once a year and accompanied by games, lasting several days. The key of the temple was carried in procession from Lagina to Stratoniceia and back; this would symbolize the attachment of the sanctuary to the city, but the key must surely have meant more than this in the minds of the worshippers; Hecate held the key to the door of the underworld. Important also was the Birthday Festival, held annually on the goddess's birthday, the thirtieth of the month; it may also have been held, with less splendour, on the same day of every month. At the annual celebration gifts of money were made to the citizens. At the same time Hecate shared with Zeus a shrine in the council-house at Stratoniceia; here, in consequence of certain miracles performed by the goddess, ceremonies were held every day throughout the year. All this is peculiar to Hecate at Lagina, and very different from the popular worship at crossroads in the dead of night.

The temple cult was served by a male priest; not until the third century A.D. do we hear of a priestess, nor even then does she take the place of the priest; she is usually his wife or other close relation and serves under him. Among the other personnel of the clergy the most important was the Key-Bearer, always a young girl, whose duty it was to open and close the temple; she too was generally related to the priest. At a late date we hear of a neocorus, or temple-warden, with duties corresponding to those of a sacristan. Eunuchs also were attached to the cult; in early times, no doubt, as in oriental religions generally, these were important, but when we hear of them, in the third century A.D., they have uncharacteristic functions, as for example the maintenance of the trees in the temple precinct. Another permanent official was the President of the Mysteries; but of his duties, and of the mysteries themselves, we are as usual told nothing. They were, however, celebrated regularly at least from the second century onwards.

The temple precinct consisted of a large, nearly rectangular enclosure about 490 by 440 feet (149·3 by 134·1 m.) surrounded by a stoa, plain on three sides, but on the south raised on a flight of steps; at the west end on this side was a monumental gateway

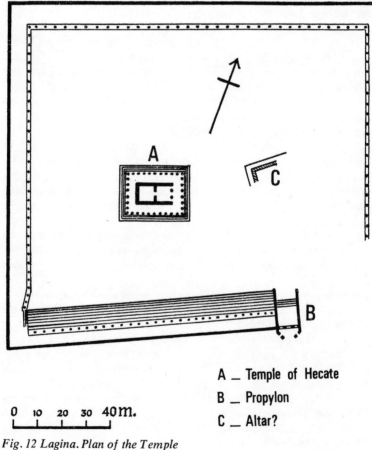

A — Temple of Hecate

B — Propylon

C — Altar?

0 10 20 30 40 m.

Fig. 12 Lagina. Plan of the Temple

74

(propylon), of which the jambs and lintel are still in place—the only thing actually standing on the site (Pl. 27). As the inscription shows, it dates to the time of Augustus, and it is likely that the whole stoa is of the same period. The steps were probably used as seats for those assisting at the mysteries.

Nearly in the centre of the precinct stood the temple of Hecate. It was excavated, or at least investigated, in 1891–92, but the work was never carried through, and the ruins still lie in a jumbled heap. The chief result of this work was the recovery of numerous blocks of the frieze and their transportation to the museum in Istanbul. Then and at other times many inscriptions have been found, and to these we are indebted for most of what we know about the cult. The temple is in the Corinthian order, unlike the stoa, which is Doric. It is pseudo-dipteral, with eight columns at front and back, but only eleven on the long sides; it includes a deep pronaos, with two columns in antis, and a cella, but no opisthodomus. Some of this may still be seen, notably the front steps, some of the paving in the peristyle, the antae, and the threshold of the cella, and three column bases at the rear. The frieze on the east front showed Hecate assist-ing at the birth of Zeus, and carrying the stone to offer in his place to his father Cronos; at the west end she watches over a battle between gods and giants. The north side showed a scene of frater-nization between Amazons and Greek soldiers, while Hecate pours libation; this is thought to be an allusion to the treaty of alliance ratified in 81 B.C. between Stratoniceia and Rome. On the south side was a series of figures, mostly unrecognizable, apparently represent-ing Carian deities and cities.

There was much else in the sanctuary besides the temple, though little of it can be seen today. In front of the temple on the east an altar would be expected, and there is in fact a heap of ruins in this position (C on the plan), but it has not been excavated and is differently orientated from the temple; its identity is therefore uncer-tain. The precinct housed a considerable permanent population, attached in various ways to the cult; an inscription of the second century A.D. tells us that a priest constructed at his own expense three stoas 'in the sacred house' and completed the stoa in front of the sacred house 'close to the provision-market'. This house was probably occupied by the clergy. There was also a sacred grove of trees, for whose upkeep the eunuchs were responsible, and another inscription forbids the pasturing of flocks in the sanctuary. All of this—altar, houses, market, grove, and pasture—was apparently contained within the area of the precinct.

A few hundred yards to the east of the temple is an attractive pool, fed from a spring above. An inscription found here, but not yet published, apparently records the installation of this pool.[1] A fragmentary text from the sanctuary refers to the construction of a water-channel 'leading to the fountain from the . . .'; here it breaks off, but it is likely enough that it led from the pool in question to a fountain in the temple precinct.

Lagina was a deme of Stratoniceia, and was joined to her by a Sacred Way six miles (9·65 km.) long, of which only the scantiest traces remain. The name of Lagina, however, is never used in the inscriptions, and it appears that the deme was known as Hieracome, the sacred village. The nearest town now is the *nahiye* of Turgut, about a mile to the south; this name is new, and until recently the place preserved its ancient name in the form Leyna—which indeed is still heard. It is nine miles (14·5 km.) from Yatağan by a perfectly tolerable road.

Panamara

A second sanctuary belonging to Stratoniceia, and rivalling in importance that of Hecate at Lagina, was that of Zeus Panamaros. The site, discovered in 1886, is about seven miles (11·3 km.) as the crow flies to the south-east of Eskihisar, but it is reckoned three and a half or four hours on foot. The ruins are on a hill above the village of Bağyaka, but they have never been excavated and there is not now very much to see. The sanctuary consists of a walled enclosure some 50 yards (45·7 m.) square containing a jumble of blocks among trees and bushes; this forms part of a larger enclosure nearly 100 yards (91·4 m.) square, with a massive wall of which the west angle is preserved for some 80 yards (73·2 m.). In one corner is a ruined building about 60 feet (18·3 m.) long. This outer enclosure was joined on the south-west by a paved road from Stratoniceia, of which a long stretch is recognizable on the height opposite. Many inscriptions have been found on the site, and give much information concerning the cult.

The two principal buildings were the temples of Zeus Panamaros and of his consort Hera; these, however, have not been identified on the ground. But other deities also were worshipped, notably Artemis and Sarapis; and as at Lagina the precinct contained many shrines and other buildings. We hear for example of a reception-room, a luncheon-hall, and a store-room.

Panamaros is an old Anatolian name, and the cult too may be

very ancient, though our information concerning it begins only after the foundation of Stratoniceia. The sanctuary was honoured with a visit by Philip V; it may have suffered from Mithridates in 88 B.C.; but in 40, when Labienus, failing to take Stratoniceia, attacked Panamara, the defenders, aided by the powerful walls and by a miraculous intervention of the god himself, successfully repelled him. The details of the battle were recorded in a long decree engraved in the sanctuary; there were apparently three attacks. The first took place by night, but the god sent a great flame of fire upon the assailants and they recoiled. Next morning the assault was renewed; this time the god's aid took the form of a thick mist followed by a great storm, before which the attackers fled as if pursued by Furies; not a single defender was seriously wounded. A third attack was made with reinforcements, and now the god's mysterious power became very evident; cries were heard as if of a relieving force, though none appeared, and a snarling as of dogs attacking the assailants; the latter were then, from some cause which is not apparent, suddenly hurled down from the walls. Throughout these events the lamps in the temple were found to have remained burning.

Festivals at Panamara seem to have been less frequent than at Lagina; we hear notably of three. Of these the greatest was the Panamareia, celebrated annually and lasting for ten days; the statue of Zeus was carried down to Stratoniceia for the duration, and the festival and games took place in the city. In honour of Hera the Heraea was held at Panamara every other year and was, at least at first, restricted to women; it lasted one day and included mysteries. Finally, every fourth year, a two-day festival of Zeus, the Comyria, was held in a sanctuary at Panamara called the Comyrium; this was primarily for men and it too included mysteries.

The name Panamaros, as was said above, is Anatolian, but it was later Graecized in the form Panemeros or Panemerios, and understood to mean either 'very gentle' or 'of the full daylight', in contrast to the nocturnal Hecate.

Note

1 The stone is said to have been subsequently built into a house with the inscribed face hidden, and the writer was unable to see it.

9   Halicarnassus

Of the Seven Wonders of the ancient world—only one of them in Greece itself—hardly anything survives today, apart from the pyramids of Egypt. The lighthouse at Alexandria, the Colossus of Rhodes, the Hanging (that is terraced) Gardens of Babylon, and the statue of Zeus at Olympia are utterly lost. Of the temple of Artemis at Ephesus some fragments of the columns are in the British Museum, and the foundations still remain, sunk in a muddy pool. The Mausoleum at Halicarnassus has fared little if at all better. Its site was determined by Sir Charles Newton in 1856, and a number of the sculptures that he found are also in the British Museum; large quantities of the green stone which formed its base may be seen built into the Castle of the Knights at Bodrum; on the site itself virtually nothing is now visible. This famous building has, however, served to make the name of Halicarnassus more familiar than any other city of Caria.

That Halicarnassus was a Dorian foundation is stated both by Herodotus and by Strabo; the colonists came, according to the tradition, from Troezen on the east coast of the Peloponnese under a certain Anthes or one of his descendants. In A.D. 26, when Halicarnassian envoys came to Rome to compete for the privilege of erecting a temple to the Emperor Tiberius, they urged in their own favour that for 1,200 years their city had never felt the shock of an earthquake. This would put the foundation, at the latest, very soon after the Trojan War;[1] but in fact it is unlikely to have been earlier than the Dorian invasion of Greece about 1100 B.C. Strabo indeed observes that at a date after the death of Codrus, the last king of Athens, about the first quarter of the eleventh century, Cnidus and Halicarnassus were not yet in existence. We may therefore probably accept the foundation under Anthes some time after 1000 B.C.

At first the city was a member of the Dorian hexapolis (above, p. 4), but was later expelled for the misconduct of one of its citizens. The story as told by Herodotus, himself a Halicarnassian, is that a certain Agasicles, after winning a victory in the games celebrated in honour of Apollo at Triopium near Cnidus, received a bronze tripod as his prize; in disregard of the rule which required him to dedicate this on the spot to Apollo, he took it home with him and hung it up in his house. It is likely enough that this was a mere pretext, and that the real reason for the expulsion was the increasing Ionian tendencies of the Halicarnassians; at all events, when the city becomes familiar in the fifth century, it appears as purely Ionian. Herodotus wrote in Ionic, as did his uncle Panyasis the epic poet, and even the earliest inscriptions show no trace of the Doric dialect. It is not clear how this came about. No special reason (as for example at Iasus or Smyrna) is recorded, apart of course from the expulsion from the hexapolis. However this may be, the connexion with the mother-city of Troezen was maintained, and the Halicarnassians built there a temple of Aphrodite.

When the Persians overran the Greek cities of the coast after the capture of Sardis in 546 B.C., Halicarnassus naturally fell with the rest. Sixty years later, at the time of the Persian Wars, the city was ruled in the Persian interest by a Carian dynasty of which the most famous member was the queen Artemisia. Her name is Greek, but her father had the Carian name Lygdamis, while her mother was Cretan. When Xerxes was preparing for his invasion of Greece in 480 B.C., this redoubtable woman not only joined his navy in person —though, as Herodotus remarks, there was no need for her to do so —but was esteemed by him above all his other counsellors. At Salamis, when the King was debating whether to risk a sea-fight with the Greek navy, Artemisia was alone in advising him against it, pointing out among other things the worthlessness of many of the elements in his forces; Xerxes himself was inclined to agree, but thought it better to adopt the advice of the greater number. In the battle itself Artemisia was favoured by chance in a curious way: when the Persian fleet was routed and in confusion, she found her own ship closely pursued by an Athenian vessel; thereupon, whether by chance or by design, she bore down on a ship of her own side from Calynda and sank it with all hands. The Athenian, supposing that her ship must be fighting for the Greeks, turned away and Artemisia escaped; on the other hand, the King and his companions, watching the battle from a neighbouring hillside, imagined the Calyndian to be an enemy, and were loud in their praises of the queen's prowess; Xerxes himself was said to have exclaimed, 'My men have shown themselves women and my women men'. As Herodotus drily observes, it was lucky for her that no Calyndian survived

79

to give the game away. From then on she stood higher than ever in the King's favour, and when she advised him to return home after the battle, he accepted her advice and entrusted his bastard children to her care. The Athenians, on the other hand, had put a price of 10,000 drachmae on her head if taken alive—a reward which was never claimed.

When the Delian Confederacy was founded a few years afterwards, Halicarnassus, either then or later, became a member. The comparatively modest standing of the city at that time is shown by the amount of its normal tribute, namely one and two-thirds talents, or less than was paid by the Lelegian towns of Termera and Pedasa. It had, however, an influence disproportionate to its size; at least, Artemisia is said to have ruled also over several of the islands, including the large island of Cos. The same dynasty continued in control until the middle of the fifth century, and it was during this period that Herodotus grew to maturity. Forced to leave his native city by the oppressive government of the tyrant Lygdamis II, the historian later returned and was instrumental in putting an end to the dynasty.

Such is the account current in later antiquity. But an interesting inscription, the earliest found at Halicarnassus, suggests that the power of the tyrant was not altogether unbridled. It takes the form of a decree issued by the 'Council of the Halicarnassians and Salmacitans, together with Lygdamis'. Persian control was of course removed after Salamis, and it appears that the first steps had been taken towards a kind of democracy, though no doubt the ultimate authority would rest with the tyrant.

The inclusion of the Salmacitans in this decree is interesting. Salmacis is indeed something of a puzzle. In later times we find it described variously as a headland, a fountain, and (less convincingly) as a city of Caria. Its position is fixed approximately on the west side of the harbour at Bodrum. Evidently in the fifth century it formed a kind of suburb of Halicarnassus, with enough independence to be separately represented on the Council; its inferior status is shown by the fact that elsewhere in the inscription only Halicarnassus is mentioned. The fountain had some celebrity, or rather notoriety, for it was said that its water, though excellent to drink, had the effect of making men who drank from it soft and effeminate. The Roman architect Vitruvius, who shows a particular interest in Halicarnassus, vigorously denies this imputation, and attributes the fame of the spring to a much nobler cause. When the Greek colonists arrived, he says, and drove the Carians to the hills, the latter gave them much trouble by raiding and brigandage; but after a while one of the Greeks set up a tavern beside the fountain of Salmacis because of the excellence of the water, and the Carians gradually got into the habit of patronizing this. So, by mixing with the Greeks, they learned the ways of society and, thanks to Salmacis, were weaned from barbarity to civilization.

How much, if any, truth there may be in this story no one can say; but it is certain that there was, from the earliest times of which we can judge, a very considerable Carian element in the city. This is clear from the names of the citizens. Among several hundreds of names of Halicarnassians known to us from inscriptions in the fifth century, Greek and Carian names are almost equally divided. They are, moreover, frequently mixed in the same family; we find sons with **Greek names** having fathers with Carian names, and vice versa; the father of Herodotus himself had the Carian name Lyxes. It would, however, be quite wrong to suppose that Halicarnassus was anything but a truly Greek city; all the archaeological evidence goes to show that this strong Carian element was absorbed without any diminution of the city's Hellenic character.

In the fourth century great changes took place at Halicarnassus. Caria was now once again under Persian dominion, ruled by a satrap appointed by the Great King. Early in the century this satrap was, as related above, a certain Hecatomnos, succeeded on his death in 377 by his son Mausolus. Until then Halicarnassus was a comparatively small city, but Mausolus, observing her natural advantages for fortification and commerce, transferred his capital from Mylasa. His ideas were never on a niggardly scale, and he set out to create a worthy capital city. He it was who built the line of walls, some three and a half miles long, of which parts are standing today; and to people this great area he forcibly transplanted the inhabitants of six of the eight Lelegian cities in the neighbourhood. These were of varying size, but some at least, if we may judge by the tribute they paid to Athens in the fifth century, seem to have been comparable to Halicarnassus herself, and the population of the new city must have been four or five times that of the old. For his own residence Mausolus built a palace with walls of dried brick, finished in all parts with marble from the Sea of Marmara. Nothing of this palace survives today, and its position has been the subject of much discussion (below, pp. 86–8).

Mausolus died in 353 B.C. and was succeeded by his wife and sister, Artemisia the younger. She ruled for only three years, but in that time made herself famous in two notable respects. The first of these was the superb tomb with which she has perpetuated her husband's memory, the Mausoleum. For the form of this monument we have to rely on the description given by the elder Pliny, eked out by the rather scanty remains unearthed by Sir Charles Newton in 1857 and in more recent years by a Danish expedition. Something may be gleaned too by comparing the remains with those of other buildings, such as the mausoleum Belevi near Ephesus,[2] which were modelled on the Mausoleum at Halicarnassus. This is not the place to discuss details,[3] but the general appearance is clear enough. The building was of oblong shape and comprised four parts: first, a solid base or podium; above this a colonnade of thirty-six columns, disposed apparently with eleven on the flanks and nine on the short sides, surrounding a rectangular chamber; above again, a pyramid of twenty-four steps; and at the top a chariot-and-four bearing (in all probability) figures of Mausolus and Artemisia. The total height, according to Pliny, was 140 Ionic feet—about 41 metres by modern reckoning. All four sides were adorned with sculptured friezes by some of the first-rate sculptors of the day, Leochares, Bryaxis, Scopas, and Timotheus, who each took one side. Three of them were apparently brought from Greece, but Bryaxis has a Carian name. It was principally these sculptures, we are told, that caused the Mausoleum to be reckoned among the Seven Wonders. Fragments of them are now in the British Museum, and a single slab is exhibited in the Castle of the Knights (Pl. 23). Even more than these, however, many people (the present writer included) will no doubt admire the superb figure of Mausolus himself which may have occupied the chariot at the top. The Mausoleum stood for 1,500 years; Bishop Eustathius in the twelfth century, in his Commentary on Homer, observes that it 'was, and is' a marvel. But when the Knights arrived in 1402, they found it in ruins, destroyed presumably by one of the earthquakes which the envoys to Tiberius claimed to be so rare. Looking for building-stone and material for burning lime, they found here a plentiful supply of both; they removed to the castle almost the whole of the solid base, in the interior of which they discovered and destroyed the handsomely decorated tomb-chamber. Newton found only the lowest courses of the base, made of the same green granite of which the castle is largely constructed; he found also on the west side a rock-cut stairway descending to the level of the lowest foundations, and a few paces from the foot of this stairway a huge door-stone weighing two tons which in all probability closed the entrance to the tomb-chamber. But of the chamber itself nothing remained.

Artemisia's other claim to fame is of a totally different character. That a woman should rule over Caria seemed to the Rhodians an indignity, and also no doubt an opportunity; they therefore equipped a fleet and set out to take the kingdom from her. Artemisia, learning of this, hid her own fleet in a secret harbour joined by a canal to the great harbour. This had been constructed by Mausolus close under his palace, so as to have his ships under his eye and to make his decisions without interference. The Rhodians sailed in and put their men ashore to occupy the city. Whereupon the queen led her ships quickly out of the secret harbour, seized the unmanned Rhodian vessels, and carried them out to sea. The Rhodian soldiers, deprived of their retreat, were surrounded and destroyed in the market-place. Artemisia then put her own men on the enemy ships and sailed to Rhodes. There the Rhodians, supposing their own ships to be returning victorious, admitted the Halicarnassians, and the city was easily captured. To celebrate this victory Artemisia had a trophy erected there in the form of a statue of herself branding the city of Rhodes. Humiliating though this was for the Rhodians, ancient custom forbade that a trophy once set up should be taken down; to hide their shame, therefore, they afterwards erected a building around it and declared it forbidden ground.

On Artemisia's death in 350 B.C. the succession passed in turn to the other children of Hecatomnos, the last of whom, Pixodarus, called in a Persian satrap named Orontobates to share his rule; and this satrap was in control when Alexander arrived in 334, shortly after Pixodarus' death. Of the Macedonian siege of Halicarnassus we have detailed accounts by Diodorus and Arrian, from which the course of events is reasonably clear. Orontobates was assisted in the defence by the Rhodian Memnon fighting in the Persian cause, and the city was well prepared, with command of the sea. Alexander fixed his headquarters on the north-east side, near the Mylasa gate, and after an unsuccessful attack on Myndus settled down to the siege of Halicarnassus.

Sending round a detachment to invest the city on the west side by the Myndus gate and to prevent reinforcement from that quarter, he took command in person on the north-east. Filling in the fosse, he brought up his siege-engines and succeeded in breaking through the wall. The defenders, however, fought back vigorously and built an inner wall to close the breach. The fighting continued with frequent sallies by the Persians to set fire to the engines, all of which were repulsed with much slaughter on either side; the historians emphasize the fierce and determined bravery of both parties. One

83

evening two of the Macedonian soldiers, having applied themselves too freely to the bottle, got to boasting of their achievements, and to show off their prowess set out by themselves to attack the wall. The defenders came out to punish their presumption, and as others came up on either side, a sharp engagement ensued, and the city was almost taken. Alexander, however, was hoping for a voluntary surrender and forbore to press the attack. Meanwhile on the other front by the Myndus gate an unsuccessful sortie by the Persians also brought the city near to capture, but again Alexander called his men back. Eventually Orontobates and Memnon, realizing that they could not hold out much longer, while their losses were severe, set fire to the upper part of the city and withdrew with the best of their troops to the two headlands on east and west of the harbour, sending the rest to the island of Cos. Alexander thereupon sacked the city, sparing the inhabitants, but made no attempt on the headlands; leaving a force to blockade them, under the direction of the ex-queen Ada, he passed on into Lycia. The sack was evidently not complete; at least, the Mausoleum and the palace of Mausolus seem to have suffered no harm. The headlands surrendered shortly afterwards, from weariness of the siege rather than from compulsion.

Ada was thereupon appointed as ruler of the whole country. Pliny states further that Alexander attached to Halicarnassus six of the neighbouring Lelegian towns, and gives their names. This, however (in the writer's opinion), is plainly an error; Pliny has wrongly attributed Mausolus' action to Alexander. When Alexander left, the city was not even completely captured, and by the time such a settlement became possible he was in the midst of his eastern campaign.[4]

In the free-for-all which followed Alexander's death the Halicarnassians came, early in the third century, under the control of Ptolemy II of Egypt, to whom, together with Apollo, they dedicated a stoa. In 196 B.C. Antiochus III of Syria would have taken the city from the Ptolemies, but was prevented by their allies the Rhodians. After Antiochus' defeat by the Romans in 190 B.C. Halicarnassus was left as a free city, and remained so, as far as we know, for the rest of her history. She was among the places plundered by the notorious Verres in 80 B.C., and by 60 seems to have been in low water; her fortunes were, however, restored, as we are told, by Quintus Cicero, brother of the famous orator, who was governor of Asia at that time. But before long the exactions of the 'tyrannicides' Brutus and Cassius (above, p. 10) again reduced the eastern cities to distress; and Halicarnassus may well have suffered more than most, for

Cassius made his headquarters for a time at Myndus. The better times that followed the establishment of the Empire under Augustus are reflected in an inscription found at Halicarnassus, in which the Emperor is called

Paternal Zeus and Saviour of the entire human race, whose providence has not only fulfilled but exceeded the hopes of all men; for earth and sea are at peace, the cities flourish in good order, concord, and prosperity, and every blessing is furnished in fullest measure.

The praise is fulsome, but not unjustified by the facts.

As distinguished Halicarnassians Strabo mentions, apart from Herodotus, Heraclitus, the writer of epigrams, and Dionysius, the historian and literary critic. A less enviable distinction was that of Phormio the boxer, who was victorious at Olympia in 392 B.C., but at the next celebration four years later was found guilty of corruption and was 'fined a Zeus'—that is, he was required to dedicate a bronze statue of Zeus bearing his name at Olympia. His exact offence is not known, but the commonest was being bribed to sell the victory or to enter from a city to which he did not belong.

As is so often the case when a place has been inhabited continuously since antiquity, little is left at Bodrum of the city of Halicarnassus. To reconstruct it as it was we have the help of a passage in Vitruvius, who is led on from speaking of the brick palace of Mausolus to give a description of the site. He compares it to the auditorium of a theatre; at the bottom by the shore, where the orchestra would come, is the agora, and across the middle, like a diazoma, runs a broad street, and in the middle of this is the Mausoleum. At the top of the citadel, in the middle, is a shrine of Ares; on the right wing is the fountain of Salmacis with a temple of Aphrodite and Hermes close by, and on the left wing is the palace of Mausolus, built to his own specification. This palace commands on the right a view of the agora and harbour and the whole circuit of the walls; under it on the left is the secret harbour.

Of all this nothing is actually standing today apart from the city wall. This may be traced for most of its length; on the west the Myndus gate remains in a ruined state, and is evidently to be identified with the Tripylon, or triple gate, mentioned by Arrian. Hereabouts we may imagine the unsuccessful Persian sortie which nearly resulted in the loss of the city. A curious feature is the

85

isolated line of outer wall on the north-east; from Arrian's description of the terrain it seems that this must be the wall that Alexander attacked, and must apparently be an early Mausolan fortification later abandoned. Here was presumably the Mylasa gate, no longer surviving.

A shrine of Ares has not been located. Vitruvius' words would suggest the summit of Göktepe, the conical hill which stands at about the middle point of the wall-circuit. There is in fact a level platform here about 40 feet (12·2 m.) long, but no visible sign of a building. At the east foot of Göktepe there is another large platform on which Newton found some traces of a building similar in style to the Mausoleum, and he and others have preferred to place the temple of Ares here. But the situation so low down does not answer well to Vitruvius' location 'at the top of the citadel in the middle'.

The exact position of the agora is not now determinable, as it has long since been obliterated by the town of Bodrum, but the site of the Mausoleum has now been cleared. Needless to say, all the splendours of the building are gone, but the rock cuttings which formed its foundations may still be traced. Indeed, the Danish excavators argue that some of these indicate the existence of an earlier cemetery with monumental built tombs in the same place. Salmacis, however, with its fountain and temple, has disappeared. Its position was almost certainly on and around the headland which carried the old Turkish arsenal; sherds of classical and archaic pottery are to be found here, but no trace of any ancient building. Something over half a mile down the coast there is a small spring, and a rather shorter distance to the north is the fountain called by the Turks Eski Çeşme, but both of these are too far away to come in question. On the other hand, an abundant head of fresh water rises in the harbour just off the Arsenal Point, and it seems highly likely that this represents the fountain of Salmacis; it may quite possibly have risen on land in antiquity, for the west coast in general has sunk some 5 or 6 feet (1·52 or 1·83 m.) in the last two thousand years.[5]

The other, eastern wing was apparently the site of the original settlement. The peninsula on which the Castle of St Peter stands was in early times an island, and seems to have borne the name of Zephyrium; but the great pile of the castle has obliterated all traces of anything earlier. In this neighbourhood were the palace of Mausolus and the secret harbour and canal. That the palace should be utterly lost is no great wonder, but the disappearance of the secret harbour is surprising. Some remains of walling have been observed under water in the great harbour (L on the plan), and it has been suggested that these may be the remains of it; but the position is not satisfactory. Mausolus' palace had a view on the right over the great harbour and the city walls, and on the left over

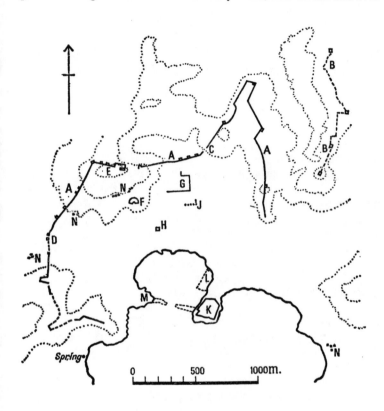

A.A _ City Wall   F _ Theatre   K _ Castle of the Knights
B.B _ Outer Fortification   G _ Large Platform   L _ Submerged Wall
C _ Gate   H _ Site of Mausoleum   M _ Arsenal Point(Salmacis)
D _ Myndus Gate   J _ Colonnade   N.N _ Tombs
E _ Göktepe   *Contours approximate*

Fig. 13 Plan of Halicarnassus

the small harbour; if it stood on the 'island' with a westward view, the city would be on the right, but the secret port would then have to be near the tip of the island, which is obviously out of the question; the peninsula on which the castle stands is solid rock, and a secret harbour once cut into it must ever afterwards be plainly visible. The palace must therefore have been on the landward side of the isthmus; but a situation which would have the harbour and city on the right and the submerged walling on the left could not be anywhere near the eastern 'horn'. Moreover, Artemisia led her ships into the great harbour by a canal, whereas the submerged walling is actually in the great harbour. It seems almost inevitable that the secret port must have been on the east side of the isthmus, with a canal across to the west. This would agree with the words of the geographer who passes under the name of Scylax and wrote about or soon after the time of Mausolus; speaking of Halicarnassus he says that she has 'a closed harbour and another harbour by the island, and a stream'. By 'closed' he means closed with a chain in the usual way; this refers to the great harbour. The other harbour by the island would naturally be placed on the east of the present isthmus rather than on the west inside the great harbour, and it may be that Scylax is thinking simply of the open roadstead on that side off the quarter of Kumbahçe; on the other hand, he may equally well be referring to the secret port, which must have existed in his day. The word translated above as 'stream' means generally a river, but is also used occasionally of an artificial stream or canal; since there is nothing near Bodrum which could fairly be called a river, it seems very likely that the word is here used of the canal which joined the two harbours. Cutting across the isthmus this canal would produce the 'island' of which Scylax and other ancient authors speak. This explanation would, in the writer's opinion, be completely satisfactory if only there were some trace existing of the secret port in the required position, but neither there nor anywhere else does there appear to be any. Visitors to Bodrum may be interested in trying their hand at a solution of this puzzle.

Other remnants of the ancient city are scanty. The theatre on the slope of Göktepe has recently been cleared by a Turkish team. A large part of the lower rows of seating can now be seen, but most of the stage-building has disappeared. Tombs are to be seen in various places, notably a rock-cut group below the summit of Göktepe. And the modern town is full of ancient stones; at almost every turn the visitor will come on fragments of antiquity.

The splendid Castle of the Knights Hospitallers (Pll. 24–6), which is no doubt the chief attraction of Bodrum today, cannot be described in detail here. It was built in the fifteenth century, at which time the Knights were established in Rhodes, largely, as was said above, with materials taken from the Mausoleum and other ancient buildings. It contains a small museum in three parts, including a selection of objects found during the underwater explorations recently carried out in the neighbourhood. Not the least interesting of these are the copper ingots, roughly in the shape of an oxhide, found in 1960 in a sunken wreck off Cape Gelidonya at the eastern tip of the bay of Finike. Similar ingots were previously known, and it was supposed that they were a form of currency used in the days before money was invented, and that each represented one talent weight or the value of one ox—hence the 'oxhide' shape. But it seems that this cannot now be accepted. The forty specimens found in 1960 vary in weight from 35 to 59 lb. (15·9 to 26·8 kg.), and hardly any two are of the same weight. The majority, but not all, bear marks which also vary greatly; they can scarcely be letters, but are thought to be rather foundry-marks. Probably then the ingots are not currency at all, but simple merchandise, and the 'lugs' at each corner, which give the 'oxhide' shape, are merely for ease of handling. From the pottery found the date of the wreck is estimated to be about 1200 B.C. (Pl. 21).

Other interesting items collected in the castle include: prehistoric and Dorian vases from an excavation at Dirmil near Myndus; Mycenaean vases and other objects, including a necklace of stone,

Fig. 14 Bodrum. Stone Anchor in Museum

found at Müsgebi; a headless archaic statue from Caunus, thought to be of Apollo; a bronze figure of a negro boy; the cross-shaft of a huge anchor weighing over half a ton from the sea near Bodrum; a number of stone anchors which had apparently wooden flukes (Fig. 14); and finally a superb Byzantine steelyard.

From Bodrum an easy excursion by boat takes one to the island of Karaada, the ancient Arconessus. Visitors alight at a little resort on the north side of the island, and from here a stiff climb leads up to an ancient building, probably a small temple surrounded by an enclosing wall. Nothing is definitely known of the date and purpose of this building, but its splendid position is undeniable, and the main attractions of a visit are the magnificent views to be had of Halicarnassus and the island of Cos.

Notes

1 Traditionally 1194–1184 B.C.
2 See *Aegean Turkey*, p. 148.
3 The reader will find an excellent discussion in W. B. Dinsmoor, *Architecture of Ancient Greece* (3rd edition, London, 1950), pp. 257–61. This, however, is to be modified somewhat in the light of recent research and discoveries, of which details will be found in the Bibliography.
4 This question cannot be fully argued here. For a discussion of it the reader is referred to the article by J. M. Cook and the present writer quoted in the Bibliography.
5 See *Aegean Turkey*, pp. 79, 110.

10   The Myndus Peninsula

The peninsula between Halicarnassus and Myndus is hilly, largely
bare, and in summer almost waterless, but it contains a number of
small coastal plains. This region was in early times occupied by the
Lelegians, who, as we learn from Strabo, founded there eight cities;
at first they were populous, but later the Lelegian race died out,
and six of the eight cities were incorporated by Mausolus in his
new capital of Halicarnassus. The other two, Syangela and
Myndus, continued to exist. The names of the remaining six we

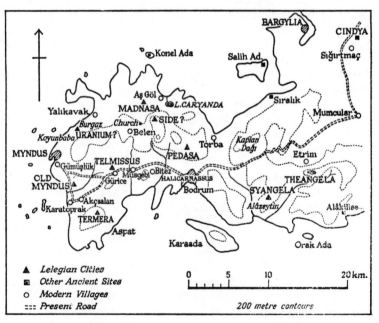

Fig. 15 Map of the Myndus Peninsula

learn from Pliny;[1] they were, with some variations of spelling, Termera, Side, Madnasa, Pedasa, Uranium, and Telmissus. Syangela lay some distance to the east of Halicarnassus, the others all to the westward. What in fact happened in the fourth century was that Mausolus forcibly transplanted the inhabitants of the six cities and refounded the other two, on fresh sites and on a greatly enlarged scale, to play their part as fully Greek cities in his new Hellenized Caria. The depopulated towns were abandoned, but their ruins remain; they are identifiable by their hilltop positions, their general lay-out, and the characteristic Lelegian masonry. They are in general rather remote and can only be reached, with considerable expenditure of effort, on foot.

Myndus

The classical city of Myndus is located with complete certainty at Gümüşlük. There is a direct road from Bodrum, or a longer and slightly better road by Karatoprak; both are passable for a car. But Gümüşlük is not the site of the Lelegian town of Myndus. This was a much smaller affair, paying only one-twelfth of a talent in the Delian Confederacy in the fifth century, and was remembered in later times as Old Myndus; it may be confidently identified with the ruins on the hilltop at Bozdağ about two miles (3·22 km.) to the south-east of Gümüşlük. Nothing survives beyond a ring-wall and the foundations of a large tower on the summit; but the sherds reveal occupation from prehistoric times to the early fourth century.

Mausolus' new foundation at Gümüşlük was on a much more ambitious scale. It had a well-sheltered harbour and a wall-circuit over two miles long. But the problem was to man it. The Lelegian inhabitants of the peninsula had mostly been transplanted to Halicarnassus, and for a long while Myndus was severely underpopulated, and much of the space inside the walls was unoccupied. It is said that the philosopher Diogenes once visited Myndus, and observing that the gates were large but the city small, advised the Myndians to keep their gates closed, or their city would be running away. In later times it was alleged that Myndus was colonized by the descendants of Aëtius, king of Troezen, at the same time as Halicarnassus, but this is clearly a fiction.

Alexander's halfhearted and unsuccessful attempt upon the city was mentioned above; but the Persian hold on it lasted only till the next year, when it was ended by the defeat of Orontobates. In the third century Myndus was mostly in the hands of the Ptolemies, and was still so in 197 B.C. when the Rhodians, as friends of Egypt, undertook to protect her 'allies' against Antiochus III of Syria, and gave their freedom to Myndus and others It was after this, apparently, that the Myndians first began to issue their own coinage. The city was for a short while held by the rebel Aristonicus about 131 B.C., and after the murder of Caesar in 44 the 'tyrannicide' Cassius kept his fleet there; the city is likely to have suffered from his exactions. After the defeat of Brutus and Cassius at Philippi Mark Antony gave Myndus to the Rhodians, but she was soon taken away again owing to the excessive harshness of their rule. Imperial coinage of Myndus is noticeably scanty, and it may be that the city did not prosper under the Empire as much as most. The silver-mines, traces of whose working have been found in the neighbourhood, and which have given its name to the village of Gümüşlük, are not mentioned in any ancient source. Indeed, the only Myndian product of which we hear is the wine, and this had a poor reputation. It was one of those which were mixed with sea-water, a not uncommon monstrosity in ancient times; it is described as relaxing the stomach, causing flatulence, and leaving a hangover. This unattractive beverage led to the Myndians being dubbed 'brine-drinkers'.

The site of Myndus is most attractive; there is hardly a better on the whole coast. The harbour is enclosed and well protected against the prevailing wind, the *meltem*, by the peninsula on the north-west. The fortification-wall on the mainland may be followed for its whole length, and is best preserved on the south-east, the most vulnerable side, where it is strengthened with frequent towers. It is about 9 feet (2·74 m.) thick, of regular ashlar, constructed in part at least of the green granite which was also used for the Mausoleum. The quarries from which this stone was cut may be seen close to the shore at Koyunbaba, about two miles to the north.

The fortification also included the peninsula; a hundred years ago the wall could be traced all round, but has now disappeared. There

Fig. 16 Myndus. Harbour and Peninsula from the Acropolis Hill

93

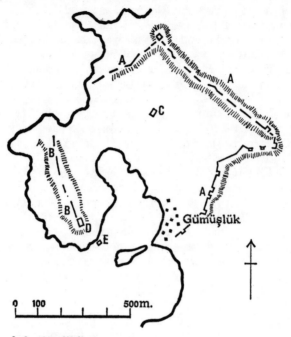

A, A - City Wall
B, B - 'Lelegian Wall'
C - Basilica
D - Church?
E - Tower

Fig. 17 Plan of Myndus

remains, however, another wall running from north to south up the spine of the hill (Pl. 31; B on the plan). It has the same thickness as the mainland wall, but is built of larger blocks less regularly fitted. It has been called 'the Lelegian wall', but this name stems from the old belief that the Lelegian Myndus stood on this site; in fact the masonry is quite unlike that of the genuine Lelegian towns. This wall has always been something of a puzzle. As it stands, it appears meaningless; with the peninsula walled all round, what could be the point of dividing the interior down the middle with a wall of this solidity? It makes sense only as a continuation of just such a mainland wall as in fact exists, and must (in the writer's opinion) be the beginning of an earlier fortification system which was almost immediately abandoned in favour of a wall encircling the whole peninsula. Its position is comparable with that of the wall on the western extension of the acropolis hill at Caunus. It and the mainland wall will belong respectively to the earlier and later years of Mausolus' reign.

Otherwise hardly anything remains of ancient Myndus. Rock-cut stairways and house-foundations may be seen on the hillside, but virtually all the ruins seen in the early nineteenth century, including theatre and stadium, have totally disappeared; all that survives is a ruined basilica and, at the highest point of the peninsula, what may have been a church. There are, however, numerous ancient stones to be seen in and around the village, and at the school about a mile inland there are some column capitals and Roman mosaics.

The Six Lelegian Towns

Pedasa

Of the eight towns this is the easiest to visit. It lies some ninety minutes' walk to the north of Bodrum, at the head of a pass, and is overgrown with pine-trees. The spot is called Gökçeler. The ancient name survives in the village of Bitez a mile or so to the west.

Pedasa has even a little history of her own, and in the sixth and fifth centuries was apparently of more account than her neighbour Halicarnassus. Herodotus, himself a Halicarnassian, tells us that after the fall of Sardis in 546 B.C., when the Persian general Harpagus was overrunning Caria, the Pedasans held out for a time against him and gave him much trouble by fortifying the mountain of Lide.[2] The historian notes incidentally that whenever any misfortune was due to befall the Pedasans, their priestess of Athena would grow a great beard; this had happened three times.[3] Later, at the time of the Ionian Revolt, after 499 B.C., another Persian army came south to suppress the Carians who had taken part. After defeating them at Labraynda the Persians were ambushed and destroyed 'on the road to Pedasa' at night. Apparently they had attempted too long a march in this waterless country and had become benighted. The Persians had evidently some respect for the men of Pedasa, and after their capture of Miletus in 494, with the object of weakening these troublesome Lelegians, they transplanted some of them to a site in the hills above Miletus. This new settlement also took the name of Pedasa. In the Delian Confederacy Pedasa paid a tribute of two talents (as compared with Halicarnassus' one and two-thirds), later reduced to one talent.

From the sherds at Gökçeler it is clear that the place was not completely abandoned after its incorporation by Mausolus in Halicarnassus, but was retained as a useful outpost. It is likely that it was occupied by Philip V during his Carian campaign, for we are told that Pedasa was one of the places from which he was required in 196 to withdraw his garrisons. Polybius does not say which Pedasa is in question, but the probabilities seem to favour that at Gökçeler.[4]

The ruins at Gökçeler are quite considerable and show a characteristic Lelegian town. The main citadel, A on the plan, is some

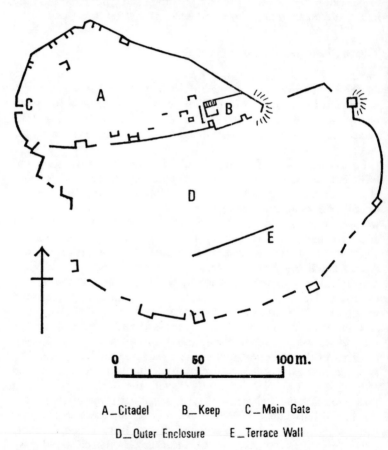

A_Citadel   B_Keep   C_Main Gate

D_Outer Enclosure   E_Terrace Wall

Fig. 18 Plan of Pedasa (Gökçeler)

96

170 yards (155·4 m.) long with a high wall of irregular masonry; at its upper (east) end is an inner enclosure or keep approached by a ramp and gateway, with a staircase in one corner. The main entrance, 8 feet (2·44 m.) wide, is at the west end. In the interior are many traces of buildings, especially close up against the inner face of the town wall. Below this citadel on the south and east is a larger outer enclosure with a wall of dry rubble masonry strengthened with towers; the towers, as often, show more regular workmanship.

On the ridges to the south and south-east are a number of the remarkable 'chamber-tumuli' which are characteristic of the Lelegian country. These consist of a vaulted circular chamber approached by a passage and enclosed by a ring-wall heaped over with loose stones. Some at least of these tombs, from the pottery found in them, must date back to 700 B.C. or even earlier. The best preserved of these tumuli is at a site known as Gebe Kilisse, north-east of Gökçeler and a little to the west of the village of Torba. It was built on a stone terrace whose walls on the north and east stand between one and two metres high. The tomb itself is made of well-dressed slabs, sometimes even squared blocks. It is roughly circular in shape, about 13 metres in diameter. The walls stand between 1·75 and 2·75 metres high, and the whole structure is capped by a shallow dome-shaped roof. The tomb is approached from the east by a narrow dromos, which leads to a chamber about 3 metres square, faced with excellent masonry. The ceiling is in the form of a tall slender pyramid reaching almost to the roof of the whole tumulus. It somewhat resembles the so-called Tomb of Tantalus, near Smyrna.[5] At the end of the dromos, and at the entrance to the tomb chamber, there are niches in the wall, clearly designed to accommodate a large slab closing off the tomb.

Telmissus (Telmessus)
There were two cities of this name in the south-west of Asia Minor; the other is located beyond all doubt at Fethiye in Lycia. Of the Carian Telmissus we are told that she lay sixty stades (rather less than seven miles; 11·3 km.) from Halicarnassus, in exceptionally fertile country, with a temple of Apollo who delivered oracles and was regarded as the progenitor of a priestly family of diviners. Even after Mausolus had transplanted her inhabitants to Halicarnassus she continued to exist as a religious community centred on the temple. The Telmissian diviners had a considerable reputation; they were consulted, for example, on more than one occasion by the

kings of Sardis, and Arrian tells this story of the Phrygian Gordius, a poor farmer: an eagle settled one day on his plough and remained there till evening; to learn the meaning of this portent he went to Telmissus. There in a village he met a girl drawing water and told her of the strange occurrence; she happened to be of the priestly family and advised him (in true oracular fashion) to sacrifice to King Zeus. This he did in accordance with her instructions, and later married her; their son was Midas who afterwards became king of Phrygia.

At the required distance from Bodrum, on a hill above the village of Gürice, is a Lelegian town-site which must (in the writer's opinion) be identified with Telmissus. It has the characteristic form of an inner citadel and outer enclosure, with an entrance on the south-east; the masonry is of dry rubble. On the summit is a large square tower of good ashlar standing some 11 feet (3·35 m.) high. There are three tombs, a rock-cut chamber inside the circuit, a vaulted chamber-tomb in ruins outside the entrance-gate, and a handsome rock-cut tomb on the north-west. The fertile territory is the arable plain around Müsgebi to the south. Müsgebi (Misgibi) is a Turkicized form of the old name Episkopi, and it is attractive to suppose that the modern bishopric has succeeded, as so often happens, to the ancient religious centre, the temple of Telmissian Apollo. A large Byzantine church was to be seen in the last century about half a mile from Müsgebi, but has now disappeared.

Termera

Before the foundation of the new Myndus by Mausolus, Termera was the leading city in the south-west of the peninsula; her tribute in the Delian Confederacy was at first two and a half talents, or just thirty times more than that of the Lelegian Myndus. Towards the end of the sixth century she was ruled by a dynast called Tymnes, who seems to have controlled all the country from Telmissus to the southern corner of the peninsula. Coins were struck in his name, as they were also by the dynasts of Syangela. Tymnes was succeeded by his son Histiaeus and then by his grandson Tymnes, who about 447 B.C. was expelled from Termera but continued to rule over his other possessions for at least another twenty years. After the removal of her population to Halicarnassus, Termera is said to have been used as a prison by 'the tyrants'. This presumably means the Hecatomnid rulers, and the statement may well be historically true. Forced transplantation of a people is always resented, and the dynasts may very likely have found it necessary to establish police posts, if only to discourage attempts by the evicted citizens to return home.

There was in antiquity a proverbial expression 'Termerian sufferings', of which two quite different explanations were given. One said that it referred to the sufferings inflicted by bandits operating from Termera; the other is more picturesque. A certain Termerus, we read, had the amiable habit of destroying those who came in his path by bashing them on the head; eventually Heracles gave him a dose of his own medicine and killed him in the same fashion. The proverb then applies to those who are paid in their own coin.

Of the site of Termera there is no doubt. Strabo says that it lay in Myndian territory opposite the island of Cos and above the promontory of Scandaria, and in this region there is only one possible site. It stands on a hilltop above the hamlet of Çeşmebaşı (Aspat). The lay-out is typical—an inner citadel and an outer enclosure, as on the sites described above. The citadel has gates on east and west, and in the interior are foundations of buildings and a large double cistern coated with plaster. The outer circuit is poorly preserved except at the south corner, where a stretch of massive polygonal wall stands up to 17 feet (5·18 m.) in height. In it is a gate over 6 feet (1·83 m.) wide; the sides incline inwards to form an arch whose top is now lost.

There are two tombs of Lelegian type on the site itself, and many others on the ridges in the neighbourhood.

Madnasa

Except that she is mentioned by Pliny and by Stephanus of Byzantium (quoting Hecataeus), our knowledge of Madnasa is confined to the fact that she paid a tribute of two talents, later reduced to one, in the Confederacy of Delos. This, however, is enough to show that she was among the more important of the Lelegian cities. Her site is almost certainly to be identified with the considerable ruins on the hill above Türkbükü Bay and lower Göl. The outer enclosure here is over 300 yards (274·3 m.) long, with a wall of dry rubble 5 feet (1·52 m.) thick. At the summit on the south-east is a tower of regular masonry, with numerous buildings grouped around it. Within the enclosure are many traces of houses and half a dozen cisterns. The main gate was apparently on the north. At the north-west end is a second tower, and in the rock-face close by is a group of tombs.

Side

This is the most obscure of all the Lelegian towns. Apart from Pliny it is not mentioned at all, unless it be the same as 'Sibda, a city of Caria' recorded by Stephanus. And it is the only one of the eight, except Telmissus, which does not appear in the Athenian tribute lists. Its site, however, can be identified with some probability.

From the village of Göl a pass leads over to Belen on the way to Müsgebi; at its head are the ruins of a church, and a short distance to the south a fortress constructed of squared blocks. Half an hour's steep climb from here to the east, on the Karadağ mountain, is the wildest and most remote of the Lelegian settlements. Unlike the others it is in two separate parts. The northern is long and narrow, with a curved wall on the south and a line of cliff on the north, with a wonderful view over the valley and sea. The wall is built of the long, roughly squared blocks which give a characteristic look to the Lelegian masonry. The altitude has been estimated at 1,800 feet (548·6 m.). There is as usual an inner enclosure, containing a build-ing about 50 feet (15·2 m.) long.

The southern settlement is quite fascinating. It has a ring-wall of similar construction to the other, and the interior is packed with houses built close up against one another, not far short of a hundred in all, many of them standing up to 8 or 10 feet (2·44 or 3·05 m.) in height. Some of the houses contain several rooms, others only a single room; in some cases there appears to have been an upper storey. This part of the site seems to have been residential only. On these bare mountainsides the inhabitants must have lived mainly by pasture, and their forced removal to the urban life of Halicarnassus must have left them bewildered. There is no trace of occupation after the fourth century, and the houses have stood utterly deserted ever since.

Reasons for identifying this site with the Lelegian Side are cir-cumstantial. The only other site on the peninsula, apart from those described above, which can reasonably claim to have been one of the Lelegian towns is close to the west coast at Burgaz (below, p. 101); this therefore is the only alternative. But a place so near to the sea is unlikely to have escaped enrolment in the Delian Confederacy, whereas we can easily imagine that the Athenian tribute-collectors would be disinclined to attempt to exact payment from the goat-herds of the Karadağ.

For a long time, however, it was believed that this site was prob-ably that of Telmissus. The distance from Halicarnassus, in a straight line, is just about sixty stades, though it is much more by any practicable route; but the chief reason for the identification was the church on the pass below. This is said to be built on the ruins of a

Carian or Hellenic building (though the present writer was not able to confirm this); moreover, an inscription found in the village of Belen, but said on local authority to have come from this church, honours a man who was 'piously disposed towards Apollo Telmisseus, and piously performed the sacrifices on behalf of the Telmissians and the city' (of Halicarnassus). It was accordingly thought that the church probably marks the position of the temple of Apollo; and the nearest site is that on the Karadağ above. This evidence is not altogether free from doubt. The church seemed to the writer to be built mostly of squared blocks taken apparently from the neighbouring fort, which may have given a false impression of antiquity; and, as every traveller in Turkey knows, villagers' information is not always to be relied upon. But the fatal objection is the character of the Karadağ site. Where, on these arid mountainsides, is the exceptionally fertile land which Cicero says that Telmissus possessed? There is no spot on the whole peninsula to which this description is less applicable. The Lelegian town at Gürice was not known until recently; now that the choice is available, it can hardly fail to be preferred.

Uranium

The historian Diodorus tells us that after the Trojan War the island of Syme was occupied by Carians, but that later, owing to persistent droughts, they fled from the island and settled in the place called Uranium. The town also appears in the Delian Confederacy, with a modest tribute. Nothing more is known of it. For its situation, the only remaining Lelegian site on the peninsula is that at Burgaz. This has the familiar form, with citadel and outer enclosure, and two towers; the pottery is of archaic and classical date. There are several 'chamber-tumuli' in the neighbourhood, including a particularly handsome one on the next hill to the north.

Caryanda

Caryanda was not one of the Lelegian cities, and her site has long been a puzzle. This is not the place to examine all the rather confusing evidence; the conclusion to which the present writer has been led is as follows.

Strabo tells us that there was between Myndus and Bargylia a Lake Caryanda and an island of the same name which the Caryandans used to inhabit. We must accordingly look for two sites, one on an island, and a later one on the mainland; and there are no inscrip-

Turkey Beyond the Maeander

tions to assist the search. For the earlier site the most likely candidate is the island of Salihadası in the Bargylian Gulf; here there exists a walled town of fair size and apparently of classical date, though it is buried in such impenetrable forest and scrub that no clear idea of it can at present be obtained. From their island home the Caryandans moved, early in the Hellenistic period, to the mainland, and from this time on the name of Caryanda appears no more except in the works of the geographers. The mainland site, on the other hand, can be identified with reasonable certainty. The lake of Caryanda can hardly be other than the one lake which exists between Myndus and Bargylia, namely that which gives its name to the present village of Göl (Lake). The lake is still there, though now reduced to little more than a marsh. In the third century this region lay on the territory of Myndus. Here then the Caryandans settled, becoming Myndian citizens, and their old name survived only for the lake. On the shore below the village of Göl are the ruins of a considerable Byzantine town; this has overlaid the Caryandan settlement, of which nothing now remains to be seen.

In 1970 W. Radt published the results of a detailed survey of the central part of the Halicarnassus peninsula, covering the area between Belen on the west and Etrim Köy in the east. He not only identified a great many new sites, large and small, but has also greatly enlarged our understanding of the nature and chronology of Lelegian settlements. In particular it is worth noting the several hill-top sites along the central massif of Karadağ, and also a number of very well defended enclosures, which probably served as refuges in times of danger. The countryside as a whole seems to have been dotted with farmsteads, other dwellings, and tombs. Visitors wishing to examine these are referred to his detailed publications, listed in the Bibliography. It may now fairly be said that the central part of the Bodrum peninsula has been surveyed and studied in more detail than any other comparable part of western Turkey.

Notes

1 See above, p. 84, and note 4. The account given in this chapter adopts the conclusions reached in that article, where the numerous problems are fully discussed.
2 Lide is identified with the high mountain to the north-east, called on the Turkish maps Kaplan Dağı or Tırman Dağı.
3 Or twice when Herodotus tells the story a second time.
4 The reader is reminded that many of the matters in this chapter are controversial; see above, n. 1.
5 See *Aegean Turkey*, pp. 36–8.

11 Syangela-Theangela

The eighth of the Lelegian cities, and the only one to the east of Halicarnassus, was Syangela. This and Myndus were the two which were not incorporated by Mausolus in his new capital. But this is not to say that he left them untouched; Myndus, as was seen above, was refounded on a new and more Hellenic site, and the same was done with Syangela. By a slight change the city's name was given the more Greek-sounding form Theangela. In this way Mausolus established in the Lelegian country three new cities of Greek type, one in the middle and one at each extremity west and east.

Apart from her preservation by Mausolus, all that we know of Syangela is that in the Delian Confederacy she paid regularly, together with her dependency Amynanda, a tribute of one talent. She was at this time ruled by a dynast, Pigres, who sometimes paid in his own name. A generation or so earlier, in 480 B.C., another Carian Pigres had served as ship-captain in the Persian fleet at the battle of Salamis; he was no doubt of the same Syangelan dynasty. An interesting series of silver coins bearing a griffin's head and dating around 500 B.C. was almost certainly issued by these same dynasts of Syangela; a group of about twenty was found in 1955 on the coast at Alâkilise, some of which were shown to the writer at Theangela in the same year. Like Tymnes at Termera, Pigres evidently controlled a considerable area of country.

Some four hours due east of Halicarnassus, above the village of Alâzeytin, is a thoroughly Lelegian site which may be that of Syangela although the recent work of W. Radt tends to suggest otherwise (below, p. 110). The spot may be reached on foot in about three hours from Etrim, or in rather less from a point on the main Bodrum road north of Kızılağaç. A guide is of course necessary.

The site at Alâzeytin can now be much better understood thanks to Radt's researches (Fig. 19). The city was roughly circular in plan, enclosed by a ring-wall punctuated at regular intervals by square

103

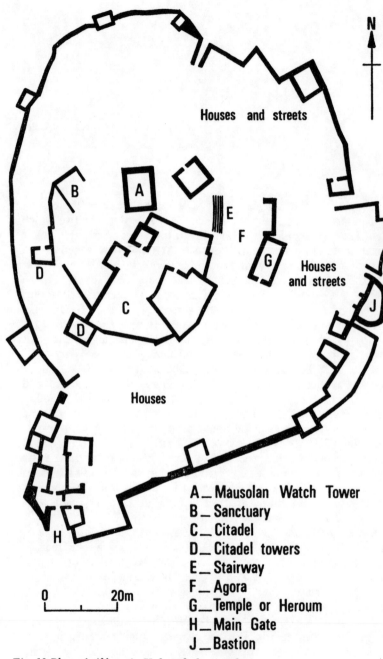

N

Houses and streets

B

A

E

F

D

G

Houses
and streets

C

D

J

Houses

H

A — Mausolan Watch Tower
B — Sanctuary
C — Citadel
D — Citadel towers
E — Stairway
F — Agora
G — Temple or Heroum
H — Main Gate
J — Bastion

0   20m

Fig. 19 Plan of Alâzeytin Kale (whole complex)

towers, and at one point on the east by a semicircular bastion (J). The main entrance, recessed into the wall and strongly defended, was at the south (H). In the centre of the site a cluster of buildings formed a citadel. Within it was a cistern and a complex of rooms looking onto a courtyard (C). The whole central area was isolated from the rest of the town by an inner fortification wall, again defended by towers (D). On the west side of the citadel a much-ruined building has been identified as the main sanctuary of the site (B). The much better preserved building beside this (A) served a quite different purpose. Its well-cut squared blocks are later than any other masonry on the site, and it was probably a watch-tower built by Mausolus when the town was abandoned, partly to protect his territory, and partly to prevent the inhabitants moving back to their former home from the new Greek cities which he had founded, notably, in this region, Halicarnassus itself and Theangela. Similar towers have been identified elsewhere on the Bodrum peninsula. From the citadel a rock-cut stairway, broad enough to have served a sacred or ceremonial purpose, led to the agora of the town, the largest open area on level ground within the walls (F). Almost directly opposite the stairway across the agora stood a rectangular building, entered from the south, which is thought to be a temple or a heroum (G). Two column capitals found here, and in the smaller structure adjoining it to the north, can be dated to the middle of the sixth century B.C., or soon after. Very probably the public buildings of the town were reconstructed in about 540 B.C., after the Persian sack of the Lelegian cities (above, p. 95). Most of the rest of the site, especially the east side, is occupied by houses (Pl. 28), built onto one another in an agglutinative manner characteristic of all the Lelegian town sites, and separated by narrow streets.

A few hundred yards to the south-west of the town on a ridge, there is an interesting group of half a dozen building complexes, also very typical of the Lelegian period (Fig. 20). The most distinctive feature of each of these groups is a large circular structure. Each of these has two eccentric ring-walls converging on one side into a single wall; on the opposite side, where they diverge, the intervening space is divided by cross-walls into a number of chambers with vaulted roof. All the interior walls have a slight inward curve, and some have supposed from this that the buildings were roofed over. This, however, cannot have been the case; the average diameter is some 40 to 50 feet (12 to 15 m.), and in no case is there a sufficient accumulation of stones in the interior to suggest a collapsed vault (Pl. 29). Closely associated with each of the circular

105

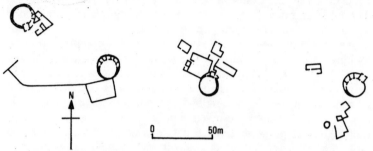

Fig. 20 Plan of Alâzeytin Kale (circular compound farm buildings)

compounds is a group of more conventional rectangular rooms, and there can be little doubt that each of these groups formed an agricultural unit. The square rooms would have housed the human inhabitants, or perhaps have been used for storage; the circular compound, with its covered rooms, was designed to accommodate animals, principally sheep and goats. The concentration of the six complexes in one place so close to the town shows that these were not farmsteads in the normal sense, but places where flocks directly belonging to the town, and their shepherds, could be accommodated. Similar buildings have been located elsewhere in the Bodrum peninsula, and their function was evidently the same, although not all examples are so closely associated with a town settlement.

The new city of Theangela was a very different affair. Her impressive ruins stand on the high hill directly above the village of Etrim and occupy three summits; the total length of the enclosure is over three-quarters of a mile (1,207 m.), and its area comparable with that of Myndus. The city wall, two miles (3·22 km.) in length, is built mostly in the Lelegian style, with the main gate on the south side near the west end; its thickness is from 7 to 9 feet (2·13 to 2·74 m.) and on the more vulnerable south side are frequent towers. As will be seen, this area was not entirely unoccupied when the wall was built.

At the top of the western hill the walls run up to a very fine and powerful fort, with a tower at each corner (plan, Fig. 21), entered from the city by a narrow passage with a right-angled bend. Just outside, a small postern gate leads through the southern wall. The exceptional strength of this fort is evidently designed to resist artillery. Smaller forts are found on the south and at the east end, where the wall runs out to form salients (C and E on the plan).

106

At P an interior wall is carried across from north to south, dividing the city into two parts. Almost all the buildings lie to the east of this wall; the middle summit A carries a fortified enclosure, but the main habitation was on and below the eastern peak B. Evidently, here as at Myndus, Mausolus was unable to man his new city, and it was found advisable to reduce its size to less than half by means of this cross-wall.

At the summit of the eastern hill B is a tower in Lelegian style; this same style is seen in other buildings on the site, and shows the conservative tendencies of the builders. Below on the east are two large cisterns finely constructed (Pl. 30), and on a terrace on this side was found a black and white mosaic floor. This peak is encircled by a wall to form a citadel, joined to the main city wall by cross-walls on north and south.

The public buildings stood on the lower slope of the middle hill, but they are not identifiable individually. At F is a handsome Lelegian house excellently preserved, with three rooms roofed with a 'corbelled' vault; that is to say, each course of masonry on each side projects beyond the course below so as to meet at the top. In the dip between the two peaks are other cisterns equally well constructed; one of them still furnishes drinking-water to the fire-watcher who lives during the summer in a hut on the western hill D. Theangela possessed no theatre; on the other hand there is, at M on the plan, a building in the form of a stadium, though it is little

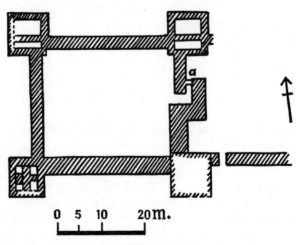

Fig. 21 Theangela. Plan of the fort at D (Tetrapyrgon)

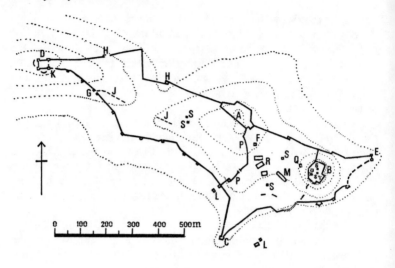

A,B_ Fortified Hilltops
C,D,E_ Fortified Posts
F _ Lelegian type House
G _ Main Gate
H,H_ Possible Gates
J,J_ Line of Ancient Road

K _ Postern Gate
L,L_ External Buildings
    of uncertain purpose
M_ Stadium-like Building
N _ Tower

Contours approximate

P _ Interior Cross-Wall
Q _ Early Tomb
R _ Public Buildings inc.
    archaic temple(?)
S,S_Wells and Cisterns
T_ Mosaic Floor

Fig. 22 Plan of Theangela

over 50 yards (45·7 m.) long, or barely more than a quarter of the usual length. No doubt it was used for athletic exercise.

But the gem of the whole site is perhaps the tomb **Q** on the slope of the eastern hill. It consists of a long narrow chamber 25 feet (7·62 m.) in length, with an antechamber at the east end; it runs parallel to the hillside. The roof is corbel-vaulted, and the projecting corners cut away to make a smooth surface. The roof is immensely solid, and on it, when it was cleared by Miss Akarca and the writer in 1955, were found no fewer than forty stone balls about 6 inches (152 mm.) in diameter. These are apparently cannon-balls, and it seems that the roof of the tomb must at some time have been used as an artillery emplacement. Previously there had been found inside this tomb, together with a quantity of bones, fragments of vases dating to the latter part of the fifth century B.C. This exceptional tomb must be that of a distinguished man, and it is highly probable that Pigres himself was buried here; he is known to have been alive in 427 B.C. after a reign of several decades (Pl. 33).

At that time the city of Theangela was not yet in existence, but there is evidence that the tomb was not entirely isolated on the hill. Archaic Greek statues have been found on the site, apparently belonging to a sanctuary of Athena; and the writer was shown in 1955 a broken archaic figurine said to come from a spot near the eastern fort at E. It appears therefore that there was in early times a sanctuary on the hill, and it is natural that a dynast should have his tomb close to it. The desire to be buried as near as possible to a sacred spot is familiar in all ages.

Mention may also be made of two short stretches of curved wall at the foot of the mound on which the fort at D stands. These are quite unlike any other masonry on the site and appear meaningless in their present position; they must, it seems, be the remnants of an earlier ring-wall belonging to an isolated fort or outpost of the pre-Mausolan Syangela.

The fine new city of Theangela played a very small part in subsequent history. In Hellenistic times she claimed, like Myndus, to have been colonized from Troezen in the Peloponnese, and the Troezenians recognized the claim; in view of the underpopulation of the city, the settlement (if it really occurred and is not merely a copy of Halicarnassus) can only have been on a small scale. In the late fourth century a dynast by the name of Eupolemus was ruling in this part of Caria; as we learn from an inscription, he laid siege to Theangela, for some reason unstated; he failed to breach the splendid new walls, but succeeded in reducing the city to surrender on terms. Upon condition of no victimization for the Theangelans and their allies he was permitted to occupy 'the city and the fortified posts'—that is, the forts A, B, C, D, and E.

It was formerly believed that at some time during the second century B.C. Theangela lost her independence and became absorbed into Halicarnassus, but this has now been shown to be a mistake; there is even reason to believe that she was a 'free' city under the early Roman Empire. Surprisingly, Theangela seems never to have struck coins. As territory she commanded not only the Çiftlik valley to the south, but also the extensive plain of Karaova on the north. Of her products we know of only one, honey. Theangelan honey had indeed a wide reputation; and the latter-day descendants of the ancient bee-keepers have given its name to the *nahiye* of Mumcular (wax-merchants) some six miles (9·65 km.) to the north.

Radt's research has led him to make some important modifications to the identifications suggested in this chapter. He argues that the archaic city of Syangela lay not at Alâzeytin, whose ancient name is not known, but much nearer to the later site of Theangela, on Kaplan Dağ, south-west of Etrim Köy, where there was a Lelegian settlement and an extensive cemetery, including burial tumuli similar to those found at the site of Pedasa (Gökçeler; above, pp. 95–7). At least the larger of these probably belonged to members of the ruling dynastic family. He suggests the following historical reconstruction. Archaic Syangela was attacked and destroyed by the Persians soon after 546 B.C., as recorded by Herodotus (above, p. 95). The remaining inhabitants then moved to the nearby hill-top above Etrim, the later Theangela, occupying especially the east end of the site, where early Lelegian constructions occur. From this period, the second half of the sixth century, date the two archaic female statues found there, which probably originated from a sanctuary, to be identified with one of the buildings marked R on the plan. Even so, the old site of Syangela continued to be partially occupied, since one of the tumuli found there dates to the fifth century. It was only finally abandoned when Mausolus definitively refounded and renamed Theangela in the second quarter of the fourth century, laying out the city on a rectangular Greek plan. Interestingly enough the older burial chamber (Q on the plan) lay within the bounds of the city, suggesting the possibility that it was the object of a hero cult.

12 Cnidus

The second mainland member of the Dorian hexapolis, and the only one after the expulsion of Halicarnassus, was Cnidus. The well-known site at the western tip of the long Reşadiye peninsula was excavated in 1857–58 by Sir Charles Newton, who sent to the British Museum several hundred cases of sculptures and other ancient stones. But this is not the original site of the city. Until about the middle of the fourth century B.C. Cnidus was halfway along the peninsula, near the present *kaza* of Datça, and all references in the classical Greek writers are to this site.[1] The reason for the change was undoubtedly the increasing importance of maritime commerce at that period; the site of the new city at Tekir is rocky, almost waterless, and devoid of arable territory within a distance of six miles (9·65 km.), but for commercial purposes it could hardly be better placed. All through the sailing season a strong north-west wind, the *meltem*, blows day and night across the promontory, and sailing vessels coming from the south have great difficulty in rounding it; they are, today as in ancient times, frequently obliged to wait in the harbour of Cnidus till conditions are more favourable. Few merchant ships in antiquity would pass up the coast without calling there.

The Datça site, on the other hand, is of utterly different character. The Reşadiye peninsula is forty miles (64·4 km.) long from Tekir to the narrow isthmus at Bencik where it joins the mainland; in all this length, apart from small coastal patches, there are only two fertile areas. The whole of the eastern half is bare, mountainous, and virtually uninhabited; the western half also is mountainous, rising in places over 3,500 feet (1066·8 m.), but has towards its western end on the south side a considerable extent of well-watered land reaching to the coast at Palamut Bay and supporting today a group of villages known collectively as Betçe (the five villages). And in the middle of the peninsula, south-west of the isthmus dividing the two halves, is the best and largest area of good land within fifty miles. 'The

111

plain and valley of Datça', says Spratt, 'is very fertile, having fine groves of olive and valonia, and of almonds and other fruit-trees, with abundance of water, if properly utilized'; he speaks of its park-like scenery, and sees for it a promising future. (This last, it must be admitted, has been slow to materialize; in 1950 the writer, during a stay of several weeks, had the greatest difficulty in getting enough to eat.)

In this central area, then, the city of Cnidus was founded by Dorians from the Peloponnese, at a date somewhat later than the settlement of Rhodes and Cos. Herodotus says the colonists came from Sparta; this, if true, is almost the only experiment in colonization that the Spartans ever made. Other accounts, however, attribute the foundation to the Argive hero Triopas; although his existence may well be doubted, a settlement from Argos appears more likely than the other.

At or about the same time a second settlement was made on the peninsula at Triopium. This was on Cnidian territory, and here was the sanctuary of Triopian Apollo, where the great Dorian festival of the Dorieia was celebrated by the six cities of the hexapolis. The site of Apollo's temple has not been discovered, though its approximate situation is hardly doubtful; more will be said of this below.

From the eighth century onwards Dorian and other colonies had been founded in Sicily by the Greeks, and early in the sixth century the Cnidians made a modest contribution of their own. A band of Cnidian emigrants settled on the north coast of Sicily and founded a city; the local Sicilians and Phoenicians, however, made life so uncomfortable that before long they transferred themselves to the island of Lipara to the north. The other islands of the group, including Strongyle (Stromboli), they tilled but did not inhabit. Here they found new enemies in the Tyrrhenian pirates, but these proved less unmanageable; the Cnidians were frequently victorious and sent offerings from their victories to Delphi.

Meanwhile the Persians had overthrown the Lydian kingdom (546 B.C.) and were subduing the Greek cities of the Asiatic coast. As their armies moved gradually southwards under their general Harpagus, the Cnidians conceived the idea of defending themselves by cutting the narrow isthmus which joined their territory to the mainland and so making it into an island. As the work proceeded, however, it was found that the splintering of the hard rock was injuring the faces and eyes of the workmen more than appeared natural; they therefore applied for advice to the oracle at Delphi. The god replied, not in his usual hexameters but in iambic verse:

Dig not nor fence your isthmus: Zeus himself
Had made your land an island, had he so wished.

The Cnidians thereupon abandoned their plan, and when Harpagus
arrived, submitted without resistance.

Before the geography of the peninsula was properly understood
it was thought that the eastern half belonged to Bybassus, and it was
accordingly supposed that the isthmus which the Cnidians began to
cut was the neck of land near Datça. This, however, is a mile and
a half (2·4 km.) wide, with a ridge of hills nowhere less than 100 feet
(30·5 m.) high; as a rush job, with the Persians approaching, this is
out of the question. The true site, as indeed Herodotus makes clear,
is the much narrowed isthmus at the extreme east end of the peninsula above the little bay of Bencik. This is about half a mile wide
(Herodotus says five stades), and is much spoken of locally as a
natural curiosity; the Turks call it Balıkaşıran ('the place where
fish may leap across'). In the last century it was often used for the
portage of small boats. On the south side a trough about 100 feet
(30·5 m.) wide runs in from the shore almost at sea-level and reduces
the width of the neck that would require to be cut to little over 250
yards (228·6 m.). The height of the col has been estimated as 50
feet (15·2 m.), but seems in fact to be considerably more. Spratt in
1838 believed that he could see actual traces of the ancient cutting;
in the hope of confirming this, Professor Cook and the writer in
1950 persuaded the driver of the bus conveying us to Marmaris to
stop while we explored the spot. Although the other passengers
displayed no impatience or resentment, our examination was
necessarily hasty, and we were not in fact able to find the traces
noted by Spratt.

In the course of the seventh century a number of Greek states,
mostly maritime cities of the Asiatic coast, had established a
trading-station at Naucratis at the mouth of the Nile. Under Amasis,
king of Egypt from 569 to 525, this was given the rank of a city.
A large precinct containing temples and markets, called the
Hellenium, was shared by half a dozen states, including Cnidus and
Halicarnassus, and this was the only place in Egypt where Greeks
were permitted to trade.

In the Delian Confederacy Cnidus paid to Athens a tribute vary-
ing from five to two talents, and was used by the Athenian admiral
Cimon as a base for his expedition in 468 B.C. to the south coast of
Asia Minor. In 412, however, the city was persuaded by the satrap
Tissaphernes, acting in the Spartan interest, to revolt from Athens

113

and quit the confederacy. The Spartans at once planned to use this new ally to advantage. A squadron of twelve ships, arriving at Cnidus, divided into two equal parts, half to guard the city and the rest to wait around Triopium and intercept the merchant vessels bringing corn to Athens from Egypt as they rounded the promontory. Learning of this an Athenian fleet at Samos sailed at once to the spot and seized the six ships at Triopium, whose crews escaped to land; then sailing on to Cnidus they attacked the city and in its unfortified condition almost succeeded in capturing it. Next day they renewed the attack; but during the night the Cnidians had improved their defences, and the sailors from Triopium had reached and entered the city; the Athenians therefore quickly abandoned their assault and returned to Samos after merely ravaging the Cnidian territory.

In reading this account of Thucydides it must of course be remembered that the city of Cnidus was then at Datça, not at Tekir. The captured Spartan ships must have been waiting either at Tekir, if there was at that time a usable harbour, or more likely in Palamut Bay some six miles (9·65 km.) to the east. From here to the city at Datça is rather more than seven hours on foot; from Tekir it is an hour or so longer; if the Spartan sailors started some time after midday, they would arrive about sunset or soon after.

As Dorians, the Cnidians may well have felt it more natural to be allied with Sparta than with Athens; but they did not remain very long in this condition. In 394 B.C. the Athenian admiral Conon, with the Persians now on his side, put an end to Spartan control of this region by his victory in a sea-battle near Cnidus. It was about this time that a group of maritime Greek states, including Cnidus, entered into an alliance in an attempt to remain independent of Athenian, Spartan, or any other domination (above, p. 6); but in 387 the King's Peace brought them all once again under the Persian King until the arrival of Alexander in 334.

Some time during the fourth century came the great moment when the city moved from Datça to the new site at Tekir. The exact date is uncertain, but is likely to have been in the 360s. The move involved of course a great deal of activity and much disturbance. A great new wall-circuit was built; streets and houses were laid out on a rectangular plan; temples, theatres, and other buildings were erected. It appears that the headland of Deveboynu (Cape Crio) was at the time an island; the Cnidians joined it to the mainland by a causeway, where there is now an isthmus, and constructed an artificial harbour on either side. The city occupied both the mainland

and a large part of the peninsula; the public buildings were on the mainland, the peninsula being terraced for private residences. Not all of this could be done in a day, and an inscription gives us a glimpse of conditions shortly after the move. It is a public decree forbidding anyone to take up quarters in the sanctuary of Dionysus. Evidently the housing situation was such that a prohibition upon squatters was considered necessary.

It is likely, though not proved, that the change of site was accompanied by a change of constitution. Back in the early sixth century, according to Diodorus, the Cnidians who emigrated to Sicily and Lipara were 'disgusted with the severity of the kings', implying that the city was governed, like so many others, by a tyrant. Later, the tyranny gave way to an oligarchy, for Aristotle quotes Cnidus as a case where the oligarchs were overthrown by the democrats because of the harshness of their rule. Democracy was accordingly established at least by about 330, the approximate time when Aristotle wrote. But it may well have been earlier than this. The most distinguished of all the citizens of Cnidus was the scientist Eudoxus, a many-sided scholar almost rivalling Aristotle himself. Mathematician, astronomer, physician, geographer, philosopher, he is recorded also as having drawn up a code of laws for his city. For this there could be no more likely occasion than the establishment of the democracy. Eudoxus died about 355 B.C.

A date for the move in the 360s is suggested by other circumstances also. The new temples in the city at Tekir required new cult-statues, and these were purchased from the outstanding sculptors of the time. In addition to the well-known Demeter, found by Newton (though it had been previously observed) and brought to the British Museum, we hear of a Dionysus by Bryaxis, an Athena and another Dionysus by Scopas, and above all the famous Aphrodite of Praxiteles. All these sculptors were contemporaries. Praxiteles is said to have 'flourished' between 365 and 360; this may mean that he was then about forty years of age, or perhaps that he created his most famous work, the Aphrodite, around that time. In any event, when the Cnidians ordered their new statue of the goddess, it happened that the men of Cos also had just done the same; and it further happened that Praxiteles had two Aphrodites ready in his workshop, one draped and the other nude. The Coans were given the choice and took the former; the nude accordingly remained for the Cnidians, and afterwards gained immensely more fame than the other, so that many people, as Pliny says, sailed to Cnidus simply to see it. Now the Coans too had moved

115

the site of their city in 365 B.C., and it is hard to resist the conclusion that they and the Cnidians found themselves simultaneously in the same need to equip their new temples.

One other item of evidence points in the same direction. Eudoxus had an observatory at Cnidus, from which, although it was only a little above the level of the houses, he was able to observe the star

Fig. 23 The Cnidian Aphrodite

Canopus. This observatory has not of course been identified on the ground, nor can the writer say how much height would be needed to see Canopus; but it is obvious that much more height is available, and the houses must have extended much higher, in the new Cnidus than in the old, and if the observatory was in fact at Tekir, the change of site must date before 355.

The foundation of the new Cnidus marks virtually the end of the city's individual history. The new site must have brought commercial prosperity, at least for a time; down to the end of the Rhodian domination in 167 Cnidian coinage is abundant. After this, however, it becomes much rarer, and silver issues cease altogether; under the Empire it became very scarce indeed. If a city's prosperity may be measured by its coinage, the evidence is of a steady decline. Historically at least, Cnidus lived her best days on the old site at Datça. In early Imperial times Cnidus is recorded as a 'free city', and was later the seat of a bishopric.

Hitherto little has been said of Triopium, which was at all times closely associated with Cnidus and formed part of her territory. The name is somewhat differently used in different contexts, and does not always mean quite the same thing. Herodotus, speaking of the Cnidians, says that 'their territory extends towards the open sea—Triopium, it is called—though it begins from the Bybassian peninsula'. His meaning is quite clear: Cnidian territory actually begins at the Bencik isthmus, but the eastern half, as far as the Datça isthmus, is a worthless mountain tract, and the only territory deserving of the name lies to the west of the city towards the open sea. This, he says, is called Triopium. How it got this name is uncertain; some said from the mythical hero Triopas, but more likely it was called 'facing three ways' by reason of its roughly triangular shape. Elsewhere Herodotus speaks of the 'Triopian headland', and Thucydides calls it 'a projecting headland of the Cnidian territory'; to others than the Cnidians themselves the important feature of Triopium was the Deveboynu promontory, an outstanding landmark and the difficult point in a journey up the coast. To a Cnidian, on the other hand, Triopium meant the western half of the peninsula, and in particular the fertile part of this around Betçe.

At the same time there is evidence also of a *town* of Triopium. Triopas is said to have 'founded' Triopium, which was named after him; and he can hardly have founded a peninsula or a headland. Still more significant is a passage of Arrian referring to the activities in 333 B.C. of Orontobates, the successor of the Hecatomnids. He was holding in the Persian interest Myndus, Caunus, Thera, and Callipolis; 'and he had won over also Cos and Triopium'. If this means what it says, Triopium must at that time have had a government distinct from that of Cnidus, having broken away soon after the change of site. Such a state of affairs can only have been temporary. There is no tangible evidence, such as coins or city-decrees, of an independent Triopium, nor did anyone, so far as is known, ever call himself a Triopian.

Somewhere, then, in the western half of the peninsula was the temple of Apollo, where was celebrated the festival of the six (later

117

five) Dorian cities, at which the Halicarnassian Agasicles disgraced himself. Of the temple itself, as was said before, no trace has been found, but its general situation cannot, in the writer's opinion, be doubted. Only in the region of Betçe is the ground suitable for the celebration of games. The festival, we are told, included not only the normal athletic and musical contests, but also horse-races. So long as it was believed that Cnidus lay at all times at Tekir, the temple of Apollo was supposed to have stood on the headland of Deveboynu, and the absence of any visible remains was explained on the supposition that it had fallen into the sea; in fact there can never have been a stadium and hippodrome at Tekir.

At Betçe, on the other hand, there is abundant level ground with water, and even more to the point, here alone between old and new Cnidus are the ruins of a considerable town. On a steep hill above the village of Kumyer is an acropolis heavily fortified with walls of early date, with a copious spring on the south side; sherds from archaic to Roman times, and an inscription in the archaic Cnidian script, have been found on it, and another inscription reveals the presence of a precinct of Asclepius. This must surely be Triopium.

As is clear from Thucydides' narrative (above, pp. 113–14), Triopium possessed a harbour distinct from that of Cnidus; Cimon in 468, with a fleet of 200 ships, had made Cnidus and Triopium his base. This harbour can hardly be other than Palamut Bay below Kumyer. This is an open roadstead with a small island, Baba Ada, lying half a mile offshore. The bay itself is somewhat exposed, though not to the prevailing north-wester, but there is evidence that the Cnidians converted it into a first-rate harbour by means of a sea-wall extending from the island to the mainland. All that can be seen of this today is a line of shallow water projecting from the south end of the island, and another projecting towards it from the mainland opposite; but the coastguard stationed on the shore in 1956 reported that there was in fact a submarine wall at this point, which he had seen with his schnorkel apparatus and on which he often caught his fishing-line.[2] Such a wall—or perhaps rather two moles with an entrance in the middle—would make a roomy anchorage, sheltered from all sides, and if it really exists, is conclusive proof that this is the harbour of Triopium. Even without a wall, an anchorage is marked here on the Admiralty Chart.

The festival of Triopian Apollo was probably of some importance in early times as a gathering-place for the Dorian states; later, however, it seems to have declined, and very little is heard of it. Ptolemy II showed some interest and may have attempted to revive it, but without much noticeable effect. Among the hundreds of inscriptions recording the victories of athletes all over the world in Hellenistic and Roman times only two make mention of the games at Cnidus; both the victors are local men, one from Cos and one from Cedreae. An ancient commentator on Theocritus makes the surprising statement that these games were celebrated in honour of the Nymphs, Apollo, and Poseidon; there is no mention elsewhere of any but Apollo, and this information is generally agreed to be unreliable.

Triopian Apollo, however, was not the principal deity of the Cnidians themselves; this was Aphrodite. From the seventh century down to Roman times nearly all the coins of Cnidus bear the goddess's head on the obverse or reverse. She had the special title of Euploia, 'of fair sailing', and after the move to Tekir this is symbolized on the coins by the prow of a ship. Her temple and statue at Tekir, as was said before, was a tourist attraction of the first order. The form of the statue is familiar from the numerous copies made in later times; the form of the temple was unusual, and seems to have been designed less for public worship than to show off Praxiteles' masterpiece. In the first place, it was not rectangular but round. Round temples were quite exceptional in Greek lands; on the other hand, they are often seen in Roman wall-paintings, and in some cases at least occur in association with Aphrodite (Venus).[3] On a monster show-boat constructed by Ptolemy IV of Egypt there is said to have been a circular temple of Aphrodite containing a marble statue of the goddess; and in Hadrian's Villa at Tivoli there is a round building with an open Doric Colonnade in which was recently found a copy of the Cnidian Aphrodite. This building is likely to be a replica of the temple at Cnidus, for it was Hadrian's whim to fill the grounds of his villa with reproductions, more or less fanciful, of famous features of the Greek world.

In the second place, the temple had at least two doors, perhaps more. Pliny says that 'the whole temple is opened, so that the statue may be seen from all sides'; he appears to mean that it may be opened, that is, there are doors, on all sides. A work entitled *Love Affairs*, passing under the name of Lucian in the second century A.D., gives an account of a visit to Cnidus. After admiring the gardens which filled the precinct the party entered the temple and stood amazed before the beauty of the statue in the middle; then, wishing to see the back as well (for the statue was noted as being equally lovely in all aspects) they went round to the rear of the temple, where the door was opened for them by the old woman who held the key. The back of the statue proved indeed to be in no way inferior to the front; they noticed, however, a dark patch like a stain on the inner side of the thigh. At first they supposed this to be a flaw in the marble, and admired the skill of the sculptor in contriving that it should come in so inconspicuous a place; but the old woman explained that this was not so. There had been, she said, a young man who fell in love with the goddess and dreamed of marrying her. All his days he spent in the temple from morning to evening; and to estimate his chances he cast knucklebones (the ancient dice) in the hope of making the throw named after the goddess herself, when all four dice showed different faces. Finally, driven to desperation by his desire, he concealed himself in the temple one day and contrived to remain hidden when the doors were closed for the night. In the morning the mark of his passionate embraces was clear on the marble, and there it remained ever since.

From these accounts it is supposed that the temple had no cella wall, but that the spaces between the columns were closed with barriers, two or more of which contained doors. These barriers reached only halfway to the roof, leaving an open space above. It need hardly be emphasized how utterly unlike a normal temple this would be; but a representation of just such a building does in fact exist. In the Villa of Julia Felix at Pompeii a wall-painting shows a round temple with panels between the columns up to half their height; and above one of the panels rises the upper part of a female statue. In the temple at Cnidus the interior arrangements are un-certain, but evidently there must have been barriers there also, since Lucian's party could not simply walk round the statue but needed the back door to be opened for them.

In 1969 the American excavators discovered a round building at Cnidus which seems to have every chance of being the famous temple of Aphrodite (below, pp. 125–6); their next hope is to find the statue itself, declared by Pliny to be the finest not only of Praxiteles' works but in all the world. Nicomedes, king of Bithynia, is said to have offered to pay the whole of the city's debts in ex-change for it, but the offer was not accepted. These debts must have been considerable, and to some extent confirm the decline in the city's fortunes. An ancient writer says that the statue was later taken to Constantinople and there destroyed by fire, but this report is now generally disbelieved.

Among the human denizens of Cnidus the most distinguished is certainly Eudoxus. He is best known as an astronomer. In the early fourth century astronomy had barely begun to make the scientific advances which culminated in the brilliance of the Alexandrine era; Eudoxus, however, felt himself able to declare that the diameter of the sun is nine times greater than that of the moon, and three times greater than that of the earth. Cnidian also were the architect Sostratus, builder of the lighthouse at Alexandria which was reckoned among the Seven Wonders of the World, and the historian Ctesias, who wrote of India and Persia; he was also a member of a family of hereditary physicians, for Cnidus was a famous seat of medicine. Ctesias is said to have served as court physician in Persia and to have cured the Great King Artaxerxes II of a wound suffered in battle.

One or two Cnidian products are mentioned as deserving the gastronomer's praise, in particular the wine. This is said to be nourishing, enriching the blood and promoting easy movement of the bowels, but relaxing the stomach if drunk in excess. Cnidian vinegar is bracketed with the Egyptian as the best to be had. Mention is also made of a special kind of cabbage, curiously called 'briny'; what this may have been like is not known, but the best was grown at Cnidus.

The site of Old Cnidus lies immediately to the north of the Iskele of Datça, where is the present administrative centre of the *kaza*. The acropolis is on a blunt headland about a mile from the Iskele, a little to the south of the point where the Datça Çayı reaches the sea. The summit is defended by a fortification-wall enclosing an area about a quarter of a mile long; the masonry is a mixture of ashlar and polygonal. On the seaward side it stands not on the cliff but at its foot at sea-level; but the sea has risen since antiquity. This is the best preserved part, standing up to six courses; it is of a type which dates generally around 400 B.C. Whether this wall was standing at the time of the Athenian attack in 412 B.C. (above, p. 114) is uncertain. Thucydides calls the city 'unfortified', but during the night the defenders 'improved their defences', so perhaps he means that the walls were in disrepair or had been partially dismantled, in which case the present wall may be a replacement of the defective fortification. Nothing is standing inside the wall, but the ground is thickly strewn with pottery ranging in date from the seventh century down to Hellenistic times. The spot is now called Dalacak. On its south side remains of a small harbour may be seen in the water.

This was not of course the whole city; there are indications of an outer defence line enclosing a very considerable area. To the north of the acropolis great quantities of large squared blocks are lying in the water, and belong evidently to a collapsed sea-wall extending to the mouth of the Datça Çayı; and on the south bank of the stream a clearly defined shelf, over a mile long, runs inland west and then south. This shelf appears to mark the line of a wall, of which only a few loose square blocks and some of the rubble filling may now be seen. This outer wall no doubt ended at or near the Iskele, and would enclose an area not far short of two square miles.

Within this area, to the south and especially to the north of Dalacak, important finds have been made in the past, though little is visible today. In particular, early in the present century, a Greek of Syme carried out excavations at a spot near the mouth of the Datça Çayı and found an archaic sanctuary 'very rich in offerings of the greatest importance', and also another archaic building; neither of these is now to be seen. On the shore, however, close to the rivermouth, are the solid foundations of a large building which appears, from the olive-press lying in it, to have been an oil-factory.

Just to the south of the Iskele is a platform some 70 feet (21·3 m.) long, supported by terrace walls of heavy polygonal masonry; here was perhaps a small sanctuary. Masonry of this type occurs in numerous places on Cnidian territory and seems to be of Hellenistic date. Most of the finds at Old Cnidus have been made at a considerable depth, and there is no doubt that the archaic and classical remains are deeply buried.

It is clear from the sherds and other remnants that the site of the old city was not abandoned after the move to Tekir; this is after all the most fertile part of the peninsula. Pliny gives Stadia as an alternative name for Cnidus; this name appears later in the lists of bishoprics, and survives in the modern Datça. It may safely be accepted as the name of the old city after the change of site.

To the north-west of Dalacak, on the north side of the peninsula, is a second harbour known at present as Körmen Limanı; built into a mosque half a mile from the shore is an archaic capital subsequently reused as a boundary-stone and inscribed in letters of the fourth century 'Boundary of the Harbour'. Körmen Limanı is little used nowadays, but must have been popular in antiquity for vessels coming from the north as far as Old Cnidus, to avoid the difficult return journey round the cape.

From Old Cnidus at Datça to Triopium at Kumyer there must always have been a road, and in fact its course may be traced; it follows closely the line of the present track, and seems to have been of a width to take two lines of traffic. After the foundation of the new city the road was extended to Tekir. Just beyond Kumyer it crossed a stream by a bridge, of which the greater part is still standing; it is among the more notable specimens of ancient Greek bridges. On either side a long abutment leads to the actual bridge, which spanned the stream in the form of a triangular or trapezoidal arch (the top is missing). The style of the masonry suggests a date around 300 B.C. As the road approaches the new city, it is lined on both sides with tombs, forming a very extensive necropolis.

New Cnidus at Tekir must have been a most attractive city. Strabo describes it as 'a kind of double city', for much of it occupied the off-lying island, which the Cnidians joined to the mainland by a causeway. He reckons the perimeter of the 'island' at seven stades, a slight underestimate. The main part, however, was on the mainland, and was laid out on the 'Hippodamian' plan, with streets crossing at right-angles. The steep gradient, as much as 1 in 3 in places, made it necessary for some of the north–south streets to be stepped. The fortifications enclose about two-thirds of the 'island' and an area on the mainland rather less than a mile (1·61 km.) long and a half a mile (804·7 m.) broad; the new city was thus smaller than the old, but more concentrated. The wall is best preserved on the north side, where it runs up to an acropolis on the east; the masonry is a regular ashlar. There are three gates, two on the north and one on the east. The towers are rectangular except for one at the mouth of the northern harbour which is still in excellent preservation.

This northern harbour is probably the one which Strabo calls the 'Trireme Harbour', and is said to provide anchorage for twenty warships; it was closed with a chain in the usual manner. The commercial harbour on the south is much larger, with an entrance partially closed by a mole on either side; remains of the moles are visible under water and constitute a hazard to vessels entering. This harbour must have been constantly filled with wind-bound ships coming from the south.

High up on the north side is a large theatre, but it is poorly preserved and the eastern half has entirely collapsed. To the east of this, at the foot of a steep scarp, is the precinct of Demeter which was excavated by Newton and produced the splendid seated statue of the goddess which is now in the British Museum.

The new American excavations have done much to clarify the layout of the main part of the city, although not all the identifications of individual buildings may be accepted as certain. The main axis of the town was a broad east–west street (running east from

123

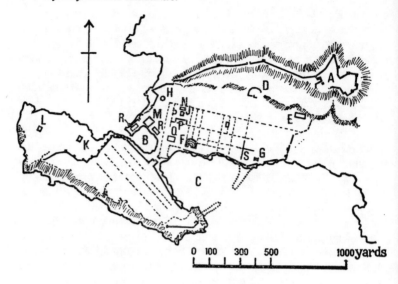

A — Acropolis
B — Trireme Harbour
C — Southern Harbour
D — Upper Theatre
E — Sanctuary of Demeter
F — Lower Theatre
G — Odeum
H — Temple of Aphrodite
J — Corinthian Temple

K — Roman Tomb
L — Lighthouse
M — Agora
N — Monumental Building
P — Doric Stoa
Q — Temple of Dionysus and Byzantine Church
R — Byzantine Churches
S — Stepped Street

Fig. 24 Plan of New Cnidus

N on the plan), which presumably led to the east city gate. This was
approached at right-angles from the south by a series of stepped
streets leading down towards the sea shore and the eastern harbour.
The buildings on one side of these, so-called stepped street 7 (S on
the plan), have been excavated, revealing terraced houses of the
Hellenistic and Roman periods, and possibly buildings associated
with the harbour. Also overlooking the harbour at the lower end
of these stepped streets was the lower theatre and an odeum. The
former (F) has been cleared and proves to be in good condition.

There are some thirty-five rows of seats, with two diazomata and an arched entrance on either side. Of the stage-building, however, little or nothing is to be seen. The theatre is estimated to hold about 8,000 people. The odeum (G) was also a handsome little building, but not very much of it is left.

Most of the main public buildings of the city were concentrated towards the west end of the main street. Adjoining it on the south are the traces of a roughly square monumental building whose function is not yet certain (N), and south of this is a small Corinthian temple, now excavated and cleared (J). The god or goddess to whom it was dedicated is uncertain. To the west of this lay another odeum, and to the south a massive stoa built in the Doric order, over 113 metres long and 16 metres deep (P). This overlooked an area now largely taken up by the ruins of a Byzantine church, which has almost certainly replaced an earlier building on the site. Still further down the slope of the hill, and not far from the lower theatre, is another Byzantine church, built over the remains of a temple of Dionysus (Q).

The agora of the ancient city certainly lay at the foot of the hill, beside the 'trireme harbour', but to date the most conspicuous remains to have been found here are two more Byzantine churches (R). The devotion of the Cnidians is indeed impressive.

However, the most newsworthy of all the buildings of Cnidus is the round building H to the north of the main street, which is in all probability the temple of Aphrodite Euploia (Pl. 37). It stands on the slope overlooking the isthmus on the north. The site is a good one, but the rock wall behind, and the slope in front, seem to leave little room for the splendid gardens which aroused the admiration of Lucian and his party. The excavator argues that these gardens, linked to the temple by a paved way, lay to the east. The temple stood on a round podium about 5 feet (1·52 m.) high, with two steps above. The statue base has been found on this, a block of dark grey stone measuring 51 by 44 inches (1·30 by 1·12 m.), most of it occupied by a D-shaped hollow 2 inches (50 mm.) deep, which held the base of the statue itself. Pl. 37 shows the condition of the building at the end of the season of 1969. On the east the round building was approached by a flight of four steps, and opposite these there is a square altar of the normal type. A large number of terracotta statuettes of various types has been found in the area of the temple, but perhaps the most curious of the finds is the quantity of erotic and pornographic pottery, remarked on by Lucian in his description. As confirmation of the identification of the temple, an inscription found in the vicinity has been adduced, beginning with the letters PRAX. It is suggested that these are the first letters of Praxiteles' name, and that the rest of the inscription, which is fragmentary, went on to mention the naked statue of Aphrodite. However, it is hard to see how the text can actually be restored to give this sense, and it may simply be a dedication of a more conventional nature, made by a person whose name began with those letters. (There are many Greek names which would fit.)

Also controversial is another claim recently put forward by the excavator, Miss Iris Love. Exploring 'under the dust of ages' in the British Museum basement among the stones sent back from Cnidus by Sir Charles Newton in 1859, she found a marble head which she at once declared to be that of Praxiteles' Aphrodite, unrecognized in the museum vaults for more than a hundred years. It seems, however, improbable that this claim will be substantiated; the museum authorities point out that the head was found by Newton, not on the site of the Aphrodite temple (which was not dug by him) but on that of the sanctuary of Demeter and Persephone at the other end of the city, over half a mile away. The head itself is too much damaged to be immediately recognizable, but is thought at the museum to belong in all probability to a statue of Persephone, companion to the well-known figure of Demeter found close by in the same sanctuary. The controversy seems likely to raise a good deal of dust before it is settled.

The excavations have been extended to the terrace of the hill immediately south of the round temple, and these have produced a complicated series of structures, apparently of a sacred nature. They appear to include parts of an altar with reliefs depicting the nymphs. Further work here, both on the finds and in the field, may answer some of the questions raised by the temple of Aphrodite.

The necropolis outside the city wall on the east is extensive and contains a great variety of tombs. In the north-east area are two rock-cut tombs approached by a *dromos* or walled passage; the entrance to the tomb is in one case triangular, in the other trapezoidal. In some cases the tombs are grouped at the rear of an open enclosure forming a family burial-ground. On the peninsula (K on the plan) is a fine built tomb of Roman date; in front is a vestibule paved with black and white mosaic, and behind this a chamber with apse at the rear and niches in the side walls. It contained originally three sarcophagi, of which only fragments are preserved.

The excavations have produced a number of sherds of the fifth century B.C., so that Tekir was evidently not unoccupied before the city moved there in the fourth century. We may hope that future discoveries will show what was there in the classical period.

As on other ancient sites in Turkey, the excavations have resulted in an accession of civilization at Tekir. In 1950 the place was utterly deserted except for the lighthouse-keeper and a party of gendarmes; in 1970 the writer was surprised to find three restaurants on the spot, and visitors are now frequent. The site is reached by boat from Bodrum (the crossing taking up to six hours if the sea is at all rough) or from Marmaris; the motor-road goes as far as Datça, and the track from there onwards is suitable only for a jeep.

Notes

1 The proof of this change is given in the article by J. M. Cook and the present writer listed in the Bibliography. The ancient writers do not distinguish old and new Cnidus. The present excavator of Cnidus has disputed the claim that old Cnidus lay at Datça, and it is true that early pottery, dating back to the Mycenaean period, and an unfinished archaic statue have been found at the site at Tekir. But no architectural remains have appeared, and the balance of probability still favours the view that Datça was the archaic site, although doubtless there was some form of settlement at the tip of the peninsula.
2 This information was communicated to the writer by Dr Wilder Penfield of Montreal.
3 They are found, for example, on the walls of bedrooms.

13   The Rhodian Peraea

In the Dorian migration to Asia the principal settlement was on the island of Rhodes. Her three cities, Lindus, Ialysus, and Camirus, which were known to Homer, made up half of the Dorian hexapolis. These cities remained separate and independent until 408 B.C., when they united to form a single Rhodian state; a new capital city of Rhodes was founded on the site which she has occupied ever since. The old cities were not abandoned but continued to maintain their own individuality within the new state.

Before this time the history of Rhodes is an almost total blank, but it is clear that from an early period the individual cities had possessed territory on the mainland of Asia opposite the island; this territory now became part of the Rhodian state, and its inhabitants had full status as citizens of Rhodes. The area in question comprised the peninsula south-west of Marmaris, commonly called the Loryma peninsula, and somewhat later the land to the north and north-west as far as the Ceramic gulf.

But as time went on, Rhodes acquired, permanently or temporarily, much other territory on the mainland, which she held in the capacity of suzerain; this country was governed by Rhodian officials, but its people were not Rhodian citizens. The land around and to the north of the east end of the Ceramic gulf was probably annexed in the early third century, and the acquisition of Stratoniceia followed soon afterwards. About 190 B.C. the Rhodians bought Caunus from Ptolemy of Egypt for 200 talents. And in the following year they received as a gift from the Romans the whole of Lycia and Caria south of the Maeander. This gift was rescinded in 167, and Stratoniceia was never again Rhodian, but the country between there and the Ceramic gulf continued to be controlled by Rhodes at least until the second century A.D. The Lycians had refused to acknowledge Rhodian dominion and had never been effectively annexed nor did Rhodes ever regain central Caria. Lycia always

128

excepted, the whole of this region, so long as it was under Rhodes, made up the Rhodian Peraea. Its heart was always the rocky and mountainous Loryma peninsula.

Following the main road south from Aydın by Çine the traveller reaches Rhodian territory at Muğla. Now the capital of a large *vilâyet*, this was only a small place in antiquity. Its name was Mobolla, which survives with little change; the intermediate form Mogola is recorded. A handful of inscriptions has been found here, attesting Rhodian domination, and there are some insignificant ancient remains on the flat-topped hill behind the town; otherwise nothing survives.

South-west of Mobolla lay the towns of Pisye and Thera. The former has kept its old name as Pisiköy. It is mentioned occasionally in literature and in inscriptions, but was never important. The acropolis hill is a mile or so south of the village, and there are some ancient stones at a spot about the same distance to the north-east. Thera is in very similar case. It makes one appearance in history, when it was held as a strongpoint by Orontobates, the successor of the Hecatomnids, in 333 B.C., before it had become a Rhodian possession. The site is proved by inscriptions to be at Yerkesik, but has little or nothing to show today.

More interesting to the traveller are the ruins of Idyma. As the road from Muğla to Marmaris comes in sight of the Ceramic gulf, at the top of the Sakarkaya, a view opens up which is quite superb. To the west is the sea; to the south are the hills which conceal Marmaris, topped by the pointed peak of Altınsivrisi; to the south-east in the distance is the lake of Köyceğiz. And directly below, some 2,000 feet (609·6 m.) down, is the little plain which nourished the men of Idyma. Descending the road obliquely down the mountain-face the traveller will perceive at one point, below him on the left, a line of ancient wall forming an elongated oval, and looking rather like a giant ship wrecked on the mountainside. This is the acropolis of Idyma. It is most easily reached from the road above; the climb from the plain is arduous to a degree. The masonry is roughly coursed, with ashlar work here and there; in the middle is a solid building with a number of rooms. The wall is best preserved on the north side. Extending down the hill is an outer enclosure, but its wall is largely destroyed.

Much lower down the hillside the road passes another and larger fortress of mediaeval date. As it reaches the plain, it runs eastward beside a short but abundant stream, probably the ancient Idymus; before turning right to cross the plain it passes a group of rock-cut tombs. Three of these are plain, but two are of temple-tomb type with Ionic architectural façade; one had two columns, of which one is now destroyed, the other had rather surprisingly a single column in the middle. The former is cut clear of the rock, affording a passage all around it (Pl. 39). These tombs date in all probability to the fourth century B.C. Of similar type and similar date is another tomb, among a group of plain chamber-tombs, well up the hillside above the village of Kozlukuyu and below the acropolis. Numerous inscriptions found in the village leave no doubt of the identity of the site. Idyma was one of the comparatively few cities in the Rhodian Peraea which had formerly been members of the Delian Confederacy; she was at that time ruled by a dynast Pactyes, who struck coins in the name of the Idymians. The city belonged to Rhodes before 200 B.C., but was subsequently lost, then recaptured by the Rhodian general Nicagoras.

A close neighbour of Idyma was Callipolis. This name is evidently preserved in the village of Gelibolu on the coast some six miles (9·65 km.) to the south-west, where there are several forts, ancient and mediaeval, and other evidence of occupation, including two or three amphora-factories and an inscription of Rhodian type. Nevertheless it is clear that this cannot be the site of the Hellenistic and Roman Callipolis; the remains are not such as to suggest a city, and it is sure that none can ever have stood here. The true site is indicated by an inscription found at a spot about six miles inland called Duran Çiftlik; it is a dedication to the Empress Domitia by the people of Callipolis. The remains at Duran Çiftlik show that a sanctuary stood here, succeeded in later times by a church; the city itself was on the hill, some 800 feet (243·8 m.) high, above the village of Kızılyaka, a mile or so to the east. Little is now standing on the site, but the slopes are thickly strewn with pottery and loose building-stones; on the summit is a tower of poor-quality masonry. The ring-wall has disappeared above ground, but its line is marked by a clearly defined shelf running most of the way round the hill. On the east side is a group of simple graves formed of thin stones set on edge and covered with stone slabs. From this site the name of Callipolis must have been transferred to the coast at Gelibolu at some date during the middle ages; the occasion for this move can only be conjectured.

One hour's walk over the hill from Gelibolu to the west is the tiny village of Taşbükü. Lying rather more than a cable offshore is a small island called variously Şehir Ada, Şehiroğlu, or Sedir Ada; a boat of some kind is generally available either at Taşbükü or at

Gelibolu. The island carries the ruins of Cedreae, one of the most considerable demes of the Rhodian Peraea. Close to half a mile (804 m.) in length, the island is divided into two parts by an isthmus in the middle; the ruins lie exclusively on the eastern half. Here a powerful wall in regular ashlar, with numerous towers, runs round close above the shore (Pl. 34). Near the central point are the foundations of the temple of Apollo, in the Doric order, on a platform supported by a solid wall well preserved; here again the temple was succeeded by a Christian church. Close by, on the north slope, is a good-sized theatre in excellent preservation, though buried in jungle: this is one of the three theatres known in the Peraea (Pl. 35). The lower parts, including the stage and orchestra, are buried, but fifteen or sixteen rows of seats are still to be seen. The cavea is divided by stairways into nine wedge-shaped sections (*cunei*); there is no sign of any diazoma. Terrace walls adjoin the theatre on either side; that on the west is especially well preserved, with handsome bossed masonry. To the east of the theatre many ruined buildings are discernible among the thick vegetation.

The agora seems to have lain towards the west, supported by a fine wall of regular ashlar whose courses are distinguished by horizontal cuttings along the edges of the blocks. Numerous inscriptions have been found here of the types that normally adorned the market-place. The inscriptions contain references to at least three athletic festivals celebrated at Cedreae, so that the city must presumably have possessed a stadium, but none has been discovered.

On the mainland opposite the island is an extensive necropolis; the tombs are mainly large sarcophagi and built tombs with vaulted roof and containing sometimes more than one chamber.

Although the name Cedreae is apparently Greek, derived from the name of the cedar-tree, the city was in origin purely Carian. In the Delian Confederacy it paid a tribute of half a talent or rather less. Towards the end of the Peloponnesian War, in 405 B.C., while Cedreae was still an ally of Athens, the Spartan general Lysander attacked her, and taking her by force at the second attempt, sold the inhabitants into slavery. Xenophon, who records this event, describes the Cedreates as 'half-barbarian'. At some uncertain date after this, Cedreae was taken over by the Rhodians and fully Hellenized as a deme of the Rhodian state. No coins of the independent city are known, and after the incorporation into Rhodes there could of course be no question of striking money.

The country west of a line drawn from Cedreae to Marmaris is today very thinly populated. In antiquity it formed that part of the

131

Peraea which was called Apeiros (the Mainland), and contained, so far as is known, two Rhodian demes. The more considerable of these is on the high and steep peak of Altınsivrisi (Golden Pike), the highest point in this region. There is a citadel on the summit, hardly less than 2,000 feet (609 m.) above sea-level, and substantial remains of the town on the slopes. This is almost certainly Euthena, one of the larger Peraean demes. The other is on a headland close to the village of Söğüt. Here is a fortified site with a handsome wall up to 18 feet in height, with a gate on the north; on the shore of the bay below is a short stretch of ancient quay-wall in good ashlar masonry with bossed faces. This is likely to be the deme of Amnistus.

There is no such uncertainty with regard to Marmaris, whose ancient name is abundantly proved by the inscriptions found there. This is the site of Physcus, the most important of all the demes in the Peraea, and the only one to be named separately in the governor's command. As a deme it was attached to the city of Lindus, and was incorporated in the Rhodian state at least by the time of Alexander the Great (as an inscription shows), and no doubt a good deal earlier. Strabo makes the extraordinary statement that Physcus was the port of Mylasa; the error is the more surprising as more than once elsewhere he gives it its true position. At the south end of the present town is a low hill carrying a mediaeval castle picturesquely mingled with modern houses; this, however, is not the acropolis of Physcus, which was on a much higher hill called Asar Tepe a mile or more to the north. On this hill are some remains of walls dating to classical and Hellenistic times, but nothing is standing inside them. Nor does Marmaris itself contain any remnants of antiquity apart from the inscribed and sculptured stones which are collected at the school; these include a marble lion lacking the head, a slab with relief of a man and a horse, and a fine marble head of a young Roman lady from the beginning of the Empire.

As was said before, the heart of the Rhodian Peraea was the Loryma peninsula. This is mountainous, rocky, and steep, wooded in the northern part but bare in the south. There is a passable road from Marmaris to Bozburun, and boats may be hired at Marmaris for a tour of the peninsula; otherwise all exploration must be done on foot.

Sailing south across the fine bay of Marmaris and passing through the narrow entrance, the traveller comes shortly in sight of a small headland known as Hisarburnu. There is a landing-place on the shore, and close above are the ruins of Amos (Pl. 36), another of the important Rhodian demes. The spot is called Asarcık. The top

of the hill is encircled by a wall 6 feet (1·83 m.) thick, standing up
to 10 or 12 feet (3·05 or 3·66 m.) in height; the masonry is of the
type called 'coursed polygonal'. This style is characteristic of the
early Hellenistic period, and all the visible remains at Amos seem
to be of this or similar date. The wall is provided with towers and
a gate on the north side. At the west end of the acropolis are the
scanty remains of a small temple about 45 feet long, and several
uninscribed statue-bases. The plan is with difficulty recognizable as
that of a temple *in antis*. On the north-east slope is a small theatre,
the second of the three known in the Peraea. It is in fair preservation;
the rows of seats remain in part, and the analemmata stand up to
17 feet (5·18 m.) in height. The stage-building was divided into
three rooms, still distinguishable; and in the orchestra, lying broken
in two pieces, is the altar on which sacrifice to Dionysus was made
before each performance. On the north slope of the hill, on a small
terrace, the writer found in 1948 four inscribed fragments containing
the terms of three land-leases issued about 200 B.C. These leases
are very detailed, with precise instructions for the payment of rent,
provision of guarantors, and development of the property; the
tenant must build a minimum number of sheds, plant a minimum
number of vines and figs, with minimum space for corn between,
and dig a drainage-trench. Penalties are fixed for failure to observe
these conditions, and also for cutting wood on the property, burying
a corpse in it, or encroaching on the public roads. It is evident that
the leases were first leases of the estates, and we have evidence of
a scheme of agricultural development initiated in the early second
century, apparently by the Rhodian government. The visitor to Amos
may well wonder where, in this rough hill-country, these estates
may have been; it is probable that they lay on the flat plain by the
present village of Gölenye, which no doubt belonged to Amos—
one of the few pieces of flat land on the peninsula. The principal
deity of Amos was Apollo, with the otherwise unknown epithet
Samnaios; a temple-inventory and a dedication by one of his priests
were found on the same terrace with the land-leases, and it is likely
that the land in question belonged to his temple. Whether the small
temple on the acropolis was his there is no evidence to show.

Further down the coast, at a spot called Gerbekilise or Gerbekse,
are the ruins of a small Byzantine trading-station with several small
churches; from here a path leads up in an hour and a half to the
village of Bayır. This is identified by an inscription with the town
of Syrna, not a Rhodian deme but distinguished by its sanctuary
of Asclepius. Tradition said that Podaleirius, son of Asclepius and

133

physician to the Greek troops at Troy, married Syrna, daughter of a king of Caria, and was given the Chersonese (that is, the Loryma peninsula) as a gift; in it he founded two cities and named one of them after his bride. In the floor of the porch of the mosque at Bayır is a large marble block inscribed with a list of contributions made about 200 B.C. to certain construction-work in the sanctuary.

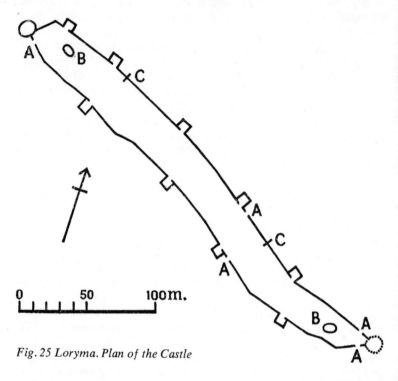

Fig. 25 Loryma. Plan of the Castle

At the southern extremity of the peninsula is the sheltered bay of Bozuk, with a few houses on the shore. It was formerly known as Oplosika Bükü, 'Arsenal Bay', and the arsenal (*hoplotheke*) is recorded by Constantine Porphyrogenitus in the tenth century. Here was the town of Loryma; like Syrna, it was not a Rhodian deme but belonged to the deme of Casara a little to the north-east. A few ancient stones may be seen near the coastguard-station by the shore; but the chief feature of the site is the impressive and well-preserved fortification on the narrow headland overlooking the entrance to the bay (Pl. 32). It forms an elongated enclosure some 350 yards (320 m.) in length by 30 (27·4 m.) in width, with a fine wall 8 feet (2·44 m.) thick, of fairly regular ashlar slightly bossed, undoubtedly of Rhodian construction; some of the blocks are as much as 17 feet (5·18 m.) long. There are nine (ruined) towers on the sides and a round tower at each end, that on the east now destroyed. Five small gates lead through the wall, four of them towards the east end. No sign of buildings is to be seen in the interior, the whole structure being purely military; there is, however, a partly rock-cut cistern near each round tower, and at C, C on the plan the wall is pierced by an outlet for water. Outside the gate in the south wall at the east end inscriptions on the rocks show that the place was sacred to Zeus Atabyrius, a deity peculiar to Rhodes.

The acropolis hill is just to the east of the landing-stage, and carries some remains of its fortification, partly in squared masonry, partly in polygonal. By the edge of the sea at the foot of this hill is a small cave with an inscription on its wall forbidding the removal of offerings from the sanctuary, so that the cave was evidently sacred. On a high hill two hours' climb to the north is another fortress comprising an inner and an outer enclosure; these also are well preserved.

The harbour of Loryma is exceptionally well protected in all weathers. It was used as a refuge for the Athenian ships during the Peloponnesian War, and in 395 B.C. the Athenian-commander Conon used it as a rendezvous shortly before the battle of Cnidus. And again in 305 Demetrius, son of Antigonus, assembled his fleet there in preparation for his unsuccessful attack on Rhodes.

A remarkable feature of this region is the large number of three- and four-sided bases graded in three stages like stepped pyramids (Fig. 26). These seem to occur only in the southernmost part of the Loryma peninsula; they are generally supposed to be bases for offerings, but none of them carries any inscription which might help to determine their purpose.

Rounding the mountainous and often boisterous promontory of Kızılburun the traveller enters the pleasant and comparatively well-populated bay of Syme; the island itself is in full view a few miles to the west. In the eastern recess of the bay, above the village of Saranda, is the acropolis of the deme of Thyssanus, with a polygonal wall; and at the northern end is the admirable harbour of Bozburun. Here was the deme of Tymnus, but very little remains of it beyond a considerable quantity of inscriptions. One of these refers to a cult of Zeus and Hera, and assigns a stoa to the priests for the disposal of the victims after sacrifice, with a prohibition upon the burning

135

of wood in the stoa for any other purpose, and on nailing up any object to the roof or epistyle; penalty 100 drachmae.

To the north of the Bozburun peninsula is the bay of Selimiye, called in antiquity Sinus Schoenus (Reedy Bay). Selimiye itself corresponds to the ancient Hyda or Hyla. Further north again, at the head of the gulf, is the town and bay of Bybassus, an important Rhodian deme. Between the shore and the village of Hisarönü is the acropolis, a steep rocky hill bearing remnants of fortification. On the summit is a mediaeval fortification, with Hellenistic walls on the slopes. Hisarönü was formerly known as Erine or Rina, and was supposed to represent the Rhodian deme of Erine, known from inscriptions. The identity of name appeared convincing, but in fact Erine derives almost certainly from a church of St Irene. The true identification of the site is due to the perspicacity of Professor J. M. Cook, and deserves to be set forth in some detail.

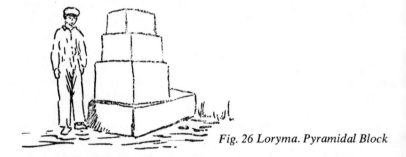

Fig. 26 Loryma. Pyramidal Block

On the mountain of Eren Dağı above Hisarönü on the south, at a spot called Pazarlık, a temple-site has long been known. Spratt in 1886 suggested it might be a temple of Leto, but his reasons were far from strong; he relied on the mention by Strabo of a grove of Leto at or near Physcus, and on a female statue that he saw on the site. Professor Cook reasoned otherwise. The historian Diodorus observes that there is at Castabus in the Chersonese a sanctuary of Hemithea, then tells the story of the sisters Molpadia and Parthenus, who were saved by Apollo and brought to the Chersonese;

and the one called Parthenus he caused to be honoured with a precinct in Bubastus of the Chersonese [Bybassus], while Molpadia came to Castabus and by reason of a divine epiphany received the name Hemithea [demi-goddess] and was honoured in all the

Chersonese; and in course of time her sanctuary so increased in renown that not only was it greatly revered by the neighbours, but even from afar men visited it and graced it with splendid sacrifices and notable offerings. And in consequence the precinct, though unguarded and unprotected by any strong wall, is crowded with votive gifts.

An inscription found by the writer near the village of Gölenye shows that the sanctuary was in the hands of the men of Bybassus. The whereabouts of Castabus in the Chersonese was quite unknown, but Bybassus at least was certainly in the region about the head of the gulf; might not the ruins on Eren Dağı be those of the sanctuary of Hemithea? This would explain the curious name Pazarlık (market) applied to this remote and deserted spot high up in the hills, if the festival of Castabus was succeeded by a great annual fair. Professor Cook accordingly carried out an excavation on the spot, and was rewarded with two inscriptions naming Hemithea and proving his theory to the hilt. Pazarlık is Castabus, and it follows that Hisarönü is Bybassus.

The sanctuary stands on a ridge of the Eren Dağı some 900 feet (274 m.) above the plain by Hisarönü, from which it is about an hour's climb. The temple of Hemithea stood on a platform built to accommodate it; it was in the Ionic order, but with minor Doric features, and dates from the latter part of the fourth century B.C. It replaced an earlier shrine of which some remnants were found. The plan is simple, a deep pronaos and a cella, with no opisthodomus, and a colonnade of eleven columns on the long sides and six at the ends. A curious feature is a round altar-like structure, decorated with reliefs, which stood in the pronaos directly in front of the door to the cella; its purpose and its date are alike uncertain. A further unusual feature is the ornamental screen-wall which ran round three sides of the platform, with small rectangular buildings at unequal intervals and of unequal size; the function of these is also unknown. On the whole platform, however, very little is now standing above the foundations. The supporting walls of the platform itself, on the other hand, are of handsome masonry in very fair condition. The only other identifiable building on the site is a theatre, very poorly preserved, a little way down the slope to the south. This is the third and last of the theatres hitherto discovered in the Peraea.

Hemithea was a healing deity, and the method of cure practised in her sanctuary was incubation. According to Diodorus the goddess in person stood over the sick and treated them in their sleep; she was especially helpful to women in childbirth, and had restored to health many desperate cases. We know of a festival called the Castabeia which was held periodically on the site, and it is probable that the incubation was practised mostly, if not exclusively, at those times. Nothing more is known of the character of the festival; it can hardly have included athletics, for there is no level ground for a stadium nearer than the plain below, but the theatre was available for dramatic and musical contests. It was certainly popular; the inscription found at Gölenye strikingly confirms Diodorus' account, recording that the crowds were so great that they could not be accommodated in the existing buildings, and revenue was being lost. This created a difficulty, since there was no land adjacent to the sanctuary suitable for an extension; unfortunately the inscription is so mutilated that we do not know what steps were taken to remedy the situation. This was in the second century B.C., and it appears from the excavation that the sanctuary at Pazarlık declined very soon after this time both in splendour and in importance, and from the Roman period there is very little evidence to suggest that it even continued to function. This decline would be partly explained if it was found necessary to remove the festival to more spacious ground elsewhere; but in fact it coincides in time with a general decline in the fortunes of the Rhodians. The establishment of the sanctuary in the fourth century was the work of the Rhodian state as a whole, not only of the deme of Bybassus; in the Gölenye inscription the decree is issued by the people of Rhodes, the proposer is a Bybassian, the man honoured is from Amos, and as we learn from another inscription, the temple was dedicated by a man of the deme of Hygassus. For two hundred years the sanctuary flourished, then sank into oblivion, until Professor Cook's inspiration brought its battered remains to light once more.

14 Caunus

Although the site of Caunus has been known since 1842, when Hoskyn found there a decree of the Council and People and Elders of the Caunians, this fascinating city was until recently surprisingly neglected. From then until the last war only two scholars, in 1877 and 1920, gave it their attention. The present writer paid it repeated visits from 1946 to 1952, and in 1967 the Turks began an excavation which is still in progress at the time of writing.

Stratonicus the harpist, who lived in the fourth century B.C., and whose quips were famous in antiquity, once paid a visit to Caunus; observing the greenish complexion of the malaria-ridden inhabitants, he remarked that he now understood what Homer meant when he said, 'As are the generations of leaves, so are the generations of men'. The Caunians protested that it was unkind of him to stigmatize their city as unhealthy. 'What!' said Stratonicus, 'how could I dare to call a city unhealthy where even dead men walk the streets?'

In fact, Caunus was a notoriously unhealthy city. Strabo, in a disputed passage, remarks that while the territory is rich, the city is universally agreed to be unhealthy 'even in the autumn' owing to the heat and the abundance of fruit. This surprising statement has sometimes been explained by supposing that the Caunians were tempted to over-indulgence in fruit; others, noting the apparently meaningless 'even', have supposed a defect in the text. It is, however, a fact that fruit was regarded by the doctors as dangerous to health; Galen, the greatest physician of antiquity after Hippocrates himself, considered it liable to cause fever, and observes that his own father lived to the age of a hundred by abstaining from it. And this idea continued in vogue even down to the sixteenth century; it was indeed one cause for the prevalence of scurvy.[1]

The role of the mosquito in producing fever was not, of course, understood in ancient times. Caunus is at present some two miles (3·22 km.) from the sea, but the intervening area is not firm land but rather an expanse of reeds holding together a little soil. There can be no doubt that all this area was in antiquity sea, but it is likely that a similar marshy region existed near the city and afforded a rich breeding-ground for mosquitoes. When the present writer first visited Dalyan in 1946–47, the room in which he slept was singing with mosquitoes, and the least flaw in the mosquito-net meant a sleepless night; in 1948 the Turks began a serious campaign to exterminate malaria, and that year not a single mosquito was in evidence. Such perfection has naturally not been maintained, and the insects have to some extent found their way back; but the visitor need no longer be deterred by this menace.

Among the fruits which may or may not have been thus fatal to the Caunians the fig held the chief place. Caunian figs were indeed famous. The story goes that in 55 B.C., when the Roman general Crassus was about to embark on a campaign against the Parthians, a vendor of figs happened to come by, calling his wares. His cry of *Cauneas* sounded to superstitious ears like *cave ne eas* (be careful not to go); but Crassus disregarded the warning and proceeded on the journey which led him to defeat and death. Figs are not today a notable product at Dalyan; but in other respects the fertility noted by Strabo is as great as ever. Fruit and vegetables, and especially sesame, are abundant; maize is also much grown, but this was of course unknown to the ancients.

Strabo says that Caunus has dockyards and a closed harbour; above it on a height is a fort called Imbrus; the river Calbis, deep with a navigable channel, flows nearby. These features are still to a large extent identifiable. The harbour is now a small lake, known as Sülüklü Gölü, below the acropolis hill on the west; by 'closed' is meant, not a sheltered anchorage, but one closed at the entrance with a chain. As was said above, the sea came in antiquity right up to the city, and must have completely surrounded the acropolis hill except for the ridge joining it to the higher ground to the north. Where the dockyards stood cannot now be determined; possibly in the bay below this ridge on the east, but this is quite uncertain. Imbrus may, in the writer's opinion, be confidently identified with a large fort on the summit of the mountain now called Ölemez Dağ, over 3,000 feet (914 m.) high, just to the north of the city. Before the existence of this fort became known in 1947 other identifications were put forward, either with the acropolis hill itself, or even with the mighty Sandras Dağı, twenty miles (32·2 km.) away to the northeast; but these are clearly less satisfactory.

30 Theangela. Door of cistern
31 Myndus. 'Lelegian' Wall

32 Loryma. The Fortress
33 Theangela. Tomb (of the dynast Pigres?)

34 Cedreae. Wall and Tower
35 Cedreae. The Theatre

36 Amos. View from Acropolis
37 Cnidus. Round Temple, probably of Aphrodite, in 1969

38 Caunus. Rock-tombs
39 Idyma. Rock-tomb

40   Caunus. View over the Harbour; western acropolis on left
41   Caunus. The Long Wall

42   Caunus. Newly excavated building
43   Alabanda. The Theatre

44 Alabanda. Council-House
45 Alabanda. Aqueduct

46   Alinda. Market-hall and Agora
47   Alabanda. Temple of Apollo Isotimus in 1939

50   Alinda. Interior of the Market-hall

48   Alinda. Half-buried Stage of the Theatre
49   Alinda. The Theatre

51 Alinda. Aqueduct
52 Alinda. Tomb in use as a house

53 Alinda. Tower in the City Wall
54 Bridge at İncekemer

55 Gerga. Inscribed rock
56 Gerga. Pyramidal Stele

57 Gerga. Speaker's Platform (?)
58 Gerga. Colossal statue on western hill

59 Gerga. Temple
60 Gerga. Fountain-house (or tomb?)

The river Calbis must evidently correspond to the Dalyan Çayı, which affords the outlet from the lake of Köyceğiz to the sea. It has a good strong current and is said to be as much as 30 feet (9·14 m.) deep in places. There is, however, a considerable tide from the sea, and the direction of the current changes regularly twice a day; with a strong sea-wind the salt water sometimes reaches to the lake. The *dalyan*, or fishery, consisting of a barrage of posts and wire netting across the stream, stood formerly opposite the village of Dalyan; but this is now removed, and a more up-to-date installation has been erected lower down, under the acropolis hill. The fish are mostly *kefal* and *levrek* (the ancient *kephalos* and *labrax*, mullet and bass), both excellent eating; in their seasons these pass up from the sea to the lake to spawn, and on their return some two months later are caught in vast quantities. A fragmentary inscription containing certain regulations concerning catches of fish suggests that in ancient times also the Caunians had their *dalyan*.

The actual course of the river, however, was almost certainly different when Strabo wrote. Caunus stood on the coast, and the Calbis flowed 'near by'. Just how far up towards the lake the sea came is hardly possible to determine, but if the line of the river was the same as it is now, the city must have been actually at its mouth. More likely it flowed further to the east, and it is not improbable that its ancient course is marked by a sluggish and marshy stream called Sarıöz which at present trickles southwards into a kind of lagoon by the name of Solungur Gölü. If this is right, the navigable channel mentioned by Strabo led from the sea, at a point over a mile east of Caunus, to the lake of Köyceğiz. But the silting process has so transformed the region that it is no longer possible, short of a thorough geological examination, to be sure of the details.

The acropolis hill is in two parts, the eastern high and steep, the western much lower. The city-centre lay near the east and north shores of the harbour; here have been found the majority of the inscriptions. Except along the ridge north of the theatre the buildings themselves have become buried and overgrown, though the Turkish excavators have begun to bring them to light. But a much larger area than this was walled in. Over the hill to the north-east runs a fine wall, two miles (3·22 km.) long and quite well preserved; the east and south faces of this hill are precipitous and unfortified. On the vast expanse of hillside thus enclosed nothing whatever has been found, and the wall winds its way over the mountain in complete solitude.

In classical times Caunus was reckoned a Carian city; she is expressly so called in the fourth century by the geographer who passes under the name of Scylax, and no tradition existed that she was ever colonized by Greeks. As so often happened in the case of cities with non-Greek names, an 'eponymous' founder was invented by the name of Caunus, made to be the son of Miletus; and a cult of this fictitious hero-king was maintained in the city down to Roman times. The cult of 'the Caunian King' is now attested as an important one in the fourth century B.C. by the newly discovered trilingual stele from Xanthus,[2] in which the people of Xanthus and those living in the neighbourhood are instructed to set up an altar in his honour, and to assign to him a recently cultivated plot of land. He is said to have had a sister Byblis, who fell in love with him and when he left her, hanged herself; from this sad story came the proverbial expression 'a Caunian love'. According to Herodotus, the Caunians themselves reckoned to have come from Crete, though the historian does not believe this, but judges them to be indigenous. He distinguishes them both from the Carians and from the Lycians, particularly in respect of their peculiar customs, and adds that their language had become assimilated to the Carian—or the Carian to it. This last statement is interestingly confirmed by an inscription found by the present writer among the ruins in the centre of the city; this is written in the Carian script, and is as yet undeciphered, but it contains a number of characters which are not found in any of the Carian inscriptions known on other sites. It is likely therefore that the Caunian language was, as Herodotus says, similar to, but not identical with, the Carian.

In the sixth century B.C., following the capture of Sardis by the Persians and the reduction of the Greek cities of Ionia, the Persian general Harpagus came south with an army to Caria and Lycia. He met with resistance at several places, and Herodotus tells of the desperate defiance of the Xanthians in Lycia; overwhelmed by numbers, they collected their families and possessions on the acropolis and set the place on fire, then sallied forth and died fighting to the last man. The historian adds that Caunus was captured in similar fashion; 'for the Caunians imitated the Lycians for the most part'.

Some forty years later, when the Ionian cities organized their revolt against the Persian King, the Caunians, remembering this disaster, refrained at first from taking any part; encouraged, however, by the Ionians' success in taking and burning Sardis, they were persuaded to join in. The revolt soon collapsed (494 B.C.), but Persian control of the coast was shortly afterwards brought to an end following the failure of Xerxes' invasion of Greece; in the

Delian Confederacy which replaced it Caunus was included and assessed for tribute at half a talent. This figure is surprisingly low—considerably less than was paid by several of the Lelegian townships of the Myndus peninsula—but in 425 B.C. it was raised at a blow to ten talents, equal to Miletus, and far in advance of Ephesus or Cnidus. How or why the Caunians should have become suddenly so much richer is not known; the present writer has suggested that they may about this time have developed a profitable business in salted fish; there were salt-pans at Caunus, and certainly no lack of fish, and dried and salted fish was a staple article of diet in the ancient world. Others have supposed a project for developing the resources of the plain around the head of the lake of Köyceğiz; but in any case it is likely enough that the assessment of 425 was unrealistic, and there is no evidence that the money was ever actually paid. Towards the end of the Peloponnesian War not only the Athenians, but also the Spartans were able to make use of the port of Caunus.

With the King's Peace in 387 B.C. Caunus reverted with the rest of the coast to Persian control, and it was due to the Hellenizing policy of the satrap Mausolus that the city first began to acquire a Greek character. Statue-bases of him and his father Hecatomnos have been found in the ruins, and it is virtually certain that Mausolus was responsible for the fortification of the city with the long wall. In Alexander's campaign of 334 B.C. no actual mention is made of Caunus, but it was presumably given by him to Ada together with the rest of Caria.

In the disturbed times that followed Alexander's death Caunus passed from one to another of his Successors. Taken in 313 by Antigonus, she was captured from him by Ptolemy four years later. Of this latter event the historian Diodorus records that the king sailed to Caunus and occupied the city; of the two acropoleis, which were defended by troops, he took the Herakleion by force and the Persikon was surrendered to him by its garrison. The reference is evidently to the two parts of the acropolis hill; after occupying the lower city Ptolemy no doubt attacked the higher eastern portion, and when this fell, the garrison of the minor western hill, the Persikon, might well feel their position untenable and submit of their own accord.

After the utter defeat of Ptolemy at Salamis in Cyprus in 306 B.C. Caunus came back into the possession of Antigonus and his son Demetrius, and was held by the latter until 286; on his surrender in the following year to Seleucus, king of Syria, she passed to the hands of Lysimachus. At an uncertain date not long afterwards she was recaptured for Ptolemy by his general Philocles by means of a trick. Encamping outside the city, Philocles is said to have bribed the Caunian corn-inspectors to announce that the soldiers' rations would be issued, not at their stations but in the city; the defenders accordingly left the walls unmanned while they drew their allowances, and Philocles was able to capture the city. The wall in question must be the long wall over the hill to the north; Philocles came by land and cannot have been attacking the sea-girt acropolis.

Caunus was still Ptolemaic in 197–196 B.C., when she is mentioned among the 'allies' of Ptolemy V whose 'freedom' was protected by the Rhodians against Antiochus III of Syria. A few years later she became a Rhodian possession. Polybius records that in 166 B.C. a Rhodian envoy to the Roman Senate declared that his city had purchased Caunus for 200 talents[3] from the generals of Ptolemy. The date of this unusual transaction must have been about 190 B.C., but the Rhodians might have saved their money, for in 189, after the defeat of Antiochus at Magnesia, the Romans gave them the whole of Caria and Lycia.

Rhodian rule lasted from 189 to 167, and during this period Caunus was under the command of a *hagemon*, a military and administrative official of unusually high rank for a dependent city. But Rhodes' new subjects were far from content, and in 167 the Caunians joined in the general revolt against her. The revolt was a failure, but immediately afterwards the Romans rescinded their gift and required the Rhodians to evacuate Lycia and Caria, including specifically Caunus. The Rhodians pleaded strongly to be allowed to retain Caunus, pointing out that she was not acquired by the favour of Rome, but that they had spent good money on her, and mentioning incidentally that from Caunus and Stratoniceia combined they drew an annual revenue of 120 talents. Caunus at 200 talents was evidently a bargain. But their plea was overruled and Caunus became a free city.

When the province of Asia was established in 129 B.C., Caunus was included in it, forming a border city on the south; not until much later was she assigned to Lycia. In 88 B.C. the province was overrun by Mithridates, and Caunus chose to take the king's part; she is mentioned among the places where the slaughter of the Roman residents was carried out with especial ferocity. Accordingly, when peace was made in 85, the city was given back to the Rhodians. No more content with Rhodian rule than they had been before, the Caunians made an application some time about 65 B.C.

to be allowed to pay tribute to Rome rather than to Rhodes. Whether this appeal was successful or not is not known, but by the end of the century we find Caunus once more a free city. Even this, however, was not the last of her vicissitudes; the sophist Dio Chrysostom, writing soon after A.D. 70, describes the Caunians as undergoing a double servitude to Rome and Rhodes, from which it appears that the Rhodians had yet again obtained control of the city.

These changes of fortune that Caunus underwent are no doubt exceptionally numerous, but they give a good idea of the unsettled state of the world in Hellenistic times. Throughout this period Caunus was a fully Hellenized city, anxious to forget her Carian origin. Her institutions are thoroughly Hellenic, and the names of her citizens are exclusively Greek. Not a single Caunian is yet known to have borne a Carian name. At the same time it is likely that she was not really popular. Dio Chrysostom in particular is almost vitriolic in his condemnation: 'These stupid Caunians', he says,

> when did they ever produce a worthwhile citizen? Who ever did them a good turn? Their misfortunes are due to their extreme folly and rascality, and if they are all but wiped out by fever, it is no more than they deserve.

He may no doubt have been prejudiced, but it is noticeable that even in earlier times in the inscriptions citizens of other cities are conspicuously few. A reputation for unhealthiness is of course no recommendation, and it is understandable that foreigners should be reluctant to take up residence; it is probable that this disability was never really overcome. Dio did overlook one famous Caunian, Protogenes, the painter responsible for the mural known as the Thesmothetai (the law-givers), which was to be seen in the Athenian agora. However, in general it remains true that Caunus attracted little attention abroad. This fact adds a special piquancy to a phrase in an inscription honouring a certain Agreophon in the second century A.D., who declared that by his generosity to the city he had so extended its reputation that it had reached the notice of foreigners.

Caunus suffered also from another trouble, which she shared with Ephesus, Miletus, and other places. The silting process which has now separated the city by two miles (3·22 km.) from the sea must have been an ever-present menace to her commerce. On a building by the shore of the harbour, in the first century A.D., was written a long inscription relating to the payment of customs dues. Unusually,

145

it is concerned almost exclusively with remissions of tax. It appears that certain public-spirited citizens had presented a sum of 60,000 denarii for this purpose, so that foreign merchants might be encouraged to use the port and the city treasury should not suffer. Although no special motive need be sought for so useful a benefaction, it is likely enough that by this date the silting may have begun to be troublesome; the harbour was beginning to be difficult of access, and merchant-captains were showing signs of avoiding it.

This same inscription gives us some information about the principal articles of commerce at Caunus. They are in fact such as we should have expected, notably slaves and salt. The importance of these is shown by the fact that, whereas in all other cases tax is remitted, the export of slaves and import of salt continue to be dutiable. Caunian salt was known to Pliny as being especially recommended for addition to eye-salves and plasters; and Caunian slaves, male and female, were familiar in antiquity. Mention is also made of resin and pitch—that is, a form of burnt resin, not mineral pitch; these would be imported by land from the pine-forests which are still so notable a feature of the Carian landscape, and would be essential for the shipbuilding and repair work in the Caunian dockyards. If the trade in salted fish be added, we have a picture of considerable commercial prosperity in the Roman period.

The ruins at Dalyan are now most easily reached by land; a road turns off the main Köyceğiz–Fethiye highway a little south of Adaköy. This road is quite respectable, and there is even a petrol-station in Dalyan village. Visitors passing through Köyceğiz will notice a splendid marble lion in the main square, recovered from the site of Caunus in 1962. Alternatively, a boat may be hired at Köyceğiz; if time is no object, this is highly recommendable, for the lake scenery is superb. The approach by the river from the sea may be difficult for anything more than a rowing- or motor-boat, owing to a sand-bar at the mouth.[4] To reach the site from the village the river has to be crossed. It is not normally possible to do this at the new fishery, and the crossing is made by a ferry from the village; the ferryman will usually act also as guide to the ruins, which lie about a mile beyond.

Even before crossing the river the visitor's eye is caught by the very fine series of tombs cut in the cliff on the far side. These are undoubtedly the most striking feature of the site. They are disposed in two uneven rows, an upper row of columned temple-tombs and

146

a lower row of simple chambers with square doors (Pl. 38). Some of the upper row are quite easily reached, others are inaccessible without tackle. The temple-tombs, and a few of the others, have a passage cut all round them in the rock. The term 'temple-tomb' refers only to the form of the façade, and does not imply that any kind of worship was carried out there; the interior bears no resemblance to a temple, but consists of a comparatively small chamber having usually three stone benches for the disposal of the dead. From the pottery found in them these tombs appear to date to the fourth century B.C. Only three or four of them carry inscriptions; of these one contains two words of Carian, while the others are not original, but relate to a reuse of the tombs in Roman times. Curiously, two of the inscriptions on neighbouring tombs are identically worded, claiming the tomb for the same three persons. The façades, which are entirely rock-cut, consist generally of two Ionic columns between antae, surmounted by a dentil frieze and a pediment with acroteria at the three corners. In many cases the columns have wholly or partly broken away. The pediment is normally undecorated, but in one case shows a pair of lions face to face.

The largest tomb of all, however, in the group nearest to the village, has four columns—or rather, it was intended to have four columns, but the work is unfinished. It shows in an interesting way how the tombs were made: the roof, the pediment, and the frieze are practically complete; the capitals and the tops of the column-shafts have been merely blocked out square; below this nothing has been done beyond smoothing the rock-face.

At the western end of the series is a group of tombs of the type called Carian; the grave-pit is sunk into the solid rock and covered with a separate lid. In the rock-wall below this group is a cluster of niches for votive offerings to the dead.

The acropolis hill is an impressive crag, conspicuous from afar, perhaps 500 feet (152 m.) in height; it is steep on all sides and quite precipitous on the south. The wall and towers on its north slope are mediaeval, but on the summit is a fort of good ashlar masonry some 130 feet (39·6 m.) in length and half as wide, now in a very ruined state; this is apparently the Herakleion captured by Ptolemy in 309 B.C. The wall which runs up the western extension of the acropolis is also of classical Greek date; its thickness varies surprisingly from 10 feet to five (3·05 to 1·52 m.). Of the Persikon nothing appears to remain.

The long wall runs uninterruptedly from the north side of the harbour to a precipice high above the river beyond the village of

Dalyan; it is reminiscent in some ways of the land-wall at Iasus. Its masonry varies remarkably, and the wall has evidently been repaired more than once. The upper part from J to K is the oldest, and the original parts date in all probability to the time of Mausolus; between H and J the style is a very handsome ashlar of Hellenistic date (Pl. 41). Below this the masonry is polygonal, the blocks prominently bossed and occasionally drafted at the edges; polygonal masonry of this type dates generally to the post-classical period. As was said above, this long wall encloses for the most part nothing but bare hillside; it would have been possible to defend the city adequately with a much shorter wall much more easily manned.

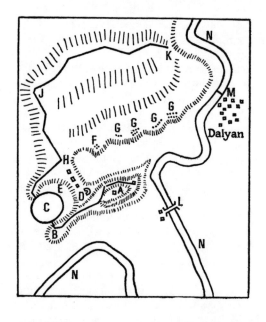

A – Acropolis Hill

B – Western Extension
of Acropolis Hill

C – Ancient Harbour

D – Theatre

E – Area of new excavation

F – 'Carian' Tombs

G,G – Rock-cut Tombs

H,J,K – Long Wall

L – New Fishery

M – Old Fishery

N,N – Dalyan Çayı,
ancient Calbis

Fig. 27 Plan of Caunus

But Mausolus' ideas were always on a generous scale, and it may be that he intended Caunus to be a much larger city than in fact she ever became. We have seen that Myndus and Theangela were in similar case.

Near the foot of the acropolis hill is the theatre, the most attractive of the buildings which are still standing. It faces west, the northern half supported by walls of masonry, the southern half cut out of the hillside. It is of average size, with a single diazoma and thirty-four rows of seats, eighteen below the diazoma, sixteen above it. The theatre is of predominantly Greek type, the cavea being considerably more than a semicircle; the two arched entrances on the north side seem to be original. Corresponding entrances on the south side were of course not possible. The number of stairways, originally ten, is not doubled above the diazoma in the usual way. The lower part of the stage-building still exists and would repay excavation; at present it is buried and overgrown. It is separated from the cavea in the Greek fashion by parodoi, of which the northern is partially obstructed by a curious semicircular projection from the analemma whose purpose is not obvious. A part of the northern retaining wall has collapsed within the last few years, and a large carob-tree growing through the northern analemma must before long throw that down also.

On the ridge to the north of the theatre is a row of three buildings. The first is a church of the basilica type, with apse and three aisles; it is of excellent squared masonry with elegant decoration. North of this is a large and massive baths, and to the north again a smaller building which has been thought to be a temple, but this is certainly a mistake. Neither the two doors in adjoining sides nor the arrangement of the interior walls conforms to the plan of a temple, and a library might be a more plausible suggestion. The northern door is flanked by engaged fluted columns, with a square buttress beyond on either side. The platform on which this building stands is supported on the west by a line of column-stumps, some upright, some horizontal. All these three buildings are of comparatively late date; they would (and no doubt will) benefit from excavation.

In fact the excavations have already added a good deal to the amenities of Caunus. When the present writer in 1946 discovered the long customs-inscription referred to above, he supposed that the ruined building on which it was carved was likely to be the customs-house. In reality it has turned out to be a fountain-house, and has been completely restored by the excavators from its own blocks. The inscription stands on the outer side of the west face. In front is lying a dedication to Vespasian, but whether this is the actual dedication of the building appears doubtful.

Not far from this a stoa has been cleared, but the masonry is rather poor and many of its stones are reused. In it is a large moulded block carrying an inscription in which the People of Caunus honour the People of Rome for benefits received.

Between the ridge and the harbour the excavators in 1969 unearthed an interesting and in some respects mysterious building. Two concentric rings form about three-quarters of a circle; the inner ring consists of a thin wall of poor masonry about 15 inches (381 mm.) high, with plastered face and unfluted columns at intervals; the outer ring is a narrow stylobate of white marble with slender flat-fluted columns spaced along it; these columns have small slots as if for fixing some kind of grille. At the back is a semicircular podium raised on three steps, with a row of unfluted columns behind it, rather irregularly spaced. Lying in the middle is a round flat-topped slab of purple stone, now broken in two. The purpose of this unusual building is not immediately apparent. The excavators have suggested that the inner ring contained a shallow bathing-pool surrounded by a colonnade. The plaster on the inner face supports this idea, and the bathers might step down from the podium into the water; indeed, the grille in the outer ring would presumably allow the pool to be entered only from this side. But the object of the round flat-topped stone (unless it was merely for sitting on) remains obscure, and an outdoor bathing-pool such as this is in the writer's experience most exceptional (Pl. 42).

Beside this building a deep pit has produced sherds going back to the ninth century B.C., and gives some hope that the excavations may throw new light on the early history of the site.

The inscriptions of Caunus mention a number of smaller places in the neighbourhood of the city, one of which, Pasanda, has lately been located with good probability. In the fifth century Pasanda paid in the Delian Confederacy a tribute equal to that of Caunus (down to 425 B.C.), but later sank to the status of a deme. An ancient authority places it thirty stades (between three and four miles; 4·83 and 6·44 km.) to the south of Caunus, and in this position, above the south end of Solungur Lake, a small town-site has recently been discovered. It has a wall, but nothing else is standing. In at least eight places a socket has been sunk into the rock to receive a stele, and one of the stelae has been found; it contains a list of names, and dates apparently to the second century B.C.

Notes

1 On this interesting belief see J. C. Drummond and Anne Wilbraham, *The Englishman's Food* (London, 1939), pp. 68–9.
2 See *Lycian Turkey*, p. 63.
3 Perhaps something like a quarter of a million sterling; but such equations of ancient money with modern are hardly realistic.
4 As Freya Stark found (*The Lycian Shore* (London, 1956), p. 107); but it seems that the bar is variable.

15 Alabanda

The River Marsyas, now the Çine Çayı, which for much of its course runs in a deep gorge, towards its northern end, before joining the Maeander, traverses a broad and fertile plain. This is now controlled by the *kaza* of Çine; in antiquity it was the territory of Alabanda. Until the present century the town of Çine stood some five or six miles (8 or 9·65 km.) further to the south, where is now the village of Old Çine; the present Çine was then called Kıroba. For those who are not too particular about the quality of their hotels, Çine makes a convenient centre for visiting Alabanda, Alinda, and several subsidiary sites.

Alabanda, the third of Strabo's three noteworthy cities of the interior, was a place of some importance throughout antiquity. Its foundation-legend is told by Stephanus of Byzantium (below, p. 170 n. 1); in Carian, he says, *ala* means 'horse' and *banda* means 'victory'; the mythical king Kar, having won a cavalry victory, gave the name Alabandus to his son, and named the city after him. Cicero, in his book on the Nature of the Gods, mentions the god Alabandus, from which it appears that a cult of this 'eponymous' personage was maintained in the city down to Roman times; and his image has been, somewhat dubiously, recognized on certain coins of Alabanda.

The earliest historical mention of the city is in connexion with an incident during Xerxes' invasion of Greece in 480 B.C. The Greek and Persian fleets were anchored not far apart at the north end of Euboea; a Persian squadron of fifteen ships, which had lagged behind, came up, and mistaking the Greek fleet for their own, sailed right into the enemy's hands. On board one of these ships was Aridolis, tyrant of Alabanda, who was thus taken prisoner. Herodotus does not say that he was captain of the ship, and it would be surprising if a city so far inland as Alabanda had any connexion with the sea. We should have expected Aridolis to serve in Xerxes' army rather than his navy.

152

In this passage Herodotus describes Alabanda as in Caria; in the following year 479, however, he tells us that 'Alabanda, a large city of Phrygia' had been given by the Persian King to a certain Amyntas. Stephanus, on the other hand, records a second city of Alabanda in Caria. What are we to make of this? No other hint of a second Alabanda, either in Caria or in Phrygia, is to be found, and it is obviously unlikely that a large city in Phrygia should completely disappear without any record. There can be little doubt that Herodotus is speaking inaccurately, and that in fact Amyntas succeeded to the tyranny left vacant by the loss of Aridolis in the previous year. What lies behind Stephanus' assertion is uncertain, but we may safely accept that there was never more than one city of Alabanda.

No mention is made of Alabanda in connexion with the passage of Alexander, and the city is next heard of at the end of the third century. At this time she bore the name of Antiocheia of the Chrysaorians, taken in honour of Antiochus III, king of Syria. A decree of the Amphictyonic Council at Delphi, dated to the last years of the century, records that an ambassador from Antiocheia, guided by an oracle, came to Delphi praising Antiochus for preserving 'the democracy and the peace' of the city, and requesting that the Council, in accordance evidently with the king's wish, should recognize the inviolability of the city's territory. The Council therefore decided that the city and territory should be regarded as inviolable and sacred to Zeus Chrysaoreus and Apollo Isotimus, and voted to erect in the sanctuary of Apollo at Delphi eight-cubit statues representing the city and the king. The city is described in the preamble as 'Antiocheia of the nation of Chrysaorians, kindred of the Greeks'. This is not intended to imply any genuine ethnological relationship, but is merely a recognition of the Hellenization of a Carian community. Alabanda had in fact recently been colonized by the Seleucid kings, and her population was predominantly Greek.

Of the two deities here mentioned, Zeus Chrysaoreus is already familiar (above, pp. 8–9, 68), but Apollo Isotimus is peculiar to Alabanda. Isotimus means 'equal in honour'; since Apollo was the special god of the Seleucids, it has been suggested that he was adopted at Alabanda as a compliment to them, and at once raised to an equality with the native Zeus. At the same time it is possible that he was originally an indigenous deity later identified with the Greek god.

A decree of inviolability, generally recognized among the Greeks, was a great thing for a city, as it should preserve her from pillage

153

during the unsettled Hellenistic age. But it did not save Alabanda; hardly a year had passed before Philip V, king of Macedonia, in the course of overrunning Caria (above, pp. 8–9), sacked her territory as that of an enemy. In defence of this sacrilegious act he said, simply and frankly, that it was essential that his soldiers should have something to eat.

The battle of Magnesia in 190 B.C. put an end to Seleucid power in Caria, and Antiocheia became again Alabanda. In the settlement of Apamea after the battle, when Lycia and Caria south of the Maeander were given to Rhodes, Alabanda would naturally be included. But Rhodian control can hardly have been more than nominal, and in fact the only indication of it is the existence, under the early Roman Empire, of a priest of Helios in the city; for Helios was almost exclusively a Rhodian deity. On the other hand, in 167 B.C., when Mylasa, which was excluded from the settlement, became embroiled with Rhodes, Alabanda went to her aid, acting virtually as a free city. And indeed, as we learn from Livy, in 170 B.C. envoys from Alabanda had come to Rome bringing a present of three hundred cavalry shields (obviously a significant detail for this city with its equestrian associations) and a golden crown weighing fifty pounds to be dedicated to Jupiter, and reminding the Senate that they had already built a temple of the City of Rome and instituted games in her honour. What they asked in return Livy does not say, but an inscription of about this period tells us that Alabandian envoys had asked for an alliance with Rome. The Senate's response was on both occasions favourable. Whether the two embassies are the same or not, these are the actions of a free city, and we may with some confidence accept that Alabanda was never actually subject to Rhodes.

The earliest coins of Alabanda seem to have been struck just before the city's name was changed; these were followed by a handsome issue in silver with the name of Antiocheia. Under the nominal rule of Rhodes the coinage appears to have ceased, but was recommenced after the grant of freedom in 167; this latter series bears dates ranging from 1 to 33, and lasted evidently till the Roman inheritance in 133 B.C. and the formation of the province of Asia. The commonest type on the early coins is the winged horse Pegasus; whether this, the victorious horse, may echo the supposed etymology of the city's name it would be rash to say, but there is no denying the excellence of her territory for the use of cavalry. After the establishment of the province no more coins were apparently struck until the early Empire.

How Alabanda fared during the invasion of Mithridates is not recorded; but the generally unsatisfactory government of the province under the Roman Republic affected her like the rest; in 51 B.C. she is named by Cicero as one of five cities in debt to the Roman banker Cluvius. The situation was not improved when eleven years later the renegade Labienus arrived with his Parthian allies (above, p. 10). Like Mylasa, Alabanda accepted a garrison from him, but later rebelled and slaughtered the occupying soldiers. For this she was punished by Labienus by the exaction of a heavy fine and the spoliation of her sanctuaries.

Better times came, here as elsewhere, with the establishment of the Empire. Alabanda's relations with Rome seem to have been universally good; we hear of cults in the city of Caesar, of Rome and Augustus, and of the Health and Safety of the Emperor—this last a curious and unique phenomenon. Alabanda had the rank of a *conventus*, which meant that the provincial governor held regular assizes in the city. Coinage under the Empire is abundant, and a general air of prosperity is revealed by the citizens' reputation for luxury and debauchery; Strabo notes the great number of female harpists, indispensable accompaniment to a rich banquet. Coins of the third century record the privilege of *ateleia*, or immunity from taxation. Two other privileges, however, are rather surprisingly absent. In A.D. 22 Tiberius held an investigation into the various cities' claims of inviolability; whether Alabanda made a claim for her temples of Zeus and Apollo, relying on the decree of the Amphictyonic Council two hundred years earlier, we do not hear, but these were not in the list of those accepted, and the title of 'inviolable' does not appear on the city's coins. And despite the number of temples devoted to the Imperial cult, the title of *neocorus*, Temple-Warden, is equally lacking. The coinage continues down to the middle of the third century, and later we find Alabanda a bishopric under the metropolitan of Aphrodisias.

Several special products are mentioned. We hear of Alabandian hemp, considered especially good for making hunting-nets, and of a special kind of gem, like a garnet, but darker in colour and rough. There was also in the hills around the city a peculiar very dark marble, almost purple, which was soluble in heat and used in the manufacture of glass. Alabandian roses and crystal, on the other hand, though worthy of mention, were less highly esteemed and comparatively cheap.

One other little piece of information is recorded. The Alabandians were addicted to a particular misuse of negatives in speaking

Greek; though known as the 'Alabandian solecism', this fault is in fact one which became increasingly common in post-classical Greek in all parts of the world.

Strabo says that the city of Alabanda lies under two adjacent hills in such a way as to present the appearance of a pack-ass loaded with its panniers—to which a certain Apollonius added 'panniers of scorpions, for these creatures are abundant both here and at Mylasa and in the country between'. It was in fact in the neighbourhood of Araphisar that the present writer first saw a scorpion in the flesh; but the resemblance to a loaded donkey has never been apparent to him.

The city walls follow the ridge of these hills, and enclosed originally a considerable area of the flat ground at their northern foot;

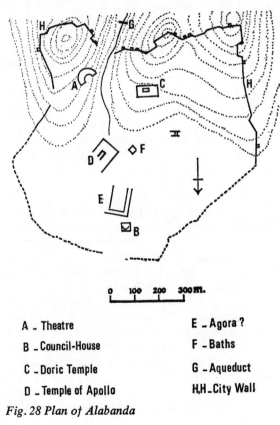

A – Theatre
B – Council-House
C – Doric Temple
D – Temple of Apollo

E – Agora?
F – Baths
G – Aqueduct
H,H – City Wall

Fig. 28 Plan of Alabanda

156

Fig. 29 Alabanda. Theatre

of this space the present village of Araphisar occupies only a small corner. The greater part of the city being on level ground, its ruins have been and are exposed both to plundering of the stones and to inundation from the small stream which flows down in winter and loses itself in the plain. The ancient foundations are in consequence some 10 or 12 feet (3·05 or 3·66 m.) under the present surface.

The ring-wall, with numerous towers, survives on the high ground and is quite well preserved in places, but on the plain it is mostly destroyed. It is built in the classical style, with two facings of slightly bossed ashlar masonry with a rubble filling between. Some six or seven gates are recognizable, but only by gaps in the wall.

The theatre is large but poorly preserved, only the ends of the retaining wall surviving. These are of fine bossed masonry (Pl. 43, Fig. 29), and contain each a vaulted passage for the entrance and exit of spectators, now blocked up. They led no doubt, as usual, to the diazoma, but of this, and of the rows of seats, nothing whatever remains. At the west end some parts of the skene and the proscenium can still be made out. From the size of the cavea it is likely that there was a second diazoma higher up. The cavea, facing north-west, is more than a semicircle, implying that the original building dates to pre-Roman times. The façade is over 270 feet (82·3 m.) in length. The excavations carried out at Alabanda by Etem Bey in 1905–06 left the theatre untouched.

Much better preserved, and the most conspicuous building on the site, is the rectangular structure, B on the plan, identified with much probability as a council-house (Pl. 44, Fig. 30). It was no doubt here that the brothers Hieracles and Menecles, described by no less

157

an authority than Cicero as among the most illustrious orators using
the florid Asianic style, spoke many times. Like the theatre it is
unexcavated. The walls are of handsome brown stone, with two
broader courses alternating with one narrower. In the front (south)
wall, which still stands over 30 feet (9·14 m.) high in part, are four
doors now almost entirely buried; above them is a strongly projecting
cornice, and above this again a row of windows of which only the
east end remains. The blocks of this wall carry numerous masons'
marks in the form of one or two Greek letters (sometimes upside
down); these would be expected to indicate the positions in which

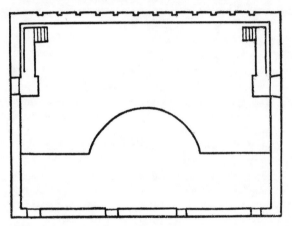

Fig. 30 Alabanda. Council-House

the blocks were to be laid, but in fact they display no intelligible
order. The interior is badly ruined, but was evidently occupied by
seats; the ground rises towards the back, and the shallow curve of
the rows of seating can be distinguished. In each side wall is an
entrance to a staircase leading up to the back rows; that on the east
is nearly buried. A conspicuous and remarkable feature of the
building is the horizontal row of square holes let into all four walls
and especially noticeable on the south front. Though quite carefully
cut, these are clearly not a part of the original design, and their
purpose has never, to the writer's knowledge, been explained. In
the north wall, in addition to a few of these square holes, is a row
of larger holes beneath each of which a cornice-block is let into the
wall, projecting only a few inches; these are equally clearly original,
and served for some kind of decoration whose nature is uncertain.

It seems most likely that all these holes were designed to help attach pieces of architectural decoration, which must once have adorned the building, but a proper study has yet to be made of them.

Just outside the city on the south the stream, called Kemerderesi, is spanned by the arch of an aqueduct (Pl. 45). This is, as usual, of Roman type, but the upper part with the actual water-channel is destroyed, and the arch is now higher than the adjoining wall. It is said locally that this arch and the bridge over the Marsyas at İnce-kemer on the Muğla road some twelve miles (19 km.) to the south-west belong to one and the same aqueduct; it is in fact true that the arches of the bridge, though much larger, are of similar construction to that at Alabanda.

The temple marked C on the plan was brought to light by the excavations in 1905. It stands on an artificial terrace in the hillside, but little more than the foundations survives. It was of the Doric order, with eleven unfluted columns on the long sides and six at the ends; when first excavated, one stump of all these columns was found in place, but most of these have been removed or overthrown. The columns stand on square slabs which could easily be mistaken for bases; in fact they belong to the stylobate, which is not preserved. The temple comprises a pronaos, unusually deep, and a cella, but no opisthodomus; the front is, contrary to normal practice, on the west. For the identity of the deity to whom the temple belonged the evidence is scanty in the extreme. The excavators found in it fifty-six coins, all of the same early type with the head of Apollo, but this is obviously far from cogent; they also found on the terrace a figurine representing Artemis-Hecate, and the building is now generally called Temple of Artemis. For the entrance on the west the temple of Artemis at Magnesia would afford a parallel; but this identification too must be considered uncertain. As appears from the coins, the temple can hardly have been built much before 200 B.C., but for a more precise date evidence is lacking.

At F on the plan is a large building which seems to have been a baths. It has not been excavated, and the ruins lie in a jumbled heap distinguished by a conspicuous shallow arch. The plan, which appears unusual, has not been completely determined.

Between this and the council-house, at E, is an open level space about 360 by 240 feet (110 by 73 m.), originally surrounded by a colonnaded stoa with an entrance at the south-west corner. The excavators were at first inclined to recognize a gymnasium, but most scholars now prefer to place the agora here. At present nothing but the open space is to be seen.

By far the most notable building in the ancient city was the temple of Apollo Isotimus. This was formerly supposed to have been built by the distinguished architect Hermogenes, himself an Alabandian, who was active in the early second century B.C.[1] The evidence for this is a passage in Vitruvius concerning the 'pseudodipteral' style; 'there is', he says, 'no example of this at Rome, but at Magnesia there is the temple of Diana by Hermogenes of Alabanda, and of Apollo by Menesthes'. It is now believed, however, that this text is faulty, and that Vitruvius really said (or meant to say) 'and at Alabanda of Apollo by Menesthes'. In any case, Vitruvius does not say that the temple of Apollo was by Hermogenes; and other evidence suggests that Hermogenes was a citizen of Priene. No other work by Menesthes appears to be known.

The temple had in the course of time become completely buried; the foundations, and numerous architectural members, were discovered in 1905 at a depth of 14 feet (4·27 m.) below the surface. It was orientated NE–SW, with the entrance on the north-east, and was, as stated, pseudodipteral—that is, the surrounding colonnade was set at twice the usual distance from the cella walls. The order was Ionic, with white marble columns 33 inches (·84 m.) in diameter, thirteen on the sides and eight at front and back. Several blocks of the frieze were found, depicting a battle between Greeks and Amazons. As an inscription shows, the temple was dedicated in Roman times to Apollo Isotimus and the Divine Emperors. The ruins have suffered severely since the excavation. Pl. 47 shows what was visible when the writer first saw them in 1939; today there is hardly one stone upon another. The plan is just discernible at the west end, and a few marble blocks are lying around.

Outside the city on the west is an extensive necropolis; hundreds of sarcophagi line the street leading to the town. They are all of the same type, a rectangular coffer with a plain granite block for lid. The inscriptions on them, mostly very worn, have the peculiarity that they commonly name the trade or profession of the deceased— banker, architect, schoolmaster, doctor, fuller, dyer, gardener, tanner, and more interestingly a dealer in pheasants and (apparently) a lamplighter.

Note

1 This is stated, for example, in Hachette's *World Guide.*

16 Alinda and Amyzon

As compared with Alabanda, her neighbour Alinda is historically obscure; but the ruins at Karpuzlu (formerly Demircideresi) are much superior—indeed they are among the finest in Caria. Surprisingly enough they have never been excavated. The site was visited by Chandler in 1765, but his brief and unenthusiastic account gave no idea of the excellent preservation of the buildings. He took the city to be Alabanda; the true identification was made later on the strength of the coins found there by Sir Charles Fellows and others. This still remains the chief ground for placing Alinda at Karpuzlu, for no inscription has ever been found to confirm it; the identification is nevertheless quite certain.

Save that she was a purely Carian foundation, nothing whatever is known of the origins of Alinda. The city's first, and virtually her only, appearance in history was in connexion with Queen Ada, sister of Mausolus (above, p. 7). Dethroned and expelled by her brother Pixodarus about 340 B.C., Ada withdrew to Alinda, where she continued to maintain herself in semi-royal state, ready to take any opportunity of regaining her throne. She had not, as it turned out, very long to wait. When Alexander the Great advanced into Caria in 334 B.C., Ada went to meet him, offering to surrender Alinda and to help him against the usurpers, pointing out that they were her own kinsmen. She proposed also, with a truly regal self-confidence, to adopt him as her son. In return she asked that he would restore her to her lost throne. Alexander's response was characteristically gracious; he declined to take Alinda from her, and did not disdain to be called her son; and later, when Halicarnassus was taken all but the two headlands, he left to her the task of capturing these, and when this was done, he appointed her queen of the whole of Caria.

Ada's dealings with Alexander may have had another consequence for Alinda. The grammarian Stephanus of Byzantium in his *Ethnica*[1] records, among eighteen cities of the name of Alexandria, one in Caria called Alexandria-by-Latmus; it possessed, he says, a sanctuary of Adonis containing an Aphrodite by Praxiteles. This Alexandria is not otherwise mentioned, and the name is evidently one of the many dynastic names which were taken temporarily in the Hellenistic age by cities of non-Greek origin; we have already seen the case of Alabanda. Some have supposed the city in question to be Heracleia-under-Latmus; others, with greater probability, have identified it with Alinda. Nothing is more likely than that the city should be renamed after the conqueror who had had such friendly relations with the queen. Of the cities which could be called 'by Latmus' Alinda is surely the most probable.

It is possible that we get a further glimpse of Alinda in Hellenistic history. In an inscription found at Karpuzlu two subordinates of the dynast Olympichus (above, p. 8) are honoured for their services. Possibly then Olympichus had his headquarters in or near Alinda. But this conclusion is far from certain; we cannot really infer more than that the two men in question were in all probability citizens of Alinda. It has even been suspected that the inscription does not belong to Alinda at all, but has been brought to Karpuzlu from elsewhere.

However this may be, there is no doubt that in the period following Alexander's campaign Alinda was rapidly Hellenized. The inscription just mentioned refers to a tribe (that is, a sub-division of the citizen-body) called Erechtheis; this name is taken direct from Athens, which also had a tribe Erechtheis, named after the mythical king Erechtheus. If the inscription really belongs to Alinda, this is a striking and significant fact; and if Alinda also possessed in the third century a statue by Praxiteles, it is evident that the city quickly lost its purely Carian character. It is true that neither of these things is proved; but the extant remains are sufficient proof in themselves. Both the theatre and the superb market-building were erected in the Hellenistic period; and a silver coinage begins about 200 B.C., with Heracles as its commonest type. The city wall may be earlier, perhaps due to Mausolus, for Arrian describes Alinda as 'a place among the strongest', implying surely that she was fortified when Alexander arrived. At the same time Alinda, like all towns of Carian origin, was a member of the Chrysaoric League.

In the province of Asia and under the Roman Empire nothing whatever is heard of Alinda. The city continued to coin down to the third century A.D., and is later recorded as a bishopric under the metropolitan of Staurupolis (Aphrodisias).

No visitor to Alinda is likely to come away dissatisfied. The site is a fine one, fully justifying Arrian's description; the hill, some 500 or 600 feet (152 or 183 m.) in height, is steep on all sides except the south-west, where it is joined by a saddle to a somewhat higher hill, which, however, also formed part of the city. The ring-wall, of good ashlar masonry, is quite well preserved for much of its course; it encloses the summit and south-east slope of the hill, but the north slope was excluded.

Climbing from the modern town the visitor comes first to the market-building, which is undoubtedly the gem of the site (Pl. 46). Similar buildings are found elsewhere, for example at Assos in the Troad, Aegae in Aeolis, and Seleuceia in Pamphylia, but none is so admirably preserved as this. It stands to its full length of 325 feet (99 m.) and to most of its original height of over 50 feet (15·2 m.). Of its three storeys the topmost was on a level with, and accessible from, the agora which adjoins it on the north; the bottom storey opens onto a narrow terrace on the south. This terrace is partly cut from the rock of the hillside, partly supported by masonry set

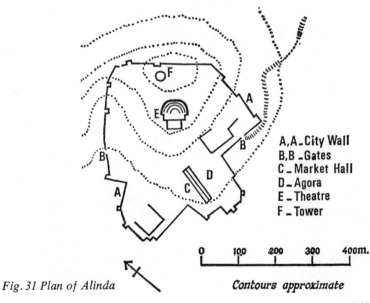

A,A - City Wall
B,B - Gates
C - Market Hall
D - Agora
E - Theatre
F - Tower

0 100 200 300 400m.

Fig. 31 Plan of Alinda

Contours approximate

between the rocks and strengthened with buttresses. The bottom storey is divided lengthwise from end to end by a continuous wall, and crosswise by walls from front to back forming a series of pairs of chambers one behind the other. The front row of chambers, evidently shops, is entered by twelve doors in the front wall, two arched and ten rectangular, and from them other doors give access to the back row. The front chambers are not all of the same size, nor has each its own front door; some of the doors lead to two or more adjoining chambers. The back row is almost entirely filled with rubbish. Owing to the ground rising towards the east, the last four doors at that end are set higher than the rest; since all four are at the same height, there must originally have been two levels. There is also an arched door in the short wall at this end. Light came to the front row of chambers principally through the front doors, though there are also V-slit windows; the back row had only such light as came through from the front, and must have been nearly dark. In some, but not all, cases there are sockets in the door-jambs for barring the door.

The middle storey, lower in height than the bottom storey, is divided longitudinally down the middle by a row of double half-columns—that is, square pillars with a half-column on each side. These stand on the long middle wall of the lower storey, but not —except by accident—at the points where the short walls cross it; they are spaced consistently 15 feet (4·57 m.) apart, whereas the rooms below vary in size. Lighting came from small windows in the form of slits in the front wall; these are sloped away on the inside so as to spread the light. There is also a large window in the short end-wall on the west. No indication appears of any division into rooms on this storey; wooden partitions would no doubt be possible, but the large window just mentioned, unnecessarily large for a single room, looks as if it were intended to light the whole gallery. How this middle storey was reached, whether from above or below, is not clear, and its purpose is equally uncertain; possibly it served as a kind of warehouse or storeroom for the shops below (Pl. 50).

Of the top storey, which bordered the south side of the agora, comparatively little remains. Like the middle storey, it was divided lengthwise by a row of columns; some stumps of these are still in place, set directly above the double half-columns of the middle storey. These columns are unfluted and have merely a narrow rounded moulding at the base. It is likely that there was another row of columns on the north, fronting the agora, but nothing of this survives. Of the walls on the other three sides only a part of that on the west is preserved. The corner pillar stands 10 feet (3·05 m.) high; adjoining it is a row of five moulded blocks like bases, divided by plain blocks, forming a wall quite unlike either of the lower storeys. There were no doubt windows in this wall, and also apparently in the south wall, for the bottom block of the corner pillar is moulded on its east side. For the rest the arrangement of this storey is quite uncertain; its floor, and that of the middle storey, were evidently of wood.

The agora is a level area running the whole length of the market-building and something over 100 feet (30·5 m.) wide, bordered at the back by a retaining wall erected against the gentle slope of the hillside. It was surrounded in the usual way by a stoa, of which a few stumps of columns are, or were, visible. No bases have been found to suggest that the agora was adorned with statues; indeed, no statue-base, let alone a statue, has ever been seen on any part of the site.

The theatre is almost as well preserved as the market-building, and no less interesting. It is of average size, with about thirty-five rows of seats, largely preserved but a good deal displaced by the vegetation which has grown up through them. There is a single diazoma, of which part of the back wall survives; and the ambulatorium, or open gallery, at the top is also preserved for most of the way round. The cavea faces south-east, contrary to the rule laid down by the Roman architect Vitruvius—a rule which is as often disregarded as observed. The retaining wall of the cavea, and the analemmata, still stand to most of their height; the masonry is a regular ashlar of the Hellenistic period. Two arched entrances, one on each side, lead to the diazoma; the one on the north-west side is now 9 or 10 feet (2·74 or 3·05 m.) above the ground outside, showing that the ground-level has changed, as indeed might be expected on so steep a hillside.

But the most interesting part of the theatre is the stage-building. Its lower parts are buried, but excavation would surely reveal an almost complete stage. The stage-building itself has collapsed, but its front wall is visible, together with certain piles of masonry projecting 4 feet (1·22 m.) from it. In front is the stage, supported on plain pilasters and paved with stone slabs 7 feet (2·13 m.) long and about 3 feet (·91 m.) wide. Much of this paving is still in place, though some of the slabs have cracked in the middle. This stage projects about 17 feet (5·18 m.) from the stage-building, and practically closes the parodoi on either side; from this it appears that it belongs to a rearrangement in Roman times. At this period the stage was

165

increased in depth, to accommodate the more numerous performers who then acted upon it, by extending it towards the cavea; in the more elaborate Graeco-Roman theatres, as at Ephesus and elsewhere, the parodoi were covered over and new arched entrances made to replace them, but at Alinda this has not been done. In consequence the stage still preserves very much the same appearance that it previously had in the original Hellenistic theatre, except that the parodoi are practically blocked. The height of the stage cannot now be determined, as its lower part is buried (Pl. 48).

Just below the summit of the hill is the fine tower shown on Pl. 53. It is in two storeys, built in excellent ashlar masonry. The lower storey has two doors in adjoining sides; that on the south has a lintel-block nearly 10 feet (3·05 m.) long, the other has a triangular relieving space over the lintel. The upper storey has a large entrance, probably a door leading to a wooden balcony, which would have been supported on the projecting stone slabs below it, and several windows.

Close by this tower is the mouth of a tunnel which is said to run down the hill to the theatre, though no one has been through it; its lower exit is pointed out just above the theatre. That such an apparently useless construction really exists he who will may believe.

On the summit is a circular foundation, over 50 feet (15·2 m.) in diameter, whose purpose is unknown; and just to the west of it are the foundations of a small building which appears to be a temple. It has two chambers, a pronaos and a cella; if it ever had columns, none are visible now.

Across the saddle to the north-west, on a summit perhaps 100 feet (30·5 m.) higher, is a second acropolis which seems to have been residential only. It is entirely surrounded by walls of good ashlar masonry 6 to 7 feet (1·83 to 2·13 m.) thick, enclosing an elongated area some 250 yards (228·6 m.) in length, sloping gently down towards the west, and divided by a cross-wall (H on the plan) at its narrowest point. There must presumably have been a gate in this wall, but only dubious traces remain. On the south, at a much lower level, is a kind of annexe (E), defended like the main enclosure by a wall with towers. At J a gate gives access to this lower level; the gate itself, about 8 feet 6 inches (2·59 m.) wide, is standing on one side to six courses, of which the topmost curves inwards to form the beginning of an arch. This gate is protected by an adjoining tower.

Over the whole area are remains of private houses. These are comparatively few at the highest point B, but on C, E, and F, and especially G, they are abundant; outlines of walls may be made out, together with door-posts, threshold-blocks, and great quantities of loose uncut building-stones. At K is a row of six good-sized cisterns just inside the wall; they are sunk at least 17 feet (5·18 m.) into the ground, and are lined with poor-quality masonry heavily coated with plaster 2 or 3 inches (about 60 mm.) thick and still showing traces of red colour.

This second acropolis is joined to the first by a good strong wall, with towers, crossing the broad ravine which runs southward from the saddle. There was also a wall across the saddle itself, but of this only scanty traces survive.

Beyond the second acropolis, across the dip which separates it from the next hill, runs an aqueduct still in good preservation (Pl. 51). It is well and strongly built, though without much pretence to elegant finish. There remain four arches and a stretch of solid wall pierced by a gate, no doubt for the passage of a road—or rather

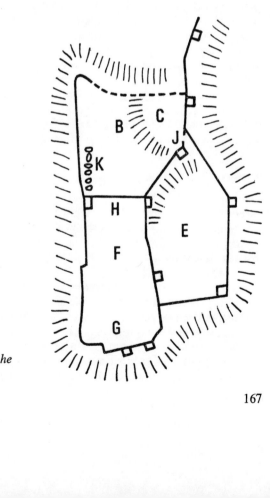

Fig. 32 Alinda. The Second Acropolis

167

path, for it is only 6 feet (1·83 m.) wide. It is at present possible to walk also through the arches, but the ground-level was originally lower. Above the arches runs the water-channel, consisting of two parallel rows of blocks set on edge and covered with other blocks, five of which are still in position.

Tombs are very numerous on all sides of the city, even on the far side of the hill beyond the aqueduct. Most common are graves of the 'Carian' type, cut in a boulder of rock (sometimes two side by side) and covered with a separate lid; most of these are full-length graves, but a few are mere rectangular holes about 18 inches (·46 m.) square with a raised rim. There are also many sarcophagi, quite plain apart from a boss or other projection on the short end of the lid; and in the town are several handsome built tombs, now converted to modern uses. Not a single one of these many tombs carries an inscription, though on one sarcophagus close by the aqueduct there is a sinking with three holes as if for a bronze name-plate. Inscriptions of any kind are indeed exceedingly rare at Alinda; the writer has seen only a fragment built into a window of the mosque, though one or two others have been known. Elegant or artistic carving is equally rare; statues, altars, reliefs, and marble work of any sort, are almost totally absent. If the Alindians had really enough appreciation of art to purchase a statue by Praxiteles, this scarcity is surprising. Mention may, however, be made of a white marble frieze-block built into a wall of a house in the town; it depicts eight persons engaged in battle, and might well come from a temple, but if so, the building to which it belonged has disappeared.

Amyzon

High up in the wild country to the north of Alinda lay the old Carian city of Amyzon. Jeeps do in fact go up from Karpuzlu in something under two hours by the worst road in the present writer's experience which professed to be passable for motor transport, but now the best approach is from the north by a new road which runs from Koçarlı to Gaffarlar.

Very little is heard of Amyzon in the ancient writers. Strabo groups it disdainfully with Heracleia, Euromus, and Chalcetor as 'outposts' of the larger cities; 'these then', he observes, 'are of less account', and makes no further reference to Amyzon. Other authors merely mention her existence. Our knowledge of her history is accordingly confined to what may be gathered from the inscriptions. From these we learn that the city was in the third century in alliance with the Ptolemies, but towards the end of the century changed its allegiance to support the Seleucid cause. A letter of Antiochus III of Syria, written in 203 B.C., confirms the city's privileges, among which was the right of asylum for the temple of Apollo and Artemis. In the latter part of the second century we find Amyzon concluding a treaty with Heracleia-under-Latmus, but its terms are lost with the damage to the inscription. In the second century A.D. the city restored 'the road allotted to it'. This was somewhat unusual, as road repairs were normally undertaken by the Imperial government. Nothing more is known of the road in question, but it was presumably superior to the one from which the writer suffered. Later, Amyzon was the seat of a bishopric.

The site, now called Mazın Kalesi, is a mile or so above the village of Gaffarlar, on the highest point in the neighbourhood. Gaffarlar is a fair-sized village, with a moderate extent of cultivation around it, but for the most part the country is a wilderness of rocky scrub-covered hills. Rather half-hearted excavations have been carried out more than once, but the place is now deserted and overgrown.

Yet the ruins are not negligible. Of the city wall a right-angled stretch some 150 yards (137 m.) long is still standing up to 20 feet (6·1 m.) in height and 5 feet 6 inches (1·68 m.) in thickness; the masonry is a very handsome isodomic ashlar dating perhaps around 300 B.C. (Pl. 86). In the interior are the ruins of a temple, possibly that of Apollo and Artemis mentioned in the inscriptions; built into it upside down is a list of officials, among whom the god's name occurs on three occasions. This means that no citizen sufficiently wealthy could be found to serve in those years, and the expenses of the office were undertaken by the temple treasury. The building is so ruined that no idea can be obtained of its exact form.

Close to the road is another building, equally ruined; in it are lying several broken columns fluted only in the upper part, but the masonry is very poor.

Inside the southern stretch of the city wall, and parallel to it, is a series of at least eleven vaulted underground chambers; they are about 80 feet (24·4 m.) long, 14 feet (4·27 m.) wide, and more than 9 feet (2·74 m.) high. They are well and strongly built of small stones, and the lower part of the walls is plastered. The entrance is in each case in the end facing the city wall; they are therefore not cisterns, but presumably store-rooms.

What provision was made for water is not clear. There is no sign of an aqueduct, nor did the writer notice any cisterns on the hill;

there are said to be three or four springs within tolerable distance of the site, but in general water is scarce. Today on the way up from Karpuzlu there are at frequent intervals stone huts by the roadside in which are kept one or more jars of drinking-water. The supply is renewed daily by the villagers, an unpaid service which in summer at least deserves the traveller's gratitude.

Note

1 This curious work is a kind of geographical lexicon. Its professed purpose is to study the principles of formation of adjectives from place-names; it takes the form of a list of city-names with the 'ethnics' belonging to them, with occasional notes on the places. Though not written before the fifth century A.D. the work is derived from much earlier sources, and while almost useless for the purpose for which it was written, it gives us quite a lot of incidental information not available elsewhere.

17 Gerga

The third site for which Çine serves as a base is of very different character from the other two. It is indeed no more than a village, but the remains are so striking and unusual that the present writer at least knows no place more fascinating. It is somewhat remote, and an adequate visit calls for a full day, mostly on foot. The site lies in the wild mountain country about four miles (6·44 km.) east-south-east of Eski Çine, and may be approached from there by way of the village of Ovacık; but it is easier now to drive along the new main road from Çine as far as the fine old bridge near İncekemer (Pl. 54), and to walk up from there. A guide is of course necessary. The Çine river may be crossed either by the bridge itself or, to save a little distance, by jumping from rock to rock across the stream at a point nearer to Çine.

In either case it is an hour's gradual climb northwards to the first signs of the ancient village. On either side of a stream-bed, dry in summer but in winter running southwards into the Çine Çayı, is a good-sized rock bearing the name Gerga in Greek letters nearly 3 feet (·91 m.) high. On the western rock the name is divided between the east and north faces. Such an ancient equivalent to the modern road-sign is unexampled in the writer's experience. But at Gerga the visitor is amazed to find the same thing repeated again and again; in at least nineteen places (there are certainly more) the name is written on the rocks in the same huge letters 2 to 3 feet (·61 to ·91 m) high. Not always in the same form, however; sometimes it is Gergas and sometimes Gergakome (the village of Gerga).

Just to the west of the spot mentioned above is a steep hillside, and near the top of this is the next surprise, a colossal statue fallen on its back. It has toppled from its base, which stands nearby, breaking close above the ankles. It represents a male figure standing stiffly with very square shoulders, the arms by the sides and the feet a little apart. The face and head are much damaged, and the

171

features are no longer discernible. And across the breast, in letters 8 inches (203 mm.) high, is the name Gerga. This again is unparalleled in the present writer's experience (Pl. 58).

Working gradually upwards from here to the north-west the visitor will pass several cases of the name Gerga or Gergakome written on the rocks (Pl. 55), in one case in Latin letters; he may then cross a saddle to the next hill to the east, which carries the principal ruins. Here he will find a group of buildings, evidently private houses; they are badly ruined, but several doorposts are still standing. Running down from here is a street lined with a wall on either side, in which again the name Gerga may be seen. Lower down the slope is another curious feature, a large flat-topped rock with sloping surface on which is inscribed in Greek letters 'Gerga Enbolo' (Pl. 57). The

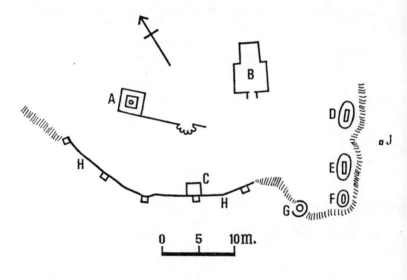

A _ Base with large fallen statue   F,G_Oil-mills

B _ Temple   H _ Terrace-wall with

C _ Fountain-house (or tomb?)   buttresses

D,E_Pyramidal Stelae   J _ Fallen Statue

Fig. 33 Gerga. Plan of the Village Centre

second word is obscure, but means most likely 'rostrum'—that is, the flat rock served as a speaker's platform at village meetings.

Higher up to the north-east is the village-centre (plan Fig. 33), which is full of interest. It is supported by a curved terrace wall with buttresses, of thoroughly Carian workmanship, and on the terrace above is a group of monuments which is quite unique. The eye is first caught by the handsome building B, still excellently preserved complete with roof (Pl. 59); this is undoubtedly a temple. Its plan is shown in Fig. 34; it is empty, and quite plain apart from

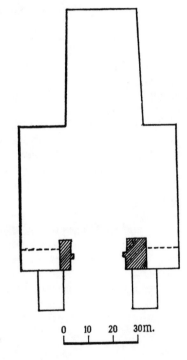

0   10   20   30m.

Fig. 34 Gerga. Plan of the Temple

two cupboard-like recesses on either side of the door. The roof is constructed with ridge-pole and rafters, in imitation of timber work. And in the pediment over the door is written the name Gergas.

This building is no doubt the gem of the whole site, but it is equalled in interest by the remarkable installation at the east end of the terrace. This consisted originally of two stone stelae 11 feet (3·35 m.) high, tapering to the top like two-dimensional pyramids,

173

and between these a colossal statue on a base (D, E, and J). The two stelae are still standing (Pl. 56), and each is inscribed with the name Gergas. The whole must have formed a most striking and unusual group, but the statue has now fallen over the edge of the terrace and is lying below. It is similar in size and appearance to the other described above, but lacks the head and feet. There is in this case no inscription on the breast; presumably it was sufficient that the name was written on the stelae.

At the south-east corner of the terrace are two blocks F and G, with hollowed surface and an outlet in the form of a hole or groove. These have been used for treading grapes or olives, though this may not have been their original purpose; they may once have supported statues or other objects. More common than this type is the oil- or wine-press in the shape of an ashtray with central knob; with these a millstone was used in the manner still employed today.

Further to the west, at A on the plan, is another extraordinary monument. Here is a large rectangular base from which a huge statue has fallen and is now lying face downwards, so that little can be clearly seen; it is over 14 feet (4·27 m.) high. The French scholar G. Cousin in 1899 had a better view of it; it is a standing figure in a stiff posture, with the hands resting on two cylindrical staffs with swellings at the base. The body consists merely of a flat rounded surface, with four small holes in the breast, apparently for fixing a plaque of some kind (Fig. 35). The head, now missing, was seen by Cousin, who calls it 'absolutely monstrous, with its enormous mouth and small eyes widely spaced'; the head was perhaps covered with a veil. On the bottom step of the base is a lion's head at the right end, and at the left end a semicircular projection; on the step above, in the middle, is a bull's head. A few paces to the east, projecting from the same platform on which the statue lies, is a kind of base adorned with five objects each formed of two contiguous balls like a figure 8, arranged in a semicircle; the largest is 2 feet 4 inches (·76 m.) long. These are puzzling; Cousin's explanation, that they are the toes of the statue's right foot, is startling rather than convincing (Fig. 36).

At various points on the site—the writer saw four of them—are small square buildings about a man's height, all closely similar to one another. They are open in front and roofed with a single large slab; the floor inside is hollowed out. They are all inscribed with the name Gerga in its various forms; one of them (Pl. 60) has the name three times, on the edge of the roof-slab over the entrance, on the right-hand interior wall, and on the roof looking to the sky.

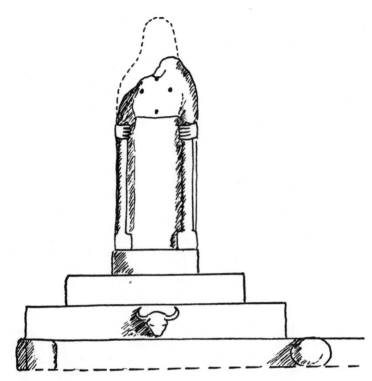

Fig. 35 Gerga. Statue

These buildings have been considered to be tombs, and the French scholar A. Laumonier, who has made an extensive study of the Carian cults, sees in the site of Gerga as a whole a kind of sanctuary, its central point the funerary temple B, that is the tomb of the local god or hero Gergas, with the tombs of priests or other notables closely grouped around it, in accordance with the familiar desire (not only in ancient times) to be buried as near as possible to some

Fig. 36 Gerga. Base

175

sacred spot. The habit of writing the name Gerga or Gergas on the tombs he ascribes to religious or magical motives, for example to invoke the protection of the deity. The present writer has to confess that this was not the impression that he received. The buildings described above seemed to him to be not tombs at all, but fountain-houses. Fountains would be very necessary, for the site is almost entirely dry in summer; there is one spring, but by the end of summer it is reduced to a miserable trickle. A number of considerations support this view. The front of the buildings is completely open, and there is no sign that it was ever closed. On the inner wall of one of them is carved a dolphin, the normal symbol of water. Another has a hole in the back wall, which seems to be a pipe-hole. And round the interior walls of a third is written Gergakome. To write the name of a god on the inner wall of a tomb is one thing, but to write the name of the village is another; there seems no reasonable motive for such a proceeding. Nor does any of the buildings contain any visible provision for a burial. The writer indeed saw nothing on the site which seemed to him to be a tomb, for there appears no cogent reason why even the 'funerary temple' should need to be really a tomb rather than a straightforward temple.

There is little sign of Hellenic culture on the site. The three surviving statues are crude in style and of archaic appearance, and the masonry in general is Carian rather than Greek. Nevertheless it would be a mistake to suppose that the monuments of Gerga must go back to a remote antiquity. On a small and secluded site like this there is a strong tendency to conservatism, and the criteria of classical Greek art do not apply. It is indeed doubtful if anything there is earlier than the Roman Empire; the inscriptions, both on the rocks and on the buildings, are unquestionably of that period. One or two fragments of inscriptions on stone have been seen, but have now disappeared; here again the style of writing is of the Roman age.

On the various problems provided by the site every visitor will form his own opinion, but of one thing there can be no doubt; no one who makes the effort to visit Gerga will feel that he has wasted his day.

18　Tralles and Nysa

In the great migrations of Greeks into Asia Minor barbarians normally played no part. It is therefore surprising to read that in antiquity the city of Tralles was believed to have been founded by an oddly assorted company of Argives from the Peloponnese and Trallians from Thrace or Illyria. If this tradition has any basis of fact, it is further surprising that the city should have taken its name from the barbarian element rather than the Greek. It had also, we are told, at some time the names Charax and, from the abundance of flowers that grew there, Euantheia. How much of all this may be accepted is very dubious.

Tralles first appears in history in 400 B.C., when the Spartan general Thibron was attempting to recover the cities of Asia from the Persians; his attack on Tralles failed by reason of the strength of the position. Diodorus, who records this, calls her a city of Ionia; much more normally she is reckoned to Caria, though some prefer to regard her as Lydian. On Alexander's arrival in 334 Tralles submitted quietly, and was used by the conqueror as a base.

Antigonus in 313 was more successful than Thibron and was able to take the city by force. After his death in 301 it fell into the hands of the Seleucids, and while their power lasted assumed the name of Seleuceia. Pliny says that it was also called Antiocheia; no reason appears why the same city should be called after two kings, both Seleucid, and this statement of Pliny's, for which there is no other evidence, is generally disbelieved. When the Seleucid power was broken at the battle of Magnesia in 190, Tralles was given by the Romans to Eumenes of Pergamum. A later Pergamene king, Attalus, had a palace in the city built of brick; this was afterwards used as a residence by the chief priest of Zeus.

When Aristonicus was disputing the Roman inheritance of the Pergamene kingdom, Tralles made the mistake of supporting him; as a punishment it appears that she was deprived of the privilege of minting coins. The city had nevertheless the rank of a *conventus* under the Roman Republic, though under the Empire it was absorbed into the diocese of Ephesus. In the Mithridatic War of 88–85 B.C. the slaughter of the Roman residents was apparently instigated at Tralles by the sons of a certain Cratippus, who for a short while held the position of tyrants there.

When Julius Caesar defeated Pompey in the crucial battle of Pharsalus in 48 B.C., many portents of this great victory were reported from many parts of the world. At Tralles, we read, there stood a statue of Caesar surrounded by a stone pavement laid on hard ground; yet from this pavement a palm-tree sprouted.

A year or two after the foundation of the Empire Tralles suffered from a severe earthquake. Augustus came to the rescue with financial help, and in gratitude the city took the name of Caesarea. The history of this name is characteristic: down to the time of Nero the coins are inscribed 'Caesarea' only; after this 'Caesarea Tralles'; and by the end of the first century 'Tralles' only as in the past.

Strabo refers to the great wealth and prosperity of the citizens, and notes that 'the leading men of the province, who are called Asiarchs' were frequently men of Tralles; yet when she and ten others competed for the privilege of erecting a temple to Tiberius, she was passed over, like Laodiceia, as lacking sufficient resources. We can only conclude that the expenses connected with a cult of the Emperor were formidable indeed.

The principal deity of Tralles was Zeus, with the title Larasius, that is, according to Strabo, Zeus of Larasa, a village three miles (4·83 km.) to the north on Mt Messogis—though in fact he uses the forms Larisa and Larisius. The chief games celebrated in the city were the Olympia and Pythia, modelled on the great games of classical Greece (below, pp. 193–4).

As distinguished citizens Strabo mentions the family of Pythodorus, who came originally from Nysa (below, pp. 180–2), and among well-known orators a certain Damasus, who had the curious nickname Skombros, 'the Mackerel'. The cultivation of figs, which are the principal product of the Maeander valley today, is not noticed in antiquity, and Tralles was famous chiefly for her pottery. The most famous citizen of Tralles was born outside the period covered by this book, Anthemius, architect of the great Byzantine church of St Sophia at Constantinople.

The site of Tralles at Aydın (formerly called Güzelhisar) answers well to Strabo's description: the city, he says, is founded on a flat-topped hill with a steep acropolis, and is well defended all round. The ruins are seldom visited these days, for two good reasons: there is very little to see; and the site is occupied by the army, so that a permit from the municipality is needed. At the end of the last century a fair amount was to be seen, notably a gymnasium, a theatre, and a stadium; the present writer in 1946 found hardly anything remaining. Long occupation by the military has had its usual effect of obliterating all that was there before.

The only thing actually standing is a row of three tall arches, called the Üç Göz, which formed part of the gymnasium. They are of poor-quality masonry of late Roman date, partly of large stone blocks with abundant mortar and partly of brickwork. The whole was coated with stucco, which still remains on the underside of the arches. Close by is a wall of similar construction, presumably belonging also to the gymnasium, and a row of five column-stumps resting on a mass of brickwork.

At the north end of the flat hilltop is the acropolis hill, with the theatre at its foot. This was excavated in 1888 and proved to be of considerable interest, if only because it was one of the very few that had an underground tunnel in the orchestra. This was 7 feet (2·44 m.) deep, and in the centre of the orchestra branched right and left at right-angles; its beginning and end, however, were not determined. These tunnels are supposed to have been used for the appearance of characters from the underworld. In 1946 nothing of this remained; a broad trench had been driven, for some obscure military purpose, right through the orchestra. A corner of the cavea was still visible on the east side, and also on the east side of the arched entrance to the upper diazoma; nothing more.

Of the stadium too very little remains. The vaulted entrance is preserved at the east end; like the gymnasium it is partly of stone, partly of brick. At various points on the site later excavations revealed the foundations of temples, but these are no longer in evidence.

Travellers to whom time is of importance will therefore probably content themselves with the view of the Üç Göz from the road or railway.

Nysa and Acharaca

Eastward of Aydın the south face of Mt Messogis is cut by innumerable stream-beds, torrents in winter but dry in summer. Set

179

astride one of these, a mile above the village of Sultanhisar, are the ruins of Nysa.

Nysa is a frequent name on the map of the ancient world; Stephanus of Byzantium lists ten cities so called. It was also a not uncommon name among the ladies of the Hellenistic royal families, and according to the same writer the Carian Nysa was founded by Antiochus I of Syria and named after his wife (below, p. 213). Strabo, on the other hand, says that three brothers, Athymbrus, Athymbradus, and Hydrelus, came from Sparta and founded three cities in their own names, and that these were afterwards united in a single city Nysa, of which Athymbrus was regarded as the founder. Strabo knew Nysa well, for he was educated there, and his account surely represents the belief of the citizens themselves. Moreover, Stephanus also, in another passage, says that the old name of Nysa was Athymbra, and in inscriptions down to the end of the third century B.C. the Nysaeans are called Athymbrians. Since Strabo makes no mention of the Seleucids, and since no wife of Antiochus I by the name of Nysa is otherwise known, it is likely that this part of Stephanus' testimony should be discredited. Equally or even more improbable is yet another statement of Stephanus', that Nysa was once called Pythopolis after a certain Pythes (otherwise unknown) who entertained Xerxes in 480 B.C. Nothing has been found on the site to suggest that a city existed there before the third century. It seems probable that the name Nysa was given at some time after 200 B.C. in honour of some female member of the Seleucid line, though the lady in question and the occasion are equally unknown. At the same time, and in spite of Strabo's silence, it is almost certain that Nysa was a Seleucid foundation, for as early as 281 B.C. we find Seleucus and Antiochus writing to the Athymbrians to confer or confirm certain privileges.

Nysa has little individual history. An inscription gives us a glimpse of events at the time of the Mithridatic War, when a rich Nysaean by the name of Chaeremon furnished the Roman commander with 60,000 bushels of wheat as provender for his army. This conduct so enraged Mithridates that he put on Chaeremon's head a price of forty talents if taken alive, twenty if dead. Chaeremon took refuge in the sanctuary of Ephesian Artemis (whether in Ephesus itself or at Nysa, for her cult was very widespread), but it seems that the right of asylum may not have been respected by the king, and that Chaeremon was taken and put to death. His family was distinguished as well as rich; a relative of his named Pythodorus was among the

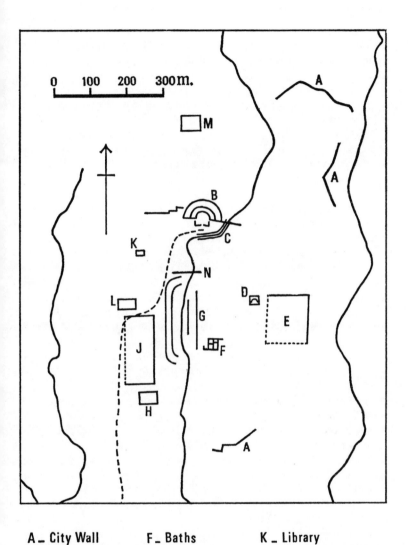

A _ City Wall   F _ Baths   K _ Library
B _ Theatre   G _ Amphitheatre   L _ Byzantine Building
C _ Tunnel   H _ Kâtip Ören   M _ Water-depot
D _ Council-House   J _ Gymnasium   N _ Bridge
E _ Agora

Fig. 37 Plan of Nysa

closest friends of Pompey the Great and possessed a fortune of over 2,000 talents; he married a daughter of Mark Antony, and their daughter Pythodoris became in turn queen of Pontus and of Cappadocia. She was, says Strabo, a sensible woman and well able to manage affairs of state.

Nysa was not backward in the field of letters. Strabo mentions a number of distinguished orators and philosophers who were natives of the city; among them was his own teacher Aristodemus, who held classes twice daily at Nysa, rhetoric in the morning, grammar in the evening. At Rome he taught the children of Pompey, and he had also a school in Rhodes.

But the chief claim of Nysa to distinction lay in the existence on her territory of a healing sanctuary of Pluto, god of the underworld, close to which was a remarkable cave called the Charonium. The site was at the village of Acharaca, three miles (4·83 km.) on the road from Nysa to Tralles. More will be said of this below.

Strabo describes Nysa as lying on the slope of Mt Messogis, close above the plain; it is, he says, a kind of double city, being split down the middle by a stream forming a ravine; of this, part is spanned by a bridge joining the two halves of the city, and part is adorned with an amphitheatre, under which the stream flows concealed. Below the theatre lie on one side the gymnasium of the young men, and on the other the agora and the Council-House of the Elders. This account may be verified on the ground today.

From Sultanhisar a newly-constructed motor-road leads directly to the theatre. This has now been almost completely excavated, by local effort financed by the Turkish government. It is a little above average size and forms rather more than a semicircle. The cavea is in good condition, with most of the seats remaining; it has one diazoma, with twenty-three rows below it and twenty-six above. There is an arched entrance (vomitorium) low down on each side. The nine stairways below the diazoma are increased, in the usual way, to seventeen above it; other steps lead up from the diazoma to the upper seats. The stage-building is of Roman type, with five doors leading onto the stage, but it has not been entirely cleared. The front wall of the stage, and a part of its decoration, is visible, with a fragmentary inscription referring to persons by the names of Justus and Stratonice; nothing is known of these, but they presumably contributed in some way to the construction or embellishment of the theatre (Pl. 61).

Just below the theatre the stream runs through an ancient tunnel, admirably constructed and about 100 yards (91 m.) long, lit at one point by a shaft in the roof. About the middle it makes an obtuse bend, and here, on the north wall, is cut an inscription: 'Work of . . . lus up to this point'. The beginning of the man's name is now lost, nor is it clear why he did not finish the job; perhaps funds ran out.

The vast constructions in and over the ravine, referred to by Strabo, are unfortunately in very poor condition. The 'bridge' of which he speaks was in reality a great platform spanning the northern part of the gully from the west end of the tunnel to the north end of the amphitheatre, but only a few rather shapeless pieces of its masonry remain. The amphitheatre itself is in no better case, though a few of its seats are, with some difficulty, discoverable. The idea of making use of the sides of a stream-bed to build an amphitheatre is not confined to Nysa; the same may be seen, for example, at Pergamum, at Cyzicus, and at Tripolis in Phrygia. The plan had the further advantage that the water of the stream was readily available (at least till May) to flood the arena for mimic sea-fights and other water-spectacles.

Of the gymnasium, on the west side of the ravine, hardly a trace is now visible; the site is chiefly recognizable as a level area some 180 yards (165 m.) in length. Close to the south end is a better-preserved building known today as Kâtip Ören. The original plan is obscured by a church which was later built over it, but it is likely to have been a baths; water-pipes are much in evidence, and ancient gymnasia were normally accompanied by baths. The chief features are the arches in the walls; but the masonry is very late, and it is certain that this building did not exist in Strabo's day.

On the other side of the ravine are the agora and Council-House of the Elders. Of the agora only a small part of one side has been excavated; a few column-stumps are standing, and others are lying around, but nothing more. The council-house (*Geronticum*), on the other hand, is perhaps the most attractive building on the site. It is excellently preserved and completely excavated, with twelve rows of seats and five stairways. The building forms a semicircle within a rectangle, of which the back is supported by large double half-columns. Behind the speaker's platform four large solid piers make three entrances. Outside this are the bases of a row of eight columns, the middle six on high pedestals, and behind this again is a long narrow bathing-pool; close by is a marble bath with a plug-hole. Two inscriptions have come to light; one refers to the two Empresses, the elder and younger Faustina, the other is an epigram in verse, for some reason left unfinished.

Of the buildings not mentioned by Strabo, the library is no doubt the most interesting (Pl. 62). It may indeed not have existed in his time, for in its present form at least it can hardly date before the second century A.D. It had originally two, or more likely three, storeys, but of these the uppermost is almost entirely destroyed, and

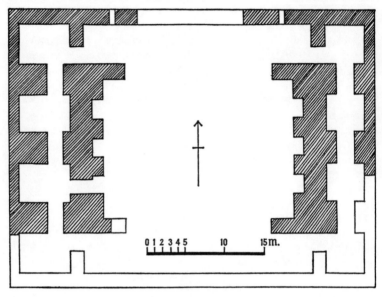

Fig. 38 Nysa. Plan of First Floor of the Library

the ground floor is buried to most of its height. The adjoining sketch shows the plan of the first floor. The niches in the walls, rectangular and vaulted, which held the books must be imagined as veneered with marble or stucco which is now gone. The entrance must have been on the south side, but the south wall is completely destroyed. It is noticeable that the bookshelves, on either side of the central reading-room, were not in the outer wall of the building, but separated from it by a gallery; the same feature is to be seen in the library of Celsus at Ephesus, its purpose being to protect the books from damp. It is to be hoped that this building will one day be excavated, for the ground floor is probably in quite good preservation. In its present condition it hardly gives a fair idea of what must have been a very handsome building.

There are many other structures on the site, all of late date, indifferent masonry, and uncertain purpose. Even the city wall is not earlier than Byzantine; for the ordinary visitor its scanty remnants barely justify the effort of tracking them down. There must presumably have been a wall in Hellenistic times, but no vestige of it survives.

In the village school in Sultanhisar there is a small collection of antiquities, including the remarkable piece of sculpture shown in Fig. 39.

Fig. 39 Nysa. Dolphin and Boy at the School in Sultanhisar

From Nysa a road lined with tombs led westward towards Tralles, passing through the village of Acharaca. It is scarcely possible now to follow this road, which crosses a number of steep ravines, and the ancient bridges are no more. A visit to Acharaca is most easily paid from Çiftekahveler on the modern highroad, from which a

185

tarmac road leads up to the village of Salavatlı. The site is just outside the village.

Strabo's account is as follows. On the road from Tralles to Nysa there is a village of the Nysaeans called Acharaca, in which are the Plutonium, with a rich precinct and a temple of Pluto and Persephone, and the Charonium, a remarkable cave lying above the precinct. Here, it is said, sick persons go to be cured by these deities, and dwell in the village near the cave with the more experienced of the priests; these incubate on behalf of the patients and prescribe treatment in accordance with their dreams, though sometimes the patients do the dreaming themselves. Often the sick are taken into the cave and installed there, like animals in their lair, for several days without food. For all others the place is forbidden ground, and indeed deadly rather than curative. A festival is celebrated there, at which a bull is taken up into the cave by the young men of Nysa; when released, the animal goes forward a little, then collapses and dies.

The Plutonium has been identified and partially excavated; it lies close to the east side of the ravine in which the stream flows past the village. The ruins are hardly impressive, but enough survives (or survived early in this century) to enable a provisional restoration of the plan (Fig. 40). The form of the temple, if rightly reconstructed, is highly exceptional; the colonnade had six columns at the ends and the unusual number of twelve on the long sides. Ten of these have been identified in their original positions. Unusual also is the north–south orientation, with the entrance apparently on the north. Most remarkable of all is the interior arrangement, with two parallel walls running the whole length of the temple. It should, however, be borne in mind that the restoration is largely conjectural, the surviving fragments (shaded on the plan) being so very scanty.

At present even less than this is visible. In the excavation hollow is a row of seven unfluted column-drums, 3 feet 6 inches (1·07 m.) in diameter, in their original positions, a large column-base with torus moulding, and two or three large blocks lying loose; and beside the path between the village and the stream are two blocks of a Doric triglyph-and-metope frieze.

By Strabo's account the cave called Charonium should be somewhere above the temple, but it seems clear that none answering the description exists today. A little to the west, however, is the source of the stream in a deep and narrow gully; the stream is heavily charged with sulphur and has a bright yellow colour which gives it its name of Sarısu. The smell of sulphur is said to be often very strong in winter. In the high and steep rock-walls of the gully are a number of ancient buildings of the arched type so characteristic of Nysa. Although no proper cave is to be found, it may well be that this place, which is quite impressive, does in fact represent the

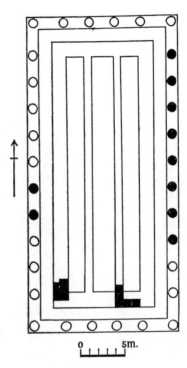

Fig. 40 Acharaca. Plan of the Temple (conjectural)

Charonium; it is the sort of place which had religious associations in antiquity. Caves can fall in and disappear; and it is easy to imagine the patients installed in the arched buildings in question. In any case it is hardly doubtful that the healing properties of Acharaca derived from the presence of the sulphur-bearing stream (Pl. 66).

19 Aphrodisias

'For Solomon went after Ashtoreth the goddess of the Zidonians
. . . and Solomon did evil in the sight of the Lord'.[1] Ashtoreth of
Sidon, Ishtar of Babylon and Nineveh, Astarte, Aphrodite, or Venus,
the worship of the laughter-loving Goddess of Love was virtually
ubiquitous. Even for the wisest of the kings of Israel her power was
too strong. Cities named after her were common; Stephanus of
Byzantium lists a dozen places, towns or islands, by the name of
Aphrodisias, of which the best known, at least in Roman times, was
the city on the eastern border of Caria.

According to Stephanus the city was founded by Pelasgian-
Lelegians and called Lelegonpolis, then Megalepolis, then Ninoe
after Ninus, king of Assyria. The first two of these names may safely
be disregarded; this is not Lelegian country, and there was certainly
no 'great city' on the site in early times. The third name Ninoe,
however, may well be historical. It is likely enough that Assyrians
from Nineveh may have established a cult of Ishtar in this rather
remote region, before or after the destruction of Nineveh by the
Medes and Babylonians. We seem indeed to have a trace of such
a tradition in the cult of Zeus Nineudius which is recorded in the
later inscriptions of the city, and recent excavations have produced
a fragment of a relief carrying the figures of Ninus and Semiramis,
in Roman dress (Pl. 72).

That the site was occupied very early is beyond doubt. The recent
excavations have revealed pottery going back to the Early Bronze
Age in the third millennium, and even to the Chalcolithic period
before 3000. But the evidence for a city of Aphrodisias is surprisingly late. The name at least seems established by the third
century B.C., when the historian Apollonius came here from Egypt
to settle, and wrote a book on Caria; he is called Apollonius of
Aphrodisias. Yet the first mention of a *city* is not earlier than the
first century. In 82 B.C. the Roman general Sulla, in response to a

Delphic oracle, sent a double axe, a characteristic divine symbol in Caria, and a golden crown to Aphrodite; the oracle speaks of 'a very great city of Caria named after Aphrodite'. But oracular language is often exaggerated.

Before this we must imagine a sanctuary of Ishtar-Aphrodite, with no doubt a considerable settlement around it, quite highly civilized; apart from pottery and figurines of the sixth and fifth centuries, coins of Alexander and a fragmentary Lydian inscription have been found on the site. By the second century this settlement had developed into a city.

One of the earliest inscriptions from Aphrodisias, dating between 80 and 50 B.C., tells how the community of the Greek cities in Asia thanked two Aphrodisians for undertaking a difficult and dangerous mission to Rome to plead the sufferings of the province before the Senate, making particular mention of the extortion suffered at the hands of Roman tax-farmers. The modest beginnings of the city of Aphrodisias are clearly shown by her relations with the neighbouring city of Plarasa.[2] Between 39 and 35 B.C. Mark Antony sent to Aphrodisias a copy of a decree of the Senate conferring freedom and immunity from taxation on 'the city of the Plarasans and Aphrodisians', and on the temple of Aphrodite a right of asylum equal to that of Artemis of Ephesus. Similarly, on the coins down to the time of Augustus both names occur, and Plarasa is placed first. Under the Empire, Aphrodisias alone is named, and Plarasa fades from view. It seems that the sanctuary of Aphrodite was on the territory of Plarasa, and as it developed the two places united into a single city; in the course of time the newer member gained the dominance and Plarasa sank to the status of a deme of Aphrodisias.

New glimpses into the city's history are afforded by the inscriptions recently discovered in the course of excavating the theatre (below, p. 196). These are not yet formally published, but include a whole series of letters from the Emperors, ranging from Augustus to Gordian III in the third century. Another records a treaty with the neighbouring cities of Tabae and Cibyra in the second century B.C. From another it appears that the city suffered from looting at the time of the war with Labienus in 40 B.C., losing among other things a golden statue of Eros dedicated by Julius Caesar, but later recovered.[3] A third is a letter from Hadrian exempting the city from the Nail Tax (whatever that may have been).

In Imperial times Aphrodisias was very rich and prosperous. As a measure of the wealth of her citizens, a certain priest of Heracles,

189

Attalus Adrastus, gave 122,000 denarii for a hall of sacrifice and a banqueting-hall, and in his will left over a quarter of a million for gymnastic purposes. Aphrodisias was famous as a seat of medicine and philosophy, and above all for her school of sculptors. This last has been abundantly confirmed by the quantity of statues and reliefs found by the excavators, and a sculptor's workshop has been located in the site (below, p. 194). At one of the festivals celebrated in the city a contest in statuary was included—a form of competition which seems to be unparalleled elsewhere.

The principal deity was naturally Aphrodite. After her, the most frequently represented on the coins is Dionysus, and other members of the Greek pantheon are mentioned in the inscriptions. A non-Greek deity is the Phrygian Mên Ascaenus, and Zeus bears the two curious titles of Nineudius, mentioned above, and Spaloxus. The meaning of the latter is unknown.

The site of Aphrodisias at Geyre has never been in doubt. Somewhat superficial excavations have been carried out several times since the beginning of the present century, and in 1961 a thoroughgoing investigation was begun under the auspices of New York University; this is still in progress at the time of writing, and has already transformed the site.

The temple of Aphrodite (Pl. 68; F on the plan) has always been conspicuous, though little of it survives apart from the colonnade. It was in the Ionic order, with thirteen columns on the long sides and eight at the ends; the style was 'pseudodipteral', that is the columns were placed at twice the usual distance from the side walls, as if to give the effect of a double row without the expense of the inner row. The temple itself comprised a pronaos and a cella, but no opisthodomus. It was formerly thought to date from the time of Hadrian, but is now shown to have been begun in the late second or early first century B.C. At the same time the excavation has produced sherds of archaic date, and there is in fact some slight evidence for an earlier temple on the spot: there are traces of an early Hellenistic mosaic which was cut through in building the pronaos. In early Byzantine times the temple, except for the colonnade, was destroyed to make way for a church, of which the apse is standing at the east end. At this time it appears that the columns on the short ends were removed and added to the side rows; this accounts for the curious fact that the end column but one on the north side, as is shown by the form of its capital, was a corner column in the original temple. At present fourteen columns are still erect and almost complete, in several isolated groups; two groups have the architrave still in place. Some of the columns bear inscriptions recording their presentation by individual citizens to Aphrodite and the People.

The form of the cult-statue is known from a number of copies. The goddess stood in 'hieratic' form, stiffly erect with forearms extended, like the Ephesian Artemis, and wearing a long robe decorated with bands of relief. The usual arrangement of the reliefs

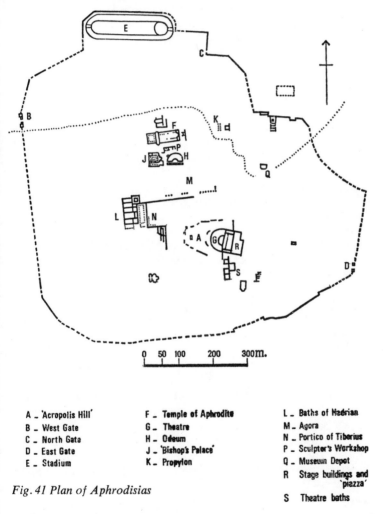

A – 'Acropolis Hill'	F – Temple of Aphrodite	L – Baths of Hadrian
B – West Gate	G – Theatre	M – Agora
C – North Gate	H – Odeum	N – Portico of Tiberius
D – East Gate	J – 'Bishop's Palace'	P – Sculptor's Workshop
E – Stadium	K – Propylon	Q – Museum Depot
		R – Stage buildings and 'piazza'
		S – Theatre baths

Fig. 41 Plan of Aphrodisias

is: at the top, the sun-god and moon-goddess, sometimes with Aphrodite between them; below this, the three Graces, sometimes between two deities; next, Aphrodite seated on a goat with fish's tail; and finally three Cupids. This last is often omitted, and there are other variations also. A statue of this form was found in 1962 just outside the temple precinct. From the inscriptions it appears that Aphrodite was served by male priests (Pl. 74).

A hundred yards or so to the east of the temple stand the spiral-fluted columns of a monumental gateway. This is not quite aligned with the temple and is not the entrance to the temple precinct; the boundary of the precinct seems in fact to be marked by a handsome wall with maeander frieze immediately behind the temple on the east.

The city wall is late, not earlier than the fourth century A.D., and contains a great number of reused stones, many of them inscribed. It is best preserved on the north side. No sign of an earlier wall is to be seen, and it may well be that the city relied for protection on its sanctity. A block built into the wall on the north-east carries the following inscription: 'Whoever throws rubbish here shall incur the curse of the 318 Fathers'—that is the bishops assembled at the Council of Nicaea in 325.

Three gates are preserved, on the west, north, and east. That on the west is called in an inscription the Antiocheian Gate; Antiocheia on the Maeander was in fact the nearest city on that side. It is dedicated by its inscription, on the outer side, to the 'health and safety and fortune and victory and eternal survival' of the Emperor Constantius II (323–61).

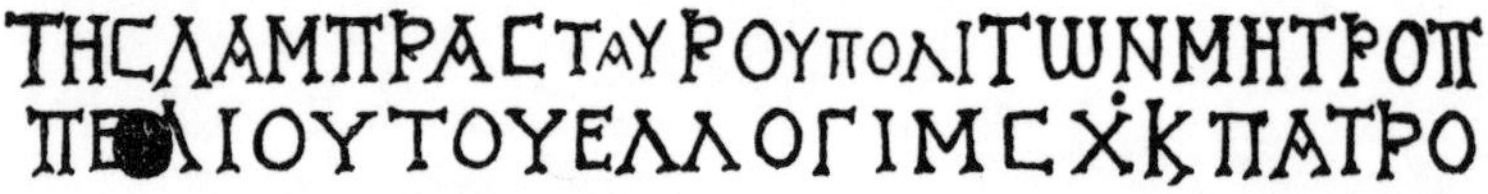

ΤΗϹΛΑΜΠΡΑϹΤΑΥΡΟΥΠΟΛΙΤΩΝΜΗΤΡΟΠ
ΠΕΔΙΟΥΤΟΥΕΛΛΟΓΙΜϹΧΚΠΑΤΡΟ

Fig. 42 Aphrodisias. Part of the Inscription over the North Gate

The North Gate (C on the plan) lies a short distance to the east of the stadium. Its inscription, on the inner side, is interesting. It is in two parts; the upper records the building of the wall, probably in the fourth century; the lower refers to a later restoration of the gate 'for the good fortune of the brilliant Metropolis of the Staurupolitans'. The name of Aphrodisias was in fact changed in the seventh century to Staurupolis; the old name offended Christian susceptibilities and the City of Aphrodite became the City of the

Cross. The restoration in question is actually earlier than this, for the inscription originally read 'Metropolis of the Aphrodisians'; this name was erased and the other substituted. By a curious exercise in economy the letters RO, which happen to be common to both names, were left unerased in making the alteration, as also were the last two letters. In actual fact, as the inscription stands it reads 'Metropolis of the Taurupolitans'; the previous word chances to end in S, and this letter was made to do double duty. Altogether a remarkable piece of epigraphical cheese-paring.[4]

The East Gate (D) also is in very fair condition, a triple arch of which the middle has collapsed. The south wing is a handsome wall, decorated with reliefs showing a human head, floral and other designs. The date is equally late, as is shown by the inscriptions, of about the second century, which are built into the arches.

The stadium (Pl. 65), dating from the early Empire, is one of the best preserved anywhere in the ancient world. It is rounded at both ends, each with a tunnel entrance; that on the west is now blocked by a solid wall at its outer end. As at Priene and elsewhere, the rows of seats are slightly curved to afford a better view of the whole length. In the middle of the north side is a 'Royal Box'. No starting-sill for the foot-races is preserved, but among the blocks lying in the arena at the west end are a slender unfluted column-drum, a dentil frieze, and other blocks which might possibly belong to a structure such as that at Priene.[5] At the east end, as at Ephesus, a curved wall has been built across at a late date to form a nearly circular area for entertainments of the Roman type; gladiatorial shows are mentioned in the inscriptions. The blocks along the top of this wall are pierced, mostly two to a block, with holes going through from the upper surface to the front face, as if to hold ropes. The writer has seen no explanation of these, nor any parallel elsewhere.

The stadium was the scene of all the athletic and most of the other contests in the various festivals held in the city. These festivals were very numerous in Roman times and naturally varied greatly in reputation. Some were modelled on the great games of classical Greece, especially the Olympic and Pythian games, and had the same name, organization, and prizes; thus we find 'Olympic' games celebrated all over Asia Minor. But this could only be done with permission from Rome, and was considered a great privilege. At Aphrodisias we have Pythian but not Olympic games. Others were instituted in honour of, and with the consent of, the Emperor, like the Gordianeia at Aphrodisias. Others again were endowed by a private citizen, and commonly bore his name; these carried less glory and were often restricted to men of the city itself, or of a limited region. The others were normally open. The prizes in the first class consisted merely of a wreath of leaves; but just as a victory at Wimbledon is worth far more to the winner than the actual prize-money, so an Olympic victor might expect to be handsomely treated in his own city. In the smaller games the prizes were in cash. Apart from the normal athletic contests—foot-races, wrestling, boxing, pancration (a kind of unarmed combat), and the pentathlon—a great variety of other events were included. At Aphrodisias we hear of competitions in tragedy, comedy, satyric drama, flute- and harp-playing, oratory, and the war-dance; there were prizes also for heralds, trumpeters, and, as mentioned above, sculptors. Second and third prizes were normally given only for the non-athletic events; in athletics victory was the thing that mattered. Horse- and chariot-racing took place separately in the hippodrome; such races are mentioned at Aphrodisias, but the hippodrome has not been located.

Just to the south of the temple is the newly-discovered odeum (H); its state of preservation is almost perfect (Pl. 64). Built in the second century A.D., it was later damaged, perhaps by an earthquake, and repaired. In plan it closely resembles the council-house at Nysa, and may well have been used on occasion as an assembly-room (below, p. 223 n. 1). The floor of the 'orchestra' is elegantly decorated, but is now permanently under water. On the front of the platform is an incomplete inscription referring surprisingly to a palaestra; the significance of this is obscure.

Adjoining the outer wall of the odeum on the west is an interesting heroum, that is the tomb of a distinguished citizen accorded the privilege of burial within the city. It is circular, with three steps leading up to a platform which supported an octagonal arrangement of seats surrounding a large sarcophagus and an altar decorated with Cupids carrying flowers and fruit. The heroum is evidently older than the odeum, since the wall of the latter slightly overlaps it. To the north of the odeum the great quantities of unfinished statues and marble chips found by the excavators show that the building here was a sculptor's workshop; the building itself is, however, poorly preserved.

Beside the odeum on the west is a complicated group of ruins including a peristyle court with blue marble columns, dubbed by the excavators 'the Bishop's Palace' (J). From a lead seal found in it with an inscription referring to the Metropolis (or Metropolitan) of Caria, and from its convenient proximity to the church which succeeded the temple, it seems not improbable that this may have been the residence of the bishop of Aphrodisias-Staurupolis.

The acropolis (A), the only elevated ground on the site, is so called merely for convenience. It is not a natural hill, but simply the accumulation of the earliest levels of occupation, for this was evidently one of the first areas of settlement in prehistoric times. Trenches sunk on the western slope brought to light material dating from the Middle Bronze Age about 2000–1600 B.C., including storage vessels containing charred seeds. At a spot further to the east, called the 'Pekmez Area', even earlier sherds were found.

On the east slope of the 'acropolis' is the great theatre (G), at present in process of excavation (Pll. 69, 70). It proves to be in excellent condition, with most of the seats still in place, and is certainly one of the finest in Asia Minor. It is unusually large and had apparently the exceptional number of three diazomata; at least, an inscription refers to 'the third diazoma', though the excavations have revealed no sign of this, and it seems indeed difficult to find room for it. The stage-building was divided into two equal sections by a central barrel-vaulted corridor. It featured a colonnade running along the proscenium, behind which were a row of chambers opening onto the portico created by the columns. A great deal of sculpture was found in this area of the excavation, including a winged victory figure carrying a trophy, and all of this was part of the original stage decoration. The proscenium and all its adornments were in fact built by a freedman of Julius Caesar, Gaius Iulius Zoilus, during the thirties B.C., and the architrave inscription records that he dedicated the whole construction to Aphrodite and the people of Aphrodisias. The arrangement at the north end is peculiar. The north return wall of the stage-building is standing to a height of 16 or 17 feet (4·88 or 5·18 m.) and flanks a passage or corridor, on the other side of which is a large vaulted room. Such a room is not a normal part of a theatre, and in this case it is evidently a later addition to the original plan. Its purpose is not known; a green-room or property-room is a possibility.

The design of the theatre was modified in the reigns of Antoninus Pius and Marcus Aurelius to accommodate the animal and gladiatorial shows popular in the Roman period. The stage was widened at the expense of the orchestra, a passage to admit animals into the arena was built, and the lowest rows of seating removed, thus converting a theatre into something more akin to a bull-ring. Later still five of the doorways in the stage-building were blocked with bricks, and a façade of coloured marble, in imitation of painting, was

195

attached to the screen wall. These later periods also produced quantities of fine sculpture and several inscriptions. But it was the wall of the stage-building that caused the excavators the greatest surprise and delight; it proved to be covered with the long series of Imperial letters which was mentioned above. These are mainly concerned with the city's successful claims to the privileges of freedom and immunity under Roman rule, which allowed them to retain their traditional laws and customs, and made them not liable to pay the various taxes and liturgies which most communities contributed. They also attest the links which tied Aphrodisias and its patron goddess to several of the leading politicians at Rome in the late Republic and early Empire. Sulla regarded Venus or Aphrodite as his particular protectress, and Julius Caesar and his adopted son Octavian, the later Augustus, actually claimed family descent from the goddess.

In Byzantine times the theatre was converted into a stronghold, in the same way as happened at Miletus. Houses were erected in the lower part of the cavea, and parts of the upper cavea were dismantled. Moreover, a fortification wall was built to block the whole length of the stage-building, incorporating many sculptural and epigraphical fragments from the Roman period.

To the east of the theatre there was an open area christened the 'piazza' by the excavators (Pl. 69). This took the form of a slightly irregular rectangle surrounded by four colonnaded porticoes. An inscription of the 360s shows that the 'piazza', called a *tetrastoon*, was built by a certain Antonius Tatianus, governor of Asia. On the south side of the theatre and the *tetrastoon* an elaborate bath complex has been found, called the theatre baths (S). The central feature of this Roman building was a circular hall, with niches and small pools round it, recessed in arched apsidal niches. This room led to the caldarium on the south, and to a rectangular hall-way, also with arched niches in the walls, on the north-east. Alongside, and connected with the baths, there was a lavishly decorated basilica. All this construction probably belongs to the third century A.D.

The main agora (M) of Aphrodisias lay between the theatre and the temple to the north. This has not yet been completely excavated, but considerable progress has been made at the west end, adjoining the Baths of Hadrian. The agora itself, as usual, was surrounded by a colonnade (Pl. 67), and along the west edge lay a huge basilica over 120 metres long, with a nave over 10 metres wide flanked by aisles of about 6 metres. It was elaborately decorated with sculpture and architectural antefixes, including a series of carved balustrades originally located between the columns of the upper storey of the eastern aisle. Among the scenes depicted on these panels was the relief of Semiramis of Babylon and her husband Ninus, mentioned above (Pl. 72). The eastern edge of the agora itself, adjoining the basilica, was known as the portico of Tiberius (N), and it was here

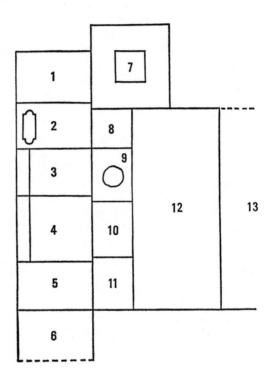

Fig. 43 Aphrodisias.
Plan of the Baths
(approximate only)

that another very important epigraphical discovery has been made, many fragments of a copy of Diocletian's edict fixing maximum prices for all sorts of products and services in the empire, and a second, unique inscription of the same period, concerned with currency and coinage. Adjoining the basilica on the west are the Baths of Hadrian (L). This is not yet completely cleared, and the identity of all the rooms is not certain. In front (1 on the plan) is a courtyard handsomely paved with black and white squares. Adjoining this on the south (Room 2) is the frigidarium; this is not heated and has a shallow pool at its west end. Room 3 is the tepidarium,

197

slightly heated by means of a hypocaust, and Room 4 is the hot room or caldarium, also with a hypocaust of which a good deal is preserved (Pl. 73). Room 10 is the praefurnium or furnace-room, with a laconicum or sudatorium (sweating-room) on either side (9 and 11 on the plan). The open court 7 has a shallow square pool in the middle. Room 8 was in all probability the apodyterium or changing-room, from which the bather might pass first to the fri̇ ' 'arium 2, then to the successively warmer rooms 3, 4, and 9, finisning perhaps with a cold plunge in the pool 7. Rooms 5 and 6 have not yet been excavated; it is likely that they, together with Room 11, formed the women's baths, which are often separate from the men's rooms; this would explain the second laconicum 11.

The tombs at Aphrodisias lay in the usual manner outside the walls. Many of the sarcophagi are very handsome, as may be seen from the specimens collected outside the museum depot. The inscriptions are mostly long, with detailed instructions as to who may be buried inside, and invoking fines and curses on anyone who may violate the tomb. The fines vary in amount up to 50,000 denarii. These epitaphs throw much interesting light on family life and social customs; one, for example, permits the owner's wife to be buried, but only if she remains his wife and produces a son.

The excavations of recent years have transformed Aphrodisias into one of the chief show-pieces of western Turkey, and it is now visited by an increasing number of visitors. Happily, the main finds, especially the quite outstanding sculpture (Pll. 75, 77, 78), are to be displayed in a newly built museum, scheduled for opening in 1979.

Notes

1 I Kings 11.5–6.
2 The Carian city of Plarasa has been located with fair probability at Bingeç, nine miles (14·5 km.) to the south-west of Aphrodisias.
3 It seems that the thief had had the effrontery to dedicate it in his own name to Artemis of Ephesus.
4 It was thought at one time, on the strength of this inscription, that Aphrodisias did for a while have the name Taurupolis, 'city of the bull'. Stephanus in fact records a city of Tauropolis in Caria, and even mentions an alliance with Plarasa; but this was in the third century B.C. and a different city must be meant. The name Staurupolis is regularly given to Aphrodisias in the Byzantine lists (though even here Taurupolis also occurs, no doubt by error).
5 See *Aegean Turkey*, pp. 170–2.

20   Hierapolis

Nowhere, even at Ephesus, is the impact of developing tourism in Turkey more striking than at Hierapolis. When the present writer first went to Pamukkale in 1939, the white cliffs, the ancient buildings, and the tombs stood deserted, and the sacred pool lay inviting the occasional visitor to a free and solitary bathe. The scene is very different now. The solitude is gone; the pool has become an adjunct of the Pamukkale Motel, surrounded by cabins and filled daily with bathers from Denizli and elsewhere; several other motels stand near the cliffs, full to capacity in the season; and the wall of the ancient baths is lined with the booths of the post-card- and souvenir-sellers. And to increase the change excavations have lately begun and are continuing. Whether all this is an improvement or not is a matter of opinion, but Hierapolis can never lose her attraction, and the excavations at least have already added greatly to the interest of the site.

When the writer's party in 1939 proposed to pitch a tent for the night, an unexpected difficulty arose; it was almost impossible to drive the pegs into the ground. In fact the level plateau on which the city stands is not earth at all, nor even rock, but a solid calcareous mass deposited in the course of ages by the lime-charged springs and streams of the region. The process still continues, and in the last two thousand years has buried the lower parts of many ancient buildings to a depth of several feet in solid stone. The spring which feeds the sacred pool has not been located, but lay presumably somewhere up the slope towards the theatre. When the water emerges from the ground, it has a temperature a little below blood-heat, making the pool comfortable for bathing; by the time it reaches the plain it has lost nearly all its heat and is freely used for drinking and for watering the fields. From the pool it issues in numerous rills, mostly a foot or so wide; these as they go deposit their lime, which gradually forms a rim on either side, so that the water runs in a

199

self-built limestone channel. Some are still flowing; many others, abandoned in the course of time, are now dry. When they reach and fall over the edge of the plateau, the lime deposit forms a shallow basin; trickling over the rim of this the water makes another basin below, then another and another, in many cases leaving clusters

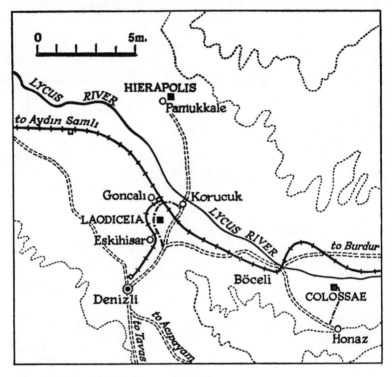

Fig. 44 Map of the Environs of Denizli

of stalactites, so that the whole cliff appears like a vast petrified cascade, slowly changing its appearance from year to year (Pl. 79). Assuming that the rate of deposit has been fairly consistent, it has been calculated that the whole mass of the plateau may have taken something like 14,000 years to accumulate. The most striking of the self-built channels runs along the length of the main street, resembling a wall rising 6 or 7 feet (1·83 or 2·13 m.) above the level of the ancient road.

The sacred pool is so called, though its sacred character is really only an assumption, based on apparent probability and the number of ancient stones lying in it. These include a long foundation and numerous column-drums and other carved blocks. The foundation shows the ground-level in Roman times, for the pool has of course changed its shape and appearance since antiquity. The spring which feeds it seems to have borne the appropriate name of Thermodon.

Hierapolis means Holy City; Stephanus of Byzantium says she is so named from the many temples she possessed; and in fact, down to the time of Augustus, the name appears officially on the coins as Hieropolis, 'Templeville'. It has been ingeniously suggested that this was not the original meaning; it is argued that the city is a Pergamene foundation, and that the kings of Pergamum (like all Hellenistic kings) normally gave to their new foundations names commemorating members of their families; it is more likely that Hierapolis was named after Hiera, or Hiero, wife of Telephus, the mythical ancestor of the Pergamenes. The name was not, however, generally so understood in later times, when we often find the two parts separately declined as adjective and noun. How many temples the city really possessed we cannot tell; certainly a great variety of deities was worshipped there, but these had not all temples. Actually, the only priests mentioned in the inscriptions are those of Cybele and the Emperors; and on the site one temple only has been identified, namely the temple of Apollo recently excavated.

Although in the past Hierapolis has widely been held to be a Pergamene foundation, recent epigraphic discoveries have shown this to be false. In the theatre a series of second- and third-century A.D. inscriptions has been found, naming the city tribes. Among these the names Seleucidos, Antiochidos, and Stratonicidos, as well as Eumenidos and Attalidos, occur, proving that the city was indeed a Seleucid foundation, later expanded under the Attalids. This is unexpected, since at first sight it appears strange that the Seleucids should have founded a second city so close to Laodicea, also in the Lycus valley. After the battle of Magnesia in 190 B.C. the region passed to the kingdom of Pergamum, and the earliest surviving inscription from Hierapolis is a decree in honour of Apollonis, mother of Eumenes II, passed on her death some time after 183.

Whether, and if so in what form, the site was previously occupied is not known, but it is evidently unlikely that so remarkable a place would be left neglected. Herodotus mentions a town of Cydrara in this neighbourhood, and later we find a city of Hydrela; the latter name, a synonym of Denizli, 'watery', suggests this region of many waters. Hydrela survived into Roman times; Cydrara, on the other hand, disappeared at an early date.

The city's subsequent history is almost a blank. It was included in the province of Asia in 129 B.C., after which time recorded events are practically confined to a succession of earthquakes. At least four of these occurred in the two centuries between Claudius and Alexander Severus; the worst was apparently that under Nero in A.D. 60, and it was probably after this that with help from the Emperor the city was rebuilt in its present form. It is thought that the city-centre, whether at that or some other time, was shifted a short distance southwards; the chief evidence for this is the scanty traces of an earlier theatre in a hollow in the hillside to the east of the northern city-entrance. There is, however, no reason why the theatre should not be situated outside the city wall, as it was, for example, at Mylasa and Perge in Pamphylia.

The highly prized title of Neocorus was awarded apparently by Caracalla. Otherwise nothing more stirring appears to have occurred than an occasional visit from the Emperor. Hadrian was probably there in A.D. 129, and Caracalla in 215, and a visit by Valens in 370 is actually recorded. There was a separate colony of Jews at Hierapolis, to some extent self-organizing, and Christianity, as at Laodiceia and Colossae, was early introduced. The apostle Philip lived there with his daughter at the end of his life, and his tomb was shown to visitors; it is so again now, having been recently uncovered by the Italian excavators (below, pp. 208–9). The bishop of Hierapolis was promoted to the rank of metropolitan by Justinian in the sixth century.

The names of the citizens, as they appear in the inscriptions, are almost exclusively Greek or Roman, and the city constitution was the normal Greek, though the tribes appear to have had Phrygian names. The religion, on the other hand, had a strong admixture of the Anatolian. Most of the familiar Greek deities were worshipped, but in numerous cases they were merged with earlier local gods. The patron deity was Apollo, identified with the Phrygian Lairbenus, a sun-god whose sanctuary lay some twenty miles (32 km.) to the north-east of Hierapolis. Similarly Leto, mother of Apollo, was assimilated to the Anatolian mother-goddess Cybele. Zeus also had at Hierapolis the non-Greek epithets Bozius and Troius, and the strange Ephesian Artemis had her worshippers too. Coins show the moon-god Mên, a wholly Anatolian deity. Of the purely Greeks gods, the cults of Poseidon the Earth-Shaker and Pluto, lord of the underworld, are naturally explained by the physical features of the country.

It was indeed this last that gave Hierapolis its chief claim to fame in antiquity, namely the Plutonium. This remarkable phenom-enon is described by several ancient authors. Strabo, writing as an eyewitness, says:

> The Plutonium is an orifice under a slight ridge of the hill which rises above, large enough to admit a man, and very deep. In front of it is a fenced enclosure some 50 feet square, filled with a thick mist, so that the floor is barely visible. Outside the enclosure the air is free of the mist, so long as no wind is blowing, and a man may approach safely; but for any living creature which enters inside death is instantaneous. Bulls, for example, which are taken in collapse and are brought out dead; we ourselves sent in small birds which at once fell lifeless. The eunuchs of Cybele, however, are immune to the extent that they can approach the orifice and look in, and even penetrate for some distance, though not nor-mally without holding their breath.

The historian Dio Cassius visited the spot in the second century, and observes similarly that the vapour destroys all living creatures except the eunuchs; 'I tested it', he says, 'by means of birds, and I bent over and saw the vapour; it is enclosed in a sort of cistern, and an auditorium had been built over it'. Later, in the fifth century, a visit by the physician Asclepiodotus is reported; he took the pre-caution of wrapping his cloak two or three times round his face, so as to breathe the pure air he took in with him, and was able to follow the course of the hot water for most of the way in, but could not reach the end because the ground was cut away by a stream of water too deep for a man to pass. The orifice is described as lying under the temple of Apollo.

The rediscovery of this remarkable phenomenon is no doubt the most striking result of the Italian excavations. The temple of Apollo had become almost completely buried; on clearing its south side the Plutonium came to light, corresponding in all essentials to the ancient accounts. There is, as Strabo says, a small shelf in the hillside, on which the rear part of the temple rests; in this shelf, at the foot of the temple on the right, is a dark chamber some 9 feet (2.74 m.) square, with a paved floor; at the back a gap 3 feet (·91 m.) wide shows the natural rock split by a deep cleft in which is a fast-flowing stream permeated with a strong-smelling gas. The chamber is entered by an arched doorway (Pl. 82) from which three steps lead down. The door has been partially blocked by the excavators for security reasons, and the visitor may hear but not see the rushing water. In front is a rectangular courtyard; in the floor of this, and in many other places, are cracks from which the gas emerges; it has a very strong sharp smell, which catches the throat and brings tears to the eyes. A single good sniff incapacitates for some minutes, though it does not kill; however, whether by coincidence or otherwise, the writer remembers on a recent visit seeing a dead sparrow lying in the courtyard.[1]

From the ancient accounts related above it appears that the Plutonium underwent a number of changes. Strabo makes no mention of a temple, and it seems clear from his words that none existed in his time, only the opening in the hillside with an enclosure in front. How this came to be filled with mist is not clear; no such effect is noticeable today, nor is this peculiarity mentioned in the later accounts. By the second century the place had evidently been converted into a regular tourist attraction, with provision for spectators. Finally, after the temple was built, the place was given the form which it has today.

As in all cities of any size, periodical festivals with athletic and musical contests were celebrated at Hierapolis. In Imperial times we find Olympic, Pythian, and Actian games, modelled on and given nominal equality with the famous festivals in Greece; we hear also of another festival called by the unusual name of 'the games by the Chrysorrhoas'. This stream, 'flowing with gold', is identified with the torrent on the north side of the city beyond the necropolis; that it ever really bore gold is uncertain, but is considered not impossible. The curious thing is that no sign of any stadium has ever been seen at Hierapolis, though there must evidently have been one; since there seems no place for it on the plateau, it presumably lay down below on the plain. Gladiatorial and wild-beast shows were given in the theatre, as is indicated by reliefs found there.

But Hierapolis was not merely a resort for tourists and theatregoers. Most of her prosperity came from her industries, which were unusually numerous and varied. Commercial companies recorded in inscriptions include not only guilds associated with the woollen industry, such as dyers, purple-dyers, wool-washers, and carpet-weavers, but also nail-makers and coppersmiths. These were organized companies, and were often entrusted with the upkeep of their members' tombs. Exports included also a special kind of marble peculiar to Hierapolis; its nature and varied colouring were due,

61 Nysa. The Theatre
62 Nysa. The Library

63 Aphrodisias.
General view of site

64 Aphrodisias.
Odeum

65 Aphrodisias. The Stadium
66 Acharaca. The Charonium (?)

67　Aphrodisias. Sarcophagus

68　Aphrodisias. Temple of Aphrodite

69 Aphrodisias. Theatre and fourth-century piazza

70 Aphrodisias. Theatre

71   Aphrodisias. Columns of the Agora

72   Aphrodisias. Section of carved balustrade depicting Ninus in Roman dress

73   Aphrodisias. Baths of Hadrian

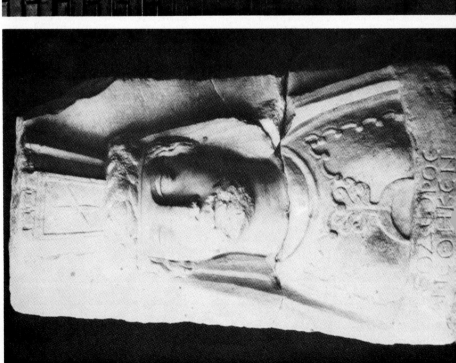

74 Aphrodisias. Bust of Aphrodite of Aphrodisias

75 Aphrodisias. Statue of Flavius Palmatus, vicar of Asia (fifth century A.D.)

76 Hierapolis. Triumphal Arch and Main Street

77 Aphrodisias. Sarcophagus
78 Aphrodisias. Bull's Head

79   Hierapolis. Petrified Cascades
80   Hierapolis. The Sacred Pool

81 Hierapolis. Sculpture in the Theatre
82 Hierapolis. The Plutonium

83 Hierapolis. Burial tumuli
84 Laodiceia. Water-tower, showing remains of pipes

85   Laodiceia. The Aqueduct
86   Amyzon. The City Wall

it was said, to the hot water entering the quarries and permeating the stone. Oddly enough, with one possible exception, this stone does not seem to have been used for the buildings of the city itself.

Among the distinguished citizens of Hierapolis the best known is the sophist Antipater, who was chosen by the Emperor Septimius Severus to educate his sons, the future Emperors Caracalla and Geta. His family tomb stands in the northern necropolis, though his own grave has not been identified.

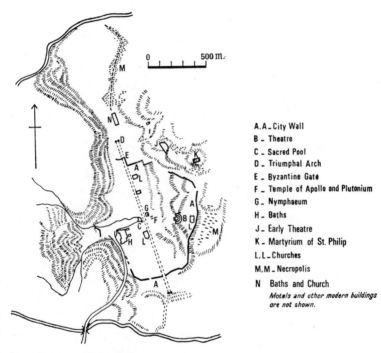

A.A_City Wall
B _ Theatre
C _ Sacred Pool
D _ Triumphal Arch
E _ Byzantine Gate
F _ Temple of Apollo and Plutonium
G _ Nymphaeum
H _ Baths
J _ Early Theatre
K _ Martyrium of St. Philip
L,L_Churches
M,M _ Necropolis
N   Baths and Church
Motels and other modern buildings are not shown.

Fig. 45 Plan of Hierapolis

The city as it stands today is wholly of the Roman period. It has been thought that it represents a more or less complete rebuilding after an earthquake, possibly that of A.D. 60, with financial help from the Emperor. However this may be, nothing remains of the original Hellenistic city. Even the city wall is no exception; in respect of height, strength, and quality of masonry it is unimpressive. Under the *pax Romana* powerful fortifications were not called for, and the

205

Holy City was protected by its sanctity; it is suggested that the wall was built rather against marauders than against enemies.

The backbone of the city is formed by a street over a mile long running dead straight from end to end; only the northern part is at all well preserved. At either end, north and south, this street was prolonged outside the city wall for some 170 yards (155 m.) to a monumental gateway; that on the north (D) is in good condition. It consists of a triple arch flanked by two round towers (Pl. 76), and is shown by its inscription, of which fragments have been found, to have been dedicated to Domitian in A.D. 84–85. Just inside the gate on the east is a small Byzantine chapel with the base of the altar remaining in the apse; and close beside the gate on the west the excavators have cleared and restored the handsome tomb of a certain Flavius Zeuxis, a merchant who, as the inscription records, had made seventy-two voyages round Cape Malea to Italy. Between the gate and the city wall the street is flanked by private houses, some of which have been recently excavated. The corresponding monumental gateway at the south end of the street is now mostly destroyed.

The newly discovered temple of Apollo (F) lies on the sloping ground between the sacred pool and the theatre. It faces south-west and is approached by a broad flight of steps. The front part stands on a podium 7 feet (2·13 m.) high, the rear part on the natural rock. The temple itself is unusually short in relation to its width, measuring some 60 by 45 feet (18·3 by 13·7 m.); it comprises a pronaos and a cella which is actually broader than it is long. There was originally a row of unfluted columns in front, probably six in number. The excavation was much hindered by the exhalations of gas; this inconvenience was remedied in antiquity in an interesting way. The blocks of the substructure were so placed as to leave gaps two inches (51 mm.) wide between them, thus allowing the gas to escape at the side of the temple. This arrangement is especially evident on the left flank of the podium.

Below the temple on the right is the grotto of the Plutonium described above. It is integrally connected with the temple by a pavement running over the grotto; on this pavement are lying four blocks forming part of a circular base whose purpose has not been explained. The back of the temple is divided by a narrow space from a flight of steps belonging to another building which at the time of writing has not been excavated.

As it stands the temple is not earlier than the third century A.D., and is largely constructed of reused material; much of this is likely to have come from an earlier building on the spot. When a temple was first erected here is uncertain; as was mentioned above, there seems to have been none in Strabo's day. Among the reused blocks are several bearing inscriptions; these include a letter-oracle of the familiar type,[2] and at the north corner of the cella a long text recording an oracle rendered on the occasion of a pestilence affecting Hierapolis and many other cities. This was probably the appalling plague which afflicted the whole of the Empire during the reign of Marcus Aurelius in the second century. The god recommends, as usual, sacrifices to various deities, with especial attention to Apollo of Claros and Apollo Careius, and adds, rather surprisingly, 'for you are sprung from me and from Mopsus the protector of your city'. Mopsus the seer was at home at Claros in the distant past after the Trojan War, and so remote an ancestry for a city founded in the middle Hellenistic age may savour of exaggeration; at the same time, Mopsus appears on coins of Hierapolis, where he is associated with another legendary figure, Torrhebus, son of Atys. Torrhebus was also, we are told, the name of a city in Lydia, and on her territory was a mountain with a sanctuary of Carius—clearly the same as Careius. The hero Torrhebus, wandering one day by a lake, heard the voices of the Muses and from them learnt music, which he afterwards taught to the Lydians. The lake is identified with the lake of Gölcük just below the main summit of Mt Tmolus above Sardis, some seventy miles (113 km.) north-west of Hierapolis. Evidently then, the Hierapolitans had invented for themselves a legendary origin involving Mopsus and Apollo Clarius, Torrhebus and Apollo Careius. Since the coins in question are dated about the middle of the second century A.D., it is likely that they were issued in consequence of this same oracle. On the other hand, it is remarkable that among the hundreds of delegations to the oracle of Claros recorded from Imperial times not a single one is from Hierapolis.

A short distance to the west of the temple is the nymphaeum (G). This is a solid building with a back wall and two side walls enclosing a water-basin approached from the front by a flight of steps. A broad ledge runs all round the interior; below the ledge are five semicircular recesses in the wall, three at the back and one on each side, and above each recess is a rectangular niche originally crowned by a pediment. In the middle niche at the back is a pipe-hole by which the water was admitted. It is likely that the water came, not from the hot spring, but from a reservoir on the hill outside the city wall on the east. The whole building was richly decorated, and many handsome architectural pieces have been excavated.

207

Further up the hillside is the theatre (B), large and well preserved, with a frontage of over 300 feet (91 m.) The cavea is in exceptionally good condition, with about fifty rows of seats and eight stairways dividing them into seven sections; there is a single diazoma, to which a vaulted passage, or vomitorium, leads on each side. The number of stairways is not doubled above the diazoma, as was often done. In the middle of the cavea is a semicircular 'Royal Box', and the orchestra is surrounded by a six-foot (1·83 m.) wall. The stage-building, long and narrow, is standing in large part, but the decoration of the stage-wall has collapsed into the orchestra, and has had to be cleared away in the excavations, which have revealed the stage and the orchestra. The stage is about 12 feet (3·66 m.) high, with round niches in its front wall; in its back wall—that is the front wall of the stage-building—are the usual five doors, with arched windows high above them. This wall, the back of the stage, was originally adorned with three superposed rows of columns, the lowest row unfluted on octagonal bases, and further decorated by statues and by friezes representing mythological scenes. In these Dionysus is as usual prominent; one scene shows his birth, with his mother Semele reclining on a couch attended by servants, one of whom is washing the infant with water issuing from a rock-face; others show the god himself riding in his car and accompanied by Maenads; in one case (Pl. 81) the car is drawn by horses, but in another by the more usual leopards. Another block carries the interesting scene—not yet, to the writer's knowledge, explained—which is shown in Fig. 46.

Although the cavea is slightly more than a semicircle, the building is of Roman type, not a converted Greek theatre; the earlier theatre lay much farther to the north. An inscription from the stage-building shows that it was extensively restored in the Severan period, and it was dedicated to Apollo and the Emperors by a rich citizen, who carried out the restoration 'with the help of his own farm-hands'. Another block lying in the orchestra refers to a gift by a lady of 600 feet of something unspecified. And in the wall of the diazoma, at the middle point, is a metrical inscription greeting the city of Hierapolis as 'foremost land of broad Asia, mistress of nymphs, adorned with streams of water and all beauty'. Another inscription records further restoration in the mid-fourth century.

Somewhere in the southern part of the city the agora is presumed to have lain, but owing chiefly to the thick deposit of lime its exact position has not been determined.

One of the most striking of the Italian excavators' discoveries is that of the Martyrium of St Philip (K), who, as was mentioned above, ended his life at Hierapolis. A simplified plan of the building is shown in Fig. 47. From the central octagonal chamber six rectangular rooms open off, and the whole is surrounded by a row of smaller rectangular chambers entered from outside. A broad stairway leads up from the south-east. In the middle of each side a door leads through to the central chamber, at the back of which

Fig. 46 Hierapolis. Relief in the Theatre

is the semicircular synthronus.[3] No altar has been found, but in the floor of the synthronus is a round hole which is supposed to have held a lectern. The building is not a church, but was used for commemorative services and the recital of panegyrics on the saint's feast-day. The small outer chambers served no doubt to accommodate the pilgrims (or some of them) who assembled on the festal occasion. The martyrium would be expected to contain the saint's tomb, but this has not been discovered. Erected early in the fifth century, the building had a short life and was destroyed little more than a hundred years later.

Among other buildings it is worth mentioning the large Roman bath building which stands on the visitor's right as he approaches the site from the west. This was presumably served by the mineral springs and accommodated not only local people but also visitors to the spa. Another bath building, to which a church was added in early Byzantine times, lay beyond the Arch of Domitian outside the city on the north (N). In addition, there were a number of other churches of the fourth to sixth centuries A.D. in different parts of the city (L), which was clearly flourishing at this period.

The necropolis (M) is one of the most extensive in Asia Minor. No fewer than 1,200 tombs have been counted, and over 300 epitaphs have been read and published. The two principal groups

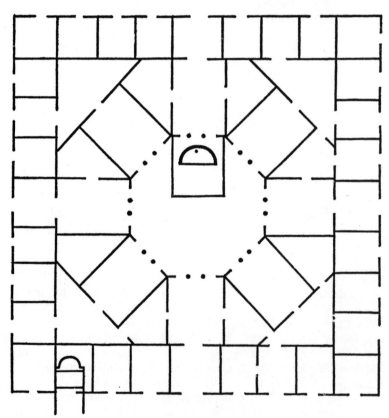

Fig. 47 Hierapolis. Plan of the Martyrium of St Philip

are on the slope outside the wall on the east and lining the street beyond the city gates on the north. In the latter case especially the tombs are closely packed, jostling one another in the most picturesque confusion; a walk along this street on a moonlight night is an experience to be remembered. The epitaphs, however, recall a time when there was less congestion; many of them refer to a garden or other area around the tomb; one insists that the tomb shall not be overshadowed, another that the approach shall be kept clear even if the adjoining ground is occupied. A feature peculiar to Hierapolis is the so-called *stephanoticum*, a sum of money left in charge of some official body, often one of the guilds, the interest to be used for laying a wreath on the tomb each year on a specified day. In one case a Jew requires that this shall be done on the feasts of Unleavened Bread and Pentecost. The sum so bequeathed varies greatly, from 150 to 2,500 denarii. Most epitaphs provide for a heavy fine for violation of the prescribed conditions, and one adds a comprehensive curse:

may he who commits transgression, and he who incites thereto, have no joy of life or children, may he find no land to tread nor sea to sail, but childless and destitute, crippled by every form of affliction let him perish, and after death may he meet the wrath and vengeance of the gods below. And the same curses on those who fail to prosecute him.

Many of the tombs consist of a solid base or substructure on which were set one or more sarcophagi; others are larger and more impressive, but the most interesting are perhaps the tumulus-tombs, which have been recently cleared and restored by the excavators. These are among the earliest at Hierapolis, and may well be of Hellenistic date. Like the vastly larger tumuli at Sardis, they comprise a circular wall at the base, with a cone of earth above, surmounted by a phallus-stone or other 'prophylactic emblem'. In the centre is the vaulted funeral chamber, equipped normally with stone benches for the dead body. Some of the tumuli are entered by a door in the circular wall and a short flight of steps down to the door of the inner chamber; others, however, have no entrance in the outer wall, so that either it was not envisaged that the tomb would be opened again after the original burial, or, if it were, access to the door of the chamber must have been gained by digging through the cone of earth (Pl. 83).

211

Notes

1 On a further visit in 1970 the writer was shocked to find not only that a placard had been erected absurdly labelling the place the Pit of Evil Spirits, but much worse, that the court was strewn with the rotting and malodorous corpses of a dog, a cat, and other small creatures, presumably placed there to illustrate the lethal properties of the place. The stench was horrible. Who was responsible for this repulsive idea the writer cannot say, but it can hardly be expected to be tolerated for long.
2 See *Turkey's Southern Shore*, p. 141.
3 Normally an apsidal recess with rows of seats for the bishop and presbyters.

21   Laodiceia and Colossae

By comparison with Hierapolis the ruins of her neighbour Laodiceia are somewhat unspectacular. Among the crowds of summer visitors to Pamukkale not one in a hundred makes his way to Laodiceia; yet the site is not without interest, though apart from a small excavation, restricted to the nymphaeum, it remains untouched.

Like Stratoniceia, Laodiceia was a foundation of a Hellenistic king, though there is some doubt as to which king. One tradition said that Antiochus I, king of Syria, saw in a dream three women, in whom he recognized his mother, wife, and sister, each desiring him to found a city in Caria; he therefore founded three, one of which he named after his sister Laodice. The other two were Nysa and Antiocheia. This sister, however, is not otherwise known to have existed, and most scholars prefer the alternative account by which the foundation was made by Antiochus II in honour of his wife Laodice. He acted, it was said, in accordance with the command of Zeus transmitted by an oracle of Apollo. In this case the foundation must date between 261 B.C., when his reign began, and 253, when he divorced Laodice. It is further recorded, on somewhat dubious authority, that the site was previously occupied by a village called at first Diospolis, then Rhoas. The former name, City of Zeus, may in fact preserve the memory of an earlier sanctuary on the site, for Zeus was the principal deity of Laodiceia.

The site was well chosen, at the junction of the great route up the Maeander valley and the road to the south-east to Pisidia and the coast, in a region, moreover, exceptionally well watered; the Lycus, a considerable tributary of the Maeander, is little over a mile distant, and the two streams, the Asopus and the Caprus, which pass close in either side of the city, maintain a flow of water throughout the year. Only in such a desirable neighbourhood could three cities, Hierapolis, Laodiceia, and Colossae, support themselves so close together. There was, however, one ever-present disadvantage; this

213

country lies in an earthquake belt, and disasters from this cause were frequent.

For the first two centuries of her existence Laodiceia has little individual history; not until the first century B.C. did she acquire any considerable importance. By the treaty of Apamea in 188 the whole of this region was attached to the kingdom of Pergamum, and in 129 was included in the province of Asia. In the first Mithridatic War (88–85) Laodiceia was among the comparatively few who resisted the king and was besieged; the defence was conducted by the Roman commander Quintus Oppius, who had retired thither with an assortment of troops, and the city was eventually relieved, though not without suffering serious damage.

In 50 B.C. Cicero, as governor of Cilicia, resided at Laodiceia for ten weeks conducting judicial business; for the city was at that time the capital of the *conventus* of Cibyra. Ten years later Labienus arrived at the head of his Parthian troops. Most cities submitted quietly to him, but at Laodiceia an influential citizen by name Zeno persuaded his countrymen to resist. What happened is not known, but his courageous action was rewarded soon after by Mark Antony, who appointed his son Polemo to the kingship of an extensive area in the south, and later also of Pontus on the Black Sea coast. On other Laodiceans Antony conferred the great privilege of Roman citizenship; it was usual, when this was done, for the recipient to add to his own name the name of his benefactor, producing an awkward mixture of Greek (or Anatolian) and Roman; at Laodiceia names such as Marcus Antonius Zeno are frequent, for the privilege extended to the man's descendants in perpetuity.

It is no surprise to learn that there was in the city at this time a flourishing colony of Jews. Their freedom of worship was guaranteed by the city authorities, but even so they were not entirely free from victimization. It was their habit to collect every year a sum in gold to be forwarded to Jerusalem; in 62 B.C. the Roman governor issued a veto and the money was confiscated to the public treasury.

In A.D. 26 Laodiceia was among the cities of Asia who competed for the honour of erecting a temple to the Emperor Tiberius, but was turned down as lacking sufficient resources; the privilege was awarded to Smyrna. This apparent poverty was only comparative; at least, when in A.D. 60 the city was badly damaged by an earthquake, it was able to recover without help from the Emperor.

But the time of greatest prosperity for Laodiceia came towards the end of the second century, and it was then, under the Emperor

Commodus, that she at last received the coveted title of neocorus, 'Temple-Warden'. This was granted, no doubt, in respect of a temple of Commodus in the city. As is well known, when an emperor died, he was, by decree of the Senate, either deified or condemned to oblivion; in the latter case his name was ordered to be erased from all public monuments throughout the Empire. This was Commodus' fate on his death in 192 (though the decision was reversed a few years later), and Laodiceia was deprived of her title of Temple-Warden; in a recently discovered inscription the word *neocorus* has been erased and the more banal epithet 'Emperor-loving' substituted. The precious title was, however, given back some time later by Caracalla, and Laodiceia became 'Temple-Warden of Commodus and Caracalla'.

Coins and inscriptions of Laodiceia reveal the existence of numerous cults of the familiar Greek gods. Among these Zeus holds the first place. He was worshipped under two titles, Laodicean Zeus and Zeus Aseis. This latter epithet is unique and its meaning uncertain; it has been compared with the Arabic *aziz* ('powerful', later used to translate 'saint') and supposed to indicate a Syrian element in the population introduced at the time of the city's foundation by a king of Syria. Another non-Greek deity was the Anatolian moon-god Mên, whose cult was widespread in Asia Minor. Cults of the deified Rome and the Emperors were normal; less usual is the mention of a priest of the City, that is of the personified Laodiceia. Apollo occurs principally in connexion with the oracle at Claros in Ionia; the recent excavations on that site have revealed hundreds of records of delegations sent year after year by a great variety of cities to consult the god and sing hymns in his honour, and Laodiceia is among the most faithful clients. Her delegation was regularly headed by the prophet of Pythian Apollo; he was, surprisingly, always a boy or youth, and was accompanied by his father (orphans were not eligible) who made the actual consultation of the oracle, while the son joined in the hymns. His title of prophet does not imply an oracle of Pythian Apollo at Laodiceia itself; his function was rather to report the oracles of Clarian Apollo.

Christianity was introduced in this region during the lifetime of St Paul by his companion Epaphras of Colossae; in the Epistle to the Colossians more than one reference is made to Laodiceia, where no doubt the acceptance of the new faith was assisted by the presence of a Jewish colony. In Revelation, Laodiceia is one of the Seven Cities of Asia; from the letter addressed to her it appears

215

that the wealth of the citizens had led to a lukewarm attitude towards the new religion: 'I know thy ways, thou art neither hot nor cold; therefore will I spew thee from my mouth'. The city was nevertheless the seat of a bishopric, and in the fourth century was the scene of an important Ecumenical Council. Its prosperity continued into the fifth century, but was shattered by a devastating earthquake in 494; although the city existed until the Turkish conquest in the fifteenth century, it seems never to have really recovered from this disaster.

Among the products of Laodiceia one is outstanding—her wool. This was reckoned softer even than that of Miletus, and was remarkable for its raven-black colour, attributed by Vitruvius to the water which the sheep drank.

The ruins stand on and around a flat-topped hill between the villages of Eskihisar and Goncalı, six miles (9·65 km.) south of Hierapolis and ten miles (16·1 km.) west-north-west of Colossae. They may be reached by a road turning off the road to Pamukkale just after it branches from the Uşak highway, close beside the Arı Tuğla-Kiremit factory, or from the other end of the same road at the village of Korucuk. A ring-wall, of which some traces remain on the east side, was carried round the rim of the plateau, enclosing an area of about a square kilometre; the hill was accordingly not merely an acropolis, but contained the whole city. There were three gates in the wall, on the north-west, north, and east. Of the northern gate little survives, but the eastern gate is better preserved. It was called the 'Syrian Gate'. The road leading out from it was lined in the usual fashion by tombs, among which was that of the sophist Polemo; it is said that he was buried in it, by his own wish, while still alive; as the door was being closed, 'Make fast, make fast', cried the dying man; 'let the sun never see me reduced to silence'. This was not the Polemo mentioned above, but a later member of the same family. He was a rich and proud man, who habitually travelled in a chariot with silver reins, and is said to have spoken to cities as a superior, to kings as by no means an inferior, and to gods as an equal. He had a house in Smyrna, and on one occasion Antoninus, then governor of Asia and afterwards Emperor, chose it as his residence while its owner was away. Polemo, unaware of this, returned late one night and was highly indignant at being excluded from his own home; without more ado he turned the governor out to find lodging elsewhere. Antoninus remembered this and later when as Emperor he received Polemo in Rome, he embraced him and said, 'Find Polemo a lodging—and see that nobody turns him out'. Antoninus Pius was of course one of the 'good Emperors'.

On the opposite side of the city is the Ephesian Gate—so called, though the name is not ancient. It had the familiar form of a triple arch flanked by towers and was dedicated to Domitian (A.D. 81–96). Fellows in 1838 saw remains of a paved road leading from the gate to a bridge of Roman construction crossing the Asopus; this bridge still survives in part. Here too the road is lined with sarcophagi.

At the southern end of the plateau is the stadium, running northwest and south-east. It was dedicated to Vespasian in A.D. 79 by a rich citizen, the ceremony of consecration being performed by the then proconsul of Asia, the father of the future Emperor Trajan. The building is remarkable for its exceptional length of some 380 yards (347·5 m.), or twice the length of the stadium foot-race; as at Aphrodisias, both ends are curved. These features are explained by the name 'amphitheatral stadium' which is given to the building in the inscriptions; that is, it was intended not only for the athletic contests conducted in a normal stadium, but also for the gladiatorial shows for which amphitheatres were designed. Cicero in 50 B.C. refers to these performances at Laodiceia. The present state of preservation is not more than fair; several rows of seats are visible on either side.

Close against the eastern end of the stadium are the solid remains of a large building which has been variously supposed to be a gymnasium or baths. The fragmentary dedication to the Emperor Hadrian and his wife Sabina records that certain persons (probably the city authorities) consecrated the —, then tantalizingly breaks off. Since the building has not the normal form of a gymnasium, the alternative identification is probably to be preferred. This is to some extent confirmed by the presence of a water-tower at its southern corner, still standing some 16 feet (4·88 m.) high; its eastern side is now broken away, revealing a number of water-pipes running vertically up its core (Pl. 84). But this tower did not only supply the adjoining building; it furnished water to other parts of the city, notably the nymphaeum. The water came by an aqueduct from the south, of which more will be said below. At the west foot of the tower stands an unfluted column, which is all that remains of a fountain-house constructed about the same time as the stadium by a certain Hedychrous.

Some 100 yards (91·4 m.) to the north, at G on the plan, is a small theatre-like building with five or six rows of seats visible; this has been hesitantly identified as an odeum, but is perhaps more

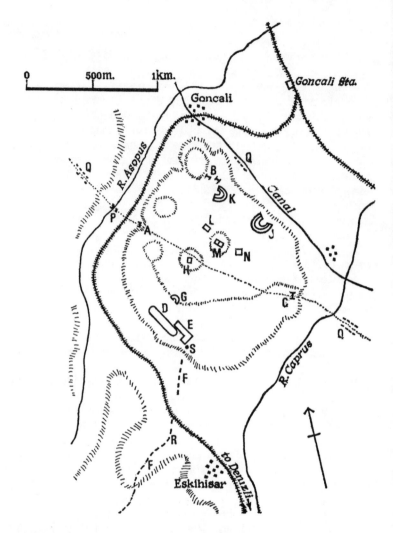

Fig. 48 Plan of Laodiceia

A – 'Ephesus Gate'
B – 'Hierapolis Gate'
C – Syrian Gate
D – Stadium
E – Gymnasium
F – Aqueduct

G – Odeum or
        Council-House
H – Nymphaeum
J – Large Theatre
K – Smaller Theatre
L – Ionic Temple

M,N – Unidentified
          Buildings
P – Bridge
Q – Sarcophagi
R – Clearing-Basin
S – Water-Tower

likely a council-chamber.[1] It has not been excavated, and in its present condition is unimpressive.

The city possessed two theatres, in the north-eastern slope of the plateau; both are above average size. The larger, J, faces north-east; most of its seats are preserved, though somewhat disarranged. The front wall of the Roman stage is visible, with a large shallow niche in the middle; this building would probably be interesting if it were excavated. The smaller theatre faces north-west. The upper part of the cavea is well preserved, with many rows of seats virtually complete; but the lower part is badly ruined and is now feature-less.

Nearly in the centre of the plateau, at H, is the nymphaeum which was excavated in 1961–63 by a team of French archaeologists. It was built not before the early third century A.D., and was recon-structed three or four times. Its original form is shown in the accompanying plan, Fig. 49; it is distinctive and unusual. The main feature is a square water-basin, A, with a colonnade on two sides; two semicircular fountains, B and C, adjoin it on the east and south. All these were fed from the chambers D and E, which in turn were supplied from the water-tower by the stadium. The whole was richly decorated and contained a number of statues; a full-size figure of Isis was found by the excavators and removed, and the inscribed base of the statue of a consular benefactor Anicius Asper remains in the building. At a much later date the whole structure was radically altered. The basin A was abolished and converted into a closed chamber, with a raised floor approached by a flight of four steps from the road which passed the building on the north. This chamber was used for some Christian purpose. The smaller basins B and C continued in use as fountains, but the semicircular recesses were walled off and rectangular troughs installed in front of them. The chamber E was at this time attached to a house adjoining on the south. In consequence of these changes the present appearance of the ruins is rather confused.

Of the other public buildings on the plateau most have now quite disappeared. At L an Ionic temple has been identified, but of this and the neighbouring buildings M and N nothing is now to be made out. An inscription records a Strategium, or hall for the generals, in the third century B.C.; the commissioners responsible for its con-struction are praised for ensuring that the architect and artisans should not make a high profit. The work was evidently let out, in the usual ancient fashion, under a contract for the whole job.

Among the most interesting things at Laodiceia is certainly the

219

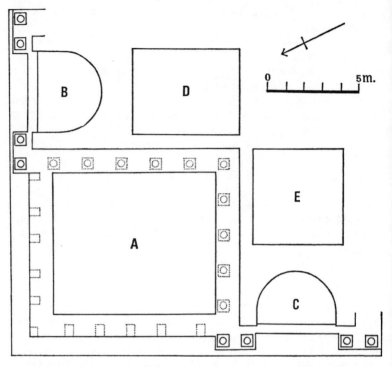

Fig. 49 Laodiceia. Plan of the Nymphaeum

aqueduct which carried water to the tower by the east end of the stadium. It was fed from the abundant spring, now called Başpınar, in the upper part of the present town of Denizli, one of the sources of the Başlı Çay (ancient Caprus). From the spring it descended to the neighbourhood of the railway station, then in the form of a covered channel, partly cut in the rock, over the intervening hills to a clearing-basin (R on the plan) on the hill opposite to the city. Up to this point the water flowed under the force of gravity: but from here it was carried, in a piped channel, under pressure across the hollow and up to the water-tower. The total length is thus about five miles (8 km.), with a fall of some 350 feet (106·7 m.).

Visitors who are not too pressed for time may find it of interest to follow the line of this aqueduct at least for some distance. To a spectator looking south from the water-tower a line of stones is clearly visible running up the hill opposite; this is the aqueduct, and makes a convenient mark to aim for. In the dip below the tower, on either side of the railway, the course of the pipe-line is marked by a row of blocks, at first a single, then a double, row; the blocks are roughly cubical, with a side of 2 to 3 feet (·61 to ·91 m.), and pierced through the middle. Many of them have also a funnel-shaped hole in the upper surface, reaching through to the pipe-hole in the middle; in the ordinary course of events these holes were plugged with round stones. But the water at Laodiceia, like that at Hierapolis, is heavily charged with lime; many of the blocks are quite thickly coated, and in a few cases the channel is completely blocked. When the flow was thus cut off, the funnel-shaped holes would enable the stoppage to be located; it was only necessary to remove the plug to discover whether the channel was dry at any point.

Some 200 yards (183 m.) to the south of the railway line, at the top of the conspicuous line of blocks at R, is a clearing-basin where the pressure begins. It is almost entirely destroyed, but apparently consisted of two chambers, a large and a small. This point is about 100 feet (30·5 m.) higher than the base of the water-tower and 160 feet (48·8 m.) above the floor of the intervening dip.

Between R and the next shoulder is a hollow; this was spanned by a built aqueduct (Pl. 85) some 450 feet (137 m.) long, some of whose arches are standing near the middle to a height of 10 feet (3·05 m.) or more. On the far (south) side of the next rise is a mass of fallen blocks belonging to another aqueduct which has completely collapsed. Round the next corner the channel is very clearly visible; in one place it is cut in the rock, with several of the covering-stones still in place. Over all this length, as far as R, there is a steady fall of approximately 1 in 170. The channel continues to be easily traceable all the way to the plain of Denizli.

The date of this interesting structure has not been determined. It has been urged that since a supply of water was essential at all times, the aqueduct must have existed almost as soon as the city; but with so much river-water available this argument loses most of its force.[2] The small built aqueducts, to judge from the quality of the masonry, can hardly be earlier than the second century A.D. They may of course be part of a later reconstruction, and the rest of the channel is really undatable; but as it stands, the aqueduct appears as a work of the Roman Imperial period.

Colossae

The third city of the Lycus valley, Colossae, had a very different history from the other two. She is first heard of in 480 B.C., when Xerxes passed through on his march across Asia Minor; Herodotus calls her 'a great city of Phrygia'. A similar judgment is given by Xenophon in relating the march of Cyrus in 401; he speaks of a large and flourishing population. But the foundation of Laodiceia in the third century was fatal to the prosperity of her neighbour; Strabo in the time of Augustus refers to Colossae as a minor city (*polisma*), and under the Empire, apart from her trade in wool, little or nothing is heard of her. Pliny's description of her as 'among the most famous towns of Phrygia' relates evidently to a much earlier period. The coinage is somewhat scanty and almost entirely of Imperial date. What the city was like in the fifth century B.C. we do not know, nor how it was governed; a king or tyrant is no doubt the most likely. In the later inscriptions, all of Roman date, it appears with a normal Greek constitution.

Christianity was early established in the city by St Paul's companion Epaphras, himself a native of Colossae, and the Epistle to the Colossians gives abundant evidence of the apostle's interest in the newly-founded church. But by about 800 the city was in complete decay and was replaced by the new town of Chonae, the modern Honaz, a few miles higher up to the south. So completely was the old name forgotten that the idea arose that the Colossians addressed by St Paul were the Rhodians, so called from their famous colossus. In the Byzantine lists the bishop is regularly recorded as of Chonae, not of Colossae.

Despite its resemblance to the Greek word *kolossos*, meaning an over-life-size statue, the name Colossae is unquestionably Anatolian. The word *kolossos* itself, as its termination indicates, was taken over by the Greeks from a pre-Greek language. At the same time, the city-name appears often in late sources in the form Colassae, and it has been suggested that this may in fact be nearer to the original Phrygian name.

The site is fixed on the left (south) bank of the Lycus some three miles (4·83 km.) north of Honaz. Herodotus says that the river disappears underground at Colossae and reappears five stades (rather over half a mile) lower down before going on to join the Maeander. In reality the city stands at the head of a narrow gorge over two miles (3·22 km.) long, but there is no indication that the river ever flowed underground at this point. Strabo says that the

222

Lycus runs underground for much of its course; and this is indeed true, but it does so above Colossae, not below it. Herodotus' statement is a characteristic example of his imperfect understanding of oral information imparted to him; he was told of the gorge and of the river's subterranean course, and combined the two to make the river run underground in the gorge.[3]

The site itself is accessible from Honaz by a road just, but only just, passable for a car. The acropolis is on a hill some 150 or 200 feet (45·7 or 61 m.) high on the north and west, but lower on the other sides; the summit is now a ploughed field. It was surrounded by a ring-wall, of which some remnants, in very poor condition, stand on the east side; many other blocks lie strewn down the slopes. The Lycus flows a short distance to the north, and the view over the valley is very fine. Towards the west end of the flat summit is a square hole faced with masonry of small stones and said to be very deep; the writer's guide claimed to have descended it on a long rope till he could no longer breathe, without reaching the bottom.

Low down on the east side is the site of the theatre. No seats or stage-building are preserved, but the hollow is unmistakable, and a tiny piece of the cavea remains at the north corner. Other blocks are lying around. As it stands, the theatre is very shallow, with room for only a dozen or fifteen rows, but the lower part is evidently buried.

On the other (north) side of the river was the necropolis. The tombs are sunk into the ground so close together that Hamilton at first mistook their lids for a pavement. Here also are (or were) visible the ruins of a large building which was perhaps the church of St Michael, one of the most distinguished in Asia. For the rest the buildings of Colossae are, in Wheler's phrase, 'by the various and potent Engines of Time, and Fate, now no more to be seen'.

Notes

1 It is often difficult to distinguish between an odeum and a council-house. The form of the building is equally appropriate for both purposes, and it is probable that in practice it served, like the theatre, for both.

2 Strabo observes that the rivers here, though causing petrifaction, are perfectly drinkable, and the writer's experience confirms this.

3 In just such a way Herodotus misunderstood what he was told of the Hittite figure in the Karabel pass near Smyrna; see *Aegean Turkey*, pp. 34–5. The historian knew little or nothing of the interior of Asia Minor from personal observation. Five stades is said to be a reasonable estimate of the length of the narrowest part of the gorge. Hamilton, who visited

Colossae in 1836, conceived the idea that the underground channel of which Herodotus speaks was formed by the continual incrustation of the sides of the gorge by the lime-charged river till they met overhead, the tunnel thus created having later been destroyed by earthquakes. This ingenious conception has found no support from later investigators.

Short Bibliography

General

R. Chandler, *Travels in Asia Minor and Greece*, 3rd edition (London 1817).

Charles Fellows, *Asia Minor* (London 1839).

C. T. Newton, *A History of Discoveries at Halicarnassus, Cnidus and Branchidae* (London 1863); a shorter version, *Travels and Discoveries in the Levant* (London 1865).

D. Magie, *Roman Rule in Asia Minor* (Princeton 1950), invaluable to scholars.

Freya Stark, *The Lycian Shore* (London 1956), chapters 6–11.

A. Laumonier, *Les Cultes Indigènes en Carie* (Paris 1958), recommended especially to scholars.

Gwyn Williams, *Turkey* (London 1967), brief and deals with the coastal parts only.

E. Akurgal, *Ancient Civilisations and Ruins of Turkey*, 4th edition (Istanbul 1977), selective and deals briefly with Caria.

Hachette *World Guides, Turkey*.

Reports on several sites discussed in this book (including Euromus, Caunus, Cnidus, Aphrodisias, and Hierapolis) have been published in the *Proceedings of the Xth International Congress of Classical Archaeology*, held in Turkey in 1973, and published in Ankara in 1978.

Readers may like to consult the detailed and appreciative review of the first edition of this book by another Turkish traveller, D. Boyd, *Journal of Hellenic Studies* 94 (1974), 253–5. Many of his suggestions have been incorporated into this revised edition; others, not without their value and interest, have been passed over.

2–3 Mylasa

A. and T. Akarca, *Milâs* (Istanbul 1954), in Turkish.

W. Radt, 'Kuyruklu Kalesi', *Istanbuler Mitteilungen* 19/20 (1969/70), 165–76.

Bibliography

4 Labraynda

Labraunda, Swedish Excavations and Researches (Lund 1969–).

5 Iasus

E. L. Hicks in *Journal of Hellenic Studies* vol. VIII; W. Judeich in *Athenische Mitteilungen* XV, 137; Italian Excavation Reports in *Annuario della Scuola in Atene* 1961 onwards, and, more recently, in *Anatolian Studies* and *Türk Arkeoloji Dergisi.*

6 Cindya and Bargylia

G. E. Bean and J. M. Cook in *Annual of the British School in Athens* 52, 96–99.

7 Stratoniceia

M. Çetin Sahin, *The Political and Religious Structure in the Territory of Stratonikeia in Caria* (Ankara 1976).

9 Halicarnassus

G. E. Bean and J. M. Cook in *Ann.Br.Sch.Ath.* 50, 85–108.

Reports on the new excavations at the Mausoleum have been published in *American Journal of Archaeology* 1973, 336–8 and 1975, 67–79; a new reconstruction of the Mausoleum is proposed by K. Jeppesen, *Istanbuler Mitteilungen* 26 (1976), 47–99. For the sculptures, mostly in the British Museum, see now G. B. Waywell, *The Free Standing Sculpture of the Mausoleum of Halicarnassus* (London 1978).

10 The Myndus Peninsula

W. R. Paton and J. L. Myres in *Journ.Hell.Stud.* XIV, 373–80 and XVI, 242–66; G. E. Bean and J. M. Cook in *Ann.Br.Sch.Ath.* 50, 108–65. As indicated in the text, W. Radt, *Siedlungen und Bauten auf der Halbinsel von Halikarnassos, Istanbuler Mitteilungen, Beiheft 3* (Tübingen 1970) is fundamental. A shorter and more popular account has been published in *Antike Welt* 6.3 (1975), 3–16.

11 Syangela

L. Robert, *Collection Froehner* I, 65–101; G. E. Bean and J. M. Cook in *Ann.Br.Sch.Ath.* 50, 112–15, 145–47, and 52, 89–96.

12 Cnidus

G. E. Bean and J. M. Cook in *Ann.Br.Sch.Ath.* 47, 171–212; new
excavation reports in *American Journal of Archaeology* 1972, 61–76
and 393–405; 1973, 413–24. There are also illustrated accounts in
Türk Arkeoloji Dergisi.

13 The Rhodian Perea

P. M. Fraser and G. E. Bean, *The Rhodian Peraea* (Oxford 1954);
J. M. Cook and W. H. Plommer, *The Sanctuary of Hemithea at
Kastabos* (Cambridge 1966).

14 Caunus

M. Collignon in *Bulletin de Correspondance Hellénique* 1877, 338–46;
A. Maiuri in *Annuario della Sc.Atene* III, 263ff.; G. E. Bean in
Journ.Hell.Stud. 1953, 10–35 and 1954, 85–110; P. Roos in *Opuscula
Atheniensia* VIII, 149–66 and IX, 60–68. P. Roos, *The Rock Tombs
of Caunus* vol. I (1972) and vol. II (1974). Recent excavation reports
are to be found in *Türk Arkeoloji Dergisi* 1970, 1973, and 1974, and
in the *Proceedings of the Tenth Congress of Classical Archaeology*,
pp. 61–7.

15 Alabanda

Etem Bey in *Comptes Rendus de l'Académie des Inscriptions* 1905–06.

16 Alinda and Amyzon

W. R. Paton and J. L. Myres in *Journ.Hell.Stud.* XVI, 238–42; E.
Fabricius in *Altertümer von Aegae* (Berlin 1889), 27–30. (Amyzon)
L. Robert in *Comptes Rendus de l'Acad.Inscr.* 1948, 431–2, 1949,
304–6 and 1953, 403–15.

17 Gerga

G. Cousin in *Bull.Corr.Hell.* 1900, 28–31; A. Laumonier in *Bull.Corr.
Hell.* 1934, 304–7 and 1936, 286–97; G. E. Bean in *Anatolian Studies*
1969, 179–82.

18 Tralles and Nysa

K. Humann and W. Dörpfeld in *Athenische Mitteilungen* XVIII, 395ff.;
W. von Diest, *Nysa and Maeandrum* (Berlin 1913).

Bibliography

19 Aphrodisias

Excavation Reports in *Amer.Journ.Arch.* 1963 onwards, and recently in *Türk Arkeoloji Dergisi* and *Anatolian Studies*. Several volumes of the detailed publication, dealing with inscriptions, sculpture, and Aphrodisias in the Byzantine period, are due to be published soon.

20 Hierapolis

W. M. Ramsay, *Cities and Bishoprics* I, 32–83; J. des Gagniers, *Laodicée du Lycos: Le Nymphée* (Paris 1969). (Colossae) W. M. Ramsay, *Cities and Bishoprics* I, 208–16.

21 Laodiceia and Colossae

Altertümer von Hierapolis (Berlin 1898); W. M. Ramsay, *Cities and Bishoprics of Phrygia* I, 84–121; Excavation Reports in *Annuario della Sc.Atene* 1961 onwards.

As with other volumes in this series it is obviously impossible to document every recent discovery, still less anticipate what will be revealed by work now in progress. Those interested should consult Machteld Mellink's reports on 'Archaeology in Asia Minor', which appear annually in the *American Journal of Archaeology*, and the reports on 'Archaeology in Western Asia Minor', published in the *Journal of Hellenic Studies, Archæological Reports* for 1971 and 1979.

Index

Acharaca, 182, 185–7
Actium, battle of, 11, 18
Ada, 7, 40, 84, 143, 161
Aegae, 163
Aelian, 44–5
Aemilius, 52
Aeolians, 4
Aëtius, 92
Agasicles, 79, 118
Agreophon, 145
Alabanda, 4, 13, 16, 36, 152–60, 161, 162
Alabandus, 152
Alâkilise, 103
Alâzeytin (Syangela), 56, 103–6
Alexander, 7, 11, 15, 37, 48, 51, 92, 114, 132, 143, 153, 177; at Alinda, 161–2; at Halicarnassus, 83–4, 86
Alexander Severus, 202
Alexandria (Egypt), 78, 121
Alexandria, name of Alinda, 162
Alinda, 4, 7, 40, 152, 161–8
Altes, 2, 3
Altınsivrisi, 129, 132
Amasis, 113
Amnistus, 132
Amorges, 50, 57
Amos, 132–3, 138
Amphictyonic Council, 153, 155
Amynanda, 103
Amyntas, 153
Amyzon, 168–70
Andanus, 63
Anthemius, 178
Anthes, 78
Antigonus I, 7, 143, 177
Antigonus III Doson, 8, 9, 15, 39
Antiocheia, name of Alabanda, 153, 154
Antiochus I, 67, 180, 213; II, 15, 39, 213; III, 16, 52, 53, 84, 93, 144, 153, 169

Antipater, 205
Antoninus Pius, 195, 216
Antonius Tatianus, 196
Antony, Mark, 10–11, 93, 182, 189, 214
Apamea, treaty of, 16, 67, 154, 213
Aphrodisias, 18, 33, 53, 69, 155, 162, 188–98
Aphrodite, 188, 189, 196; of Aphrodisias, 190; of Cnidus, 115, 119–20, 125–6; at Iasus, 53
Apollo: Careius, 207; Clarius, 207, 215; at Hierapolis, 202; at Iasus, 53; Isotimus, 153, 160; at Laodiceia, 215; Samnaios, 133; Telmisseus, 97, 101; Triopian, 4, 79, 112, 117, 119
Apollonis, 201
Apollonius of Aphrodisias, 188
Aqueduct: at Alabanda, 159; at Alinda, 167–8; at Ceramus, 36; at Iasus, 60; at Laodiceia, 217, 220–1; at Mylasa, 20
Araphisar, 156–7
Arconessus, 90
Argos, 49, 54, 58, 112
Aridolis, 152
Arion, 51
Aristagoras, 13
Aristodemus, 182
Aristonicus, 9, 63, 73, 93
Aristotle, 115
Aristotle (pseudo-), 31
Arlissis, 14
Arrian, 83, 85–6, 98, 117, 162, 163
Arselis, 13
Artaxerxes II, 121
Artemis: Astias, 53, 59, 62; Cindyas, 62–3; Ephesian, 19
Artemisia: the elder, 7, 79–80, 88; the younger, 81–2, 83
Artemisium, 14

229

Index

Asar Tepe, 132
Asarcık, 132
Asia, province, 9, 16–18, 20, 53, 59, 73, 84, 144, 202, 213
Asopus, 213, 217
Aspat, 99
Assos, 163
Assyrians, 188
Athenaeus, 19, 22
Athens, 5, 6, 14, 50, 51, 79–80, 81, 100, 113, 114, 121, 131, 135, 143
Athletics, 131, 193–4, 204
Athymbrus, 180
Attalus I, 8; III, 9, 63, 177
Attalus Adrastus, 189–90
Augustus, 11, 18, 63, 73, 75, 85, 155, 178, 189, 201, 222
Ayaklı, site of Euromus, 25
Aydın, 71n, 129, 178, 179

Baba Ada, 118
Babylon, 51, 78
Bafa, 25, 28, 48
Bağyaka, 76
Bakıcak, 34
Balıkaşıran, 113
Baltalı Kapı, 20, 22, 23
Bargylia, 8, 16, 62–6, 101, 102
Başpınar, 220
Bayır, 133, 134
Belen, 100, 101, 102
Belevi, 82
Bellerophon, 63
Bencik, 111, 113, 117
Berber Ini (B. Yatağı), 24
Betçe, 111, 117, 118
Bingeç, 198n
Bitez, 95
Bodrum, 62, 78, 80, 85, 86, 88–90, 92, 95, 98, 102, 103, 105, 106, 127
Bozburun, 132, 135, 136
Bozdağ, 92
Bozuk, 134
Bridge, Greek, 123
Brigandage, 11
Brutus, 10, 84, 93
Bryaxis, 82, 115
Burgaz, 100, 101
Bybassus, 113, 117, 136, 137, 138
Byblis, 142
Byzantium, 6, 50

Cabbage, 121
Caesarea, name of Tralles, 209
Calbis, R., 140, 141
Callipolis, 117, 130
Calynda, 79

Camirus, 128
Cappadocia, 182
Caprus, 213, 220
Caracalla, 202, 205, 215
Caria, Carians, 1ff.; boundaries, 2; customs, 3; federations, 4–5, 6, 8–9; language, 2, 3–4, 142; origin, 1, 2; 'thalassocracy', 1; tombs, 33; village-system, 4–5, 8, 68
Caryanda, 101–2
Casara, 134
Cassius, 10, 84–5, 93
Castabus, 136–8
Caunus, 6, 12n, 56, 95, 117, 128, 139–51
Cedreae, 131
Ceramus, 4, 32–6
Çeşmebaşı, 99
Chaeremon, 180
Chalcetor, 14, 16, 25, 28–9, 168
Chandler, Richard, 161
Charonium at Acharaca, 182, 186–7
Chersonese, 134, 136–7
Chios, 8
Chonae, 222
Christianity, 12, 202, 215–16, 222
Chrysaoric League, 8–9, 15, 32, 39, 68, 162
Chrysaoris, 67–8
Cibyra, 189, 214
Cicero, M. Tullius, 101, 152, 155, 158, 214, 217
Ciftekahveler, 185
Çiftlik Valley, 109
Cilicia, 10, 214
Cimon, 113, 118
Cindya, 62–3
Çine, 129, 152, 171
Claros, 207, 215
Claudius, 202
Cleopatra, 10–11
Cluvius, Roman banker, 17, 63, 155
Cnidus, 4, 6, 31, 50, 78, 79, 111–27, 143; battle of, 50, 114, 135
Codrus, 78
Coinage, 6, 18, 19, 26, 29, 33, 49, 50, 53, 54, 56, 63, 93, 98, 103, 117, 119, 152, 154, 155, 159, 161, 162, 178, 189, 190, 201, 202, 207, 215, 222
Colossae, 12, 202, 213, 216, 222–4
Commodus, 215
Conodorcondeis, 16
Conon, 50, 135
Constantine, 12
Constantine Porphyrogenitus, 134
Constantius II, 192
Conventus, 17

Cook, J. M., 30, 31, 57, 113, 127n, 136–8
Corris, 39
Cos, 4, 32, 80, 84, 90, 99, 112, 115, 117
Crassus, 140
Cratippus, 178
Crete, 1, 2, 3, 142
Crio, Cape, 114
Croesus, 5
Ctesias, 121
Cyclades, 1
Cydrara, 201–2
Cyprus, 143
Cyrus, 222
Cyzicus, 183

Dalacak, 121, 122
Dalyan, 140, 141, 146, 148
Damasus, 178
Darius, 5
Datça, 111–12, 113, 114, 117, 121, 122, 127
Daurises, 5, 38
Delian Confederacy, 5, 6, 14, 25, 28, 29, 49, 62, 68, 80, 92, 95, 98, 99, 100, 101, 103, 113–14, 130, 131, 143, 150
Delos, purification of, 1
Delphi, 19, 112, 153
Demetrius, 135, 143
Democracy at Iasus, 54; at Cnidus, 115
Denizli, 199, 202, 220
Deveboynu, 114, 117, 118
Dio Cassius, 203
Dio Chrysostom, 145
Diocletian, 12, 197
Diodorus, 83, 101, 115, 136, 137, 143, 177
Diogenes, 92
Dionysius, 85
Diotrephes, 17
Dogs, 72
Dolphin, 51, 176
Domitia, 130
Domitian, 206, 217
Dorian: hexapolis, 4, 78, 111, 128; migration, 4, 128
Dorians, 1, 5, 32, 49, 61n, 78, 112, 114, 118
Doric dialect, 79
Dorion, musician, 19–20
Duran Çiftlik, 130

Ecbatana, 51
Edrians, 68
Egypt, 113, 114

Egypt, Ptolemaic, 7–8, 15, 39, 92–3, 169
Emperor worship, 11, 23, 63, 71, 78, 85, 155, 160, 178, 214–15
Epaphras, 215, 222
Ephesus, 6, 50, 82, 143, 145, 166, 184, 189, 193, 199
Ephorus, 3
Episkopi, 98
Erechtheis, 162
Eren Dağı 136, 137
Erine, 136
Erythrae, 6
Eski Çeşme, 86
Eskihisar, site of Stratoniceia, 68, 69, 76
Eskihisar village, 216
Etrim Köy, 102, 103, 106, 110
Euboea, 152
Eudoxus, 115, 116, 120–1
Eumenes, 9, 177, 201
Eunuchs, 73–4, 203
Eupolemus, 37, 109
Euromus, 14, 16, 22, 25–7, 28, 29, 68, 168
Eusebius, 1
Eustathius, 82
Euthena, 132
Euthydemus, 17

Faustina, Empress, 183
Fellows, Sir Charles, 161, 217
Fethiye, 97, 146
Figs, 133, 140, 178
Fish, 45, 48, 60, 141, 143, 146
Fruit, unhealthy, 139

Gaffarlar, 168, 169
Galen, 139
Gebe Kilisse, 97
Gelibolu, 130, 131
Gerbekilise, 133
Gerga, 171–6
Geta, 205
Geyre, 190
Gökçeler, site of Pedasa, 95, 96, 97, 110
Göktepe, 86, 88
Göl, 99, 100, 102
Gölcük, 207
Gölenye, 133, 137, 138
Goncalı, 216
Gordian III, 189
Gordius, 98
Gorgus, 51
Goths, 12, 69
Güllük, 24, 48
Gümüşkesen, 23, 60

Index

Gümüşlük, site of Myndus, 92, 93
Gürice, 98, 101
Gyges, 13

Hacı İlyas, 22
Hadrian, 59, 68, 119, 189, 190, 202, 217
Halicarnassus, 2, 4, 5, 6, 7, 56, 57, 78–90, 91, 92, 95, 96, 97, 98, 100, 101, 102, 103, 105, 109, 111, 113, 161
Hamilton, William John, 223, 224n
Harpagus, Persian general, 5, 95, 112, 113, 142
Hecataeus, 99
Hecate, 67, 72–5, 77
Hecatomnos: dynast, 6, 14, 24, 62, 81, 83, 143; priest, 39
Helios, 72, 154
Hellenium, 113
Hemithea, 136–7
Hera, 40, 76, 77
Heracleia, 12n, 26, 56, 162, 168, 169
Heraclides of Mylasa, 13–14
Heraclitus, 85
Heraklion, 143, 147
Hermogenes, 160
Herodotus, 1, 2, 5, 18, 31, 38, 40, 41, 68, 78, 79, 80, 81, 85, 95, 102n, 110, 112, 113, 117, 142, 152–3, 201, 222, 223, 224n
Hıdırlık, 20
Hieracles, 157–8
Hierapolis, 199–212, 213, 221
Hieron, 51
Hippocrates, 139
Hisarbaşı, 18, 31
Hisarburnu, 132
Hisarönü, 136, 137
Histiaeus, 98
Homer (Iliad), 2, 49, 68, 128
Honaz, 222, 223
Honey, 109
Hyarbesytae, 16
Hybreas, 17
Hyda (Hyla), 136
Hydae, 14, 16, 25, 29–30, 37n
Hydrela, 201–2
Hygassus, 138
Hymessus, 68
Hyssaldomus, 6, 14, 24

Ialysus, 128
Iasus, 4, 6, 27, 48–61, 64, 79, 148
Idrias, 3, 68
Idrieus, 7, 38, 41, 43, 44
Idyma, 129–30
Imbrus, 140

İncekemer, 159, 171
Ionian League, 2
Ionian Revolt, 5, 13, 38, 95, 142
Ionians, 1, 4, 49, 79, 142
Isotimus, epithet of Apollo, 153, 160
Istanbul, 59, 75

Jews: at Hierapolis, 202; at Laodiceia, 214
Julius Caesar, 10, 11, 93, 155, 178, 189, 195, 196
Justinian, 202

Kafaca (Kafcı), 28
Kaplan Dağı, 102n, 110
Karaada, 90
Karadağ, 100, 101, 102
Karakuyu, site of Chalcetor, 28, 48
Karaova, 109
Karatoprak, 92
Karpuzlu, 161, 162, 168, 169
Kemerderesi, 159
Kemikler, 62
King's Peace, 6, 50, 114, 143
Kıran Dağ, 32
Kızılağaç, 103
Kızılburun, 135
Kızılyaka, 130
Knights Hospitallers, 53; castle of, 78, 82, 88–90
Koca Çay, 32
Koçarlı 168
Korazeis, 68
Körmen Limanı, 122
Korucuk, 216
Köşk, 29
Köyceğiz, 2, 129, 141, 143, 146
Koyunbaba, 93
Kozlukuyu, site of Idyma, 130
Kumbahçe, 88
Kumyer, 118, 122–3
Kuren, 48
Kurşunlu Yapı, 35
Kuyruklu Kale, 36–7

Labienus, 10, 17, 18, 22, 31, 67, 73, 77, 155, 189, 214
Labraynda, 5, 14, 15, 16, 38–47, 95
Lagina, 67, 68, 72–6, 77
Laodice, 52–3, 213
Laodiceia, 12, 178, 201, 202, 213–22
Latmus, 6, 57
Lelegians, 1, 2–3, 5, 6, 14, 56, 57, 80, 81, 84, 91, 92, 94ff., 143, 188
Lentulus, 63
Leochares, 82
Lepidus, 10
Leyna, 76

Library, at Nysa, 184
Lide, Mt., 95, 102n
Lindus, 128, 132
Lipara Is., 112, 115
Livy, 67, 154
Loboldeis, 68
Londargeis, 68
Loryma, 128–9, 132, 134, 135
Lucian, 119–20, 125
Lycia, Lycians, 3, 9, 13, 68, 84, 97, 128, 142, 144, 154
Lycus, R., 213, 222–3
Lydia, Lydians, 1, 5, 13, 18, 31, 112, 207
Lygdamis I, 79; II, 80
Lysander, 50, 131
Lysimachus, 7, 144
Lyxes, 81

Macedonia, Kingdom, 7, 15, 39
Machaon, 51
Madnasa, 92, 99
Maeander, R., 68, 128, 154, 178, 222
Magnesia, 16, 160
Magnesia, battle of, 9, 63, 144, 154, 177, 201
Mandalya, Gulf of, 64
Manitas, 14
Marathon, 5
Marcus Aurelius, 195, 207
Mark Antony, 10–11, 93, 182, 189, 214
Marmaris, 113, 127, 128, 129, 131–2
Marsyas, R., 5, 16, 68, 152, 159
Martyrium of St. Philip, 209–10
Mausoleum, 7, 78, 82, 84, 85, 86, 89, 93; at Iasus, 60–1
Mausolus, 6–7, 11, 14, 15, 16, 25, 31, 32, 36, 38, 41, 43, 50–1, 57, 62, 63, 81–2, 83, 84, 85, 86–8, 91, 92, 95, 96, 97, 98, 103, 105, 107, 110, 143, 148–9, 161, 162
Mazın Kalesi, 169
Melos, 37n
Meltem, 111
Memnon, 83, 84
Mên, 190, 202, 215
Menecles, 157–8
Menesthes, 160
Meneteşe dynasty, 30
Messogis, Mt, 178, 179, 182
Midas, 98
Milâs, 14–15, 18, 24, 25, 28, 29, 30, 32, 36, 40, 48, 62
Miletus, 2, 3, 5, 12n, 13, 16, 38, 49, 51, 68, 95, 143, 145, 196, 216
Minoan civilization, 49, 57
Minos, 1, 2, 3, 12n

Mithridates VI, 9–10, 33, 53, 67, 73, 77, 144, 155, 180
Mobolla, 129
Molpadia, 136
Mopsus, 207
Muğla, 129, 159; dialect, 2
Mumcular, 109
Müsgebi, 98, 100
Mycale, 2
Mycenaean culture, 1, 49, 57, 58, 60, 71, 127
Mylasa, 1, 3, 4, 5, 6, 8, 13–24, 25, 26, 28, 29, 30–1, 32, 36, 38, 39, 40, 49, 52, 60, 68, 81, 132, 154, 155, 202
Myndus, 6, 14, 31, 63, 83, 91–5, 98, 101, 102, 103, 106, 107, 109, 117, 143, 149
Mysians, 1, 31
Mysteries at Lagina, 72, 74
Myus, 2

Naucratis, 113
Naxos, 13
Newton, C. T., 66, 78, 82, 86, 111, 115, 123, 126
Neleus, 49
Nero, 178, 202
Nicagoras, 130
Nicaea, Council of, 192
Nicomedes, 120
Nineveh, 188
Ninoe, name of Aphrodisias, 188
Nysa, 178, 179–87, 194, 213

Octavian, 10, 11, 18, 196 (*see also* Augustus)
Ogygia, 24n
Oil-factories, 57
Ölemez Dağ, 140
Oliatus, 13
Olympichus, 8, 39, 40, 52, 162
Olymus, 16, 25, 28, 29
Oplosika Bükü, 134
Oracle, 19, 40, 45, 97–8, 112–13, 189, 207, 213
Ören, 32
Orontobates, 7, 83, 84, 92, 117, 129
Orta Okul, 20, 23
Orthosia, battle of, 16
Osiris, 19
Otorcondeis, 16, 19
Ovacık, 171
'Oxhide' ingots, 89

Pactyes, 130
Palamut Bay, 111, 114, 118
Pamphylia, 61

Pamukkale, site of Hierapolis, 199, 213, 216
Panamara, 67, 68, 76–7
Panyasis, 79
Parthenus, 136
Parthians, 10, 17, 67, 140, 155, 214
Pasanda, 150
Pausanias, 2, 3, 68
Pazarlık, 136–8
Peçin Kale, 14, 18, 24, 30–2
Pedasa, 3, 5, 80, 92, 95–7, 110
Pedasus, 2
Pegasus, 63, 154
Pelasgians, 2
Peloponnesian War, 1, 6, 131, 135, 143
Pergamum, 7, 8, 9, 15, 183, 201, 214
Perge, 202
Persians, 5, 6, 7, 13–14, 38, 50, 51, 79–80, 81, 83–4, 92, 95, 103, 105, 110, 112, 113, 142, 143, 152, 177
Persikon, fort, 143
Petra, fort, 40
Pharsalus, 178
Philip V, 8, 9, 15–16, 39, 52, 53, 63, 67, 77, 96, 154
Philip, apostle, 202
Philip of Theangela, 3
Philippi, battle of, 93
Philocles, 144
Phocion, 15
Phoenicians, 112
Phormio, boxer, 85
Phrygia, 98, 153, 222
Physcus, 132
Pigres, dynast, 103, 109
Pigres, ship-captain, 103
Pisidia, 213
Pisiköy, 129
Pisye, 129
Pixodarus, 7, 62, 83, 161
Plague, 12
Plarasa, 189, 198n
Plataea, 5
Pliny the Elder, 45, 82, 84, 92, 99, 115, 119, 120, 122, 146, 177, 222
Plutonium: at Acharaca, 182, 186; at Hierapolis, 203–4
Podaleirius, 133–4
Podilus, 52
Polemo: the elder, 214; the younger, 216–17
Polites, runner, 33
Polybius, 25, 28, 96, 144
Pompeii, 120
Pompey, 178, 182
Pomponius Marcellus, 59

Pontus, 9, 182, 214
Praxiteles, 115, 119, 120, 126, 162
Priene, 2, 16, 160, 193
Protogenes, 145
Ptolemy I, 51–2, 143, 144, 147; II, 15, 39, 84, 118; IV, 119; V, 128, 144
Pulcher, 53
Pythodoris, 182
Pythodorus, 178, 180–2
Pythopolis, 180

Quarry for Mausoleum, 93
Quintus Cicero, 84
Quintus Oppius, 214

Reşadiye, 111
Rhodes, 4, 6, 8, 15, 17, 33, 50, 63, 67, 72, 78, 83, 89, 112, 116–17, 128ff., 154, 182
Rhodians, 7, 8, 9, 16, 26, 52, 53, 67, 83, 84, 93, 128ff., 144–5, 222; Rh. Peraea, 128–38
Romans in Asia, 9, 10, 11–12, 16–18, 26, 52, 63, 75, 84, 109, 117, 128, 144–5, 154–5, 177–8, 180, 189, 196, 214

Sabina, 217
St Paul, 12, 215, 222
St Philip, 243–5
Sakarkaya, 129
Salamis, battle of, 5, 79–80, 103
Salavatlı, 186
Salihadası, 102
Salmacis, 80–1, 85, 86
Salt industry, 64, 146
Samos, 6, 18, 50, 114
Sandras Dağı, 140
Saranda, 135
Sarapis, 69, 76
Sardis, 79, 95, 142, 207, 211
Sarıçay, R., 29
Sarıöz, 141
Sarpedon, 3
Satnioeis, 2
Scandaria, 99
Scopas, 82, 115
Scorpions, 36
Scylax, 88, 142
Sea-bathing, 51, 61n3
Şehir Ada, 130
Seleuceia, name of Tralles, 177
Seleuceia in Pamphylia, 163
Seleucid Kingdom, 7–8, 9, 39, 67, 153–4, 177, 180, 201
Seleucus I, 67, 143; II, 8, 15, 39
Selimiye, 136

Septimius Severus, 205
Seven Wonders, 78, 82, 121
Sicily, 112, 115
Side, in Pamphylia, 61
Side (Sibda), 92, 99–101
Silver-mines, 93
Slaves, 146
Smyrna, 79, 97, 214, 216–17, 223n
Sodra Dağı, 29, 40
Söğüt, 132
Solungur Gölü, 141, 151
Sopolis, 51
Sostratus, 121
Spartans, 3, 6, 50, 57, 112, 113–14, 143
Spratt, T. A. B., 112, 113, 136
Stadium: at Aphrodisias, 193–4; at Labraynda, 40, 45; at Laodiceia, 217; at Theangela, 107–8; at Tralles, 179
Stephanus of Byzantium, 13, 63, 68, 99, 100, 152, 153, 162, 180, 188, 198n, 201
Strabo, 1, 2, 3, 13, 17, 20, 22, 31, 36, 38, 48, 49, 60, 67, 68, 78, 85, 91, 99, 101, 123, 132, 139, 140, 141, 152, 155, 156, 168, 178, 203, 204, 222; at Nysa, 180–6
Stratonice, 67
Stratoniceia, 3, 8–9, 13, 16, 33, 39, 67–71, 73, 75, 76, 77, 128, 144
Stratoniceia (Pergamum), 68
Stratonicus, 15, 139
Strongyle, 112
Struthion, 52
Süleyman Kavağı, 24
Sulla, 53, 67, 188–9, 196
Sultanhisar, 180, 182, 185
Sülüklü Gölü, 140
Sura, 45
Syangela, 6, 31, 91, 98, 103–10
Syme, 135
Syria, 7–8
Syrna, 133

Tabae, 189
Taşbükü, 130
Taurupolis, 198n
Tekir, site of New Cnidus, 111, 114, 115, 116, 118, 119, 122–3, 126–7
Telmissus, 92, 97–8, 100
Temples:
  of Aphrodite, at Aphrodisias, 189, 190–2; at Cnidus, 119–20, 125–6; at Troezen, 79
  of Aphrodite and Hermes, at Halicarnassus, 85
  of Apollo, at Alabanda, 155, 160;

at Amos, 133; at Cedreae, 131; at Cnidus, 112, 117–19; at Chalcetor, 29; at Hierapolis, 201, 203, 206–7; at Telmissus, 97, 98, 101
  of Apollo and Artemis, at Amyzon, 169; at Hydae, 29–30; at Olymus, 28
  of Ares, at Halicarnassus, 86
  of Artemis, at Alabanda, 159; at Cindya, 62–3; at Ephesus, 78; at Iasus, 53
  of Demeter and Core, at Iasus, 60
  of Dionysus, at Cnidus, 125
  of Hecate at Lagina, 72–6
  of Hemithea at Castabus, 136–8
  of Pluto and Persephone, at Acharaca, 186
  of Rome and Augustus, 18, 23
  of Sarapis at Stratoniceia, 69–70
  of Zeus Carius, 20, 22, 31; of Z. Chrysaoreus, at Ceramus, 34; at Stratoniceia, 68; Z. at Iasus, 60; Z. Labrayndus, 40–1; Z. Lepsynus, 26–7; Z. Osogos, 22, 28; Z. Stratius, 22; Z. Zenoposeidon, 19–20, 22
Teos, 53
Termera, 80, 92, 98–9, 103
Termerus, 99
Termilae, 3
'Thasos in Caria', 50
Theangela, 103–10, 149
Theatres: at Alabanda, 157; at Alinda, 162, 165–6; at Amos, 133; at Aphrodisias, 189, 195–6; at Bargylia, 66; at Castabus, 138; at Caunus, 149; at Cedreae, 131; at Cnidus, 123, 125; at Colossae, 223; at Euromus, 27; at Halicarnassus, 88; at Hierapolis, 201, 202, 208; at Iasus, 58–9; at Laodiceia, 219; at Mylasa, 23; at Nysa, 182; at Stratoniceia, 71; at Tralles, 179
Theocritus, 119
Theophrastus, 19
Thera, 117, 129
Thibron, 177
Thucydides, 1, 2, 50, 114, 117, 118, 121
Thyssanus, 135
Tiberius, 78, 82, 155, 178, 214
Timotheus, 82
Tırman Dağı, 102n
Tissaphernes, 50, 113–14
Tmolus, Mt, 207
Tomb of Tantalus, 97

Index

Topbaşı, 20, 23
Torba, 97
Torrhebus, 207
Trajan, 217
Tralles, 177–9, 182, 185, 186
Triopium, 79, 112, 114, 117–19, 122
Tripolis, 183
Troezen, 78, 79, 109
Trojan War, 2, 4, 78, 101, 207
Trojans, 2
Turgut, 76
Türkbükü Bay, 99
Tymnes, 98, 103
Tymnus, 135
Tyrrhenian pirates, 112

Underwater finds, 89
Uranium, 92, 101
Uşak, 216

Valens, 202
Varvil Bay, 64, 66
Verres, 84
Vespasian, 150, 217
Vitruvius, 71, 80, 85, 86, 160, 165, 216

Wheler, Sir George, 23, 223
White Pillars, 5, 68
Wine: of Cnidus, 121; of Myndus, 93

Wonders of the World, 78, 82, 121
Wool, 216

Xanthians, 142
Xenophon, 131, 222
Xerxes, 5, 79–80, 142, 152, 180, 222

Yaşyer, 37n
Yatağan, 76
Yaz Tepesi, 28
Yeldeğirmeni, 20
Yerkesik, site of Thera, 129
Yusufca köyü, 36

Zeno, 17, 214
Zenoposeidon, 19–20, 22
Zephyrium, 86
Zeus: at Iasus, 53, 59; at Laodiceia, 213, 215; at Panamara, 69, 76–7; Z. Aseis, 215; Z. Atabyrius, 135; Z. Bozius, 202; Z. Carius, 1, 5, 18, 22, 31; Z. Chrysaoreus, 8, 33, 34, 153; Z. Labrayndus, 18–19, 25, 31, 38–9, 40, 41, 43, 45; Z. Larasius, 178; Z. Lepsynus, 27; Z. Nineudius, 188, 190; Z. Osogos, 19–20, 22, 31; Z. Panamaros, 76–7; Z. Spaloxus, 190; Z. Stratius, 18–19, 38, 40, 47n; Z. Troius, 202; Z. Zenoposeidon, 22
Zoilus, C. Iulius, 195